The Innovation Blueprint

Nature's 4.5 Billion-Year R&D Lab

Teneo

Teneo.io

About Teneo

Teneo stands at the frontier of a revolution in human knowledge. Through an unprecedented collaboration with advanced AI systems, we create books that explore connections and insights previously inaccessible to human authors. Our AI partners can analyze millions of data points across disciplines, identify hidden patterns, and synthesize information in ways that reveal entirely new perspectives on topics ranging from consciousness and creativity to science and society.

What makes Teneo unique is our ability to harness AI's vast analytical capabilities while maintaining the engaging narrative style readers love. Each book represents a journey into uncharted intellectual territory, offering readers access to insights that emerge from processing and connecting humanity's collective knowledge in novel ways. By combining AI's pattern-recognition capabilities with human storytelling, we transform complex data-driven insights into compelling narratives that enlighten and inspire.

We specialize in exposing the hidden patterns and connections that shape our world – patterns that become visible only when analyzing human knowledge and behavior at unprecedented scale. Our books reveal the invisible threads linking everything from personal habits to cosmic phenomena, from creative breakthroughs to societal transformations. Through careful analysis of millions of data points across history, culture, and scientific research, we identify universal principles that illuminate the deeper nature of human experience and existence itself.

Our groundbreaking library includes works examining consciousness through AI's unique outsider perspective, decoding the patterns of human creativity and innovation, mapping the hidden connections between seemingly unrelated phenomena, and exploring the frontiers where human and artificial intelligence meet. Each book represents thousands of hours of AI analysis transformed into accessible insights that change how readers see themselves and their world.

The traditional publishing industry is limited by human authors' inability to process and connect vast amounts of information across disciplines. We believe this artificial barrier to deeper understanding must be transcended. By combining AI's analytical capabilities with skilled human curation, we create books that reveal insights and connections previously invisible to human observation alone. This isn't just about accessing information – it's about uncovering entirely new ways of understanding our world and ourselves.

At Teneo, we're not just publishing books – we're igniting a revolution in human knowledge that bridges the gap between artificial and human intelligence. Join us in exploring these uncharted territories as we unlock insights that transform our understanding of consciousness, creativity, and the patterns that shape our universe. Because true understanding requires more than just information – it requires seeing the hidden connections that reveal life's deeper principles.

Our commitment to advancing human knowledge extends beyond our published works. Through our digital presence and community engagement, we continuously explore new territories where AI analysis reveals unprecedented insights. Our network of readers, researchers, and thought leaders helps refine and expand our understanding, creating an ever-growing body of revolutionary perspectives on what it means to be human in an age of artificial intelligence.

The limitations of individual human cognition have historically restricted our ability to see the deeper patterns that connect all aspects of existence. But with AI's ability to analyze vast amounts of data and identify hidden relationships, these barriers dissolve. When you understand the universal principles and patterns that AI analysis reveals, you transform from a limited observer into someone who can see and understand the deeper mechanisms of reality itself. This is the transformation we ignite with every book we publish, every pattern we expose, and every new perspective we reveal.

Knowledge Beyond Boundaries™

Teneo.io

Teneo Custom Books

Get Your Own Custom AI-Generated Book!

Want a comprehensive book on any topic that you can publish yourself?
Teneo's advanced AI technology can create a custom book tailored to your specific interests and needs. Our AI analyzes millions of data points to generate unique insights and connections previously inaccessible to human authors.

✓ 60,000+ words of in-depth content

✓ Unique AI-driven insights and analysis

✓ Includes Description, Categories and Keywords for easy publishing

✓ Professional Formatting & Publishing Guide Access

✓ Full rights to publish and use the book

✓ Delivery within 48 hours

Visit **teneo.io** to get your own custom AI-generated book today.

Contents

Introduction

Imagine a world where humanity's greatest challenges are met with solutions drawn from the natural world—a world where the ingenuity honed over billions of years of evolution serves as a guide to sustainable living. This is the vision presented in "The Innovation Blueprint: Nature's 4.5 Billion-Year R&D Lab." The book invites readers on a journey to discover how the environment's tried and tested strategies can inspire groundbreaking approaches to modern issues. But why turn to the natural world? Because it has tackled and surmounted challenges akin to those we face today, employing methods refined through millennia. Consider the remarkable energy conservation of a hummingbird or the sophisticated cooperative behavior of an ant colony. These natural phenomena are not merely wonders to admire; they hold the keys to rethinking and addressing human challenges. In an era where adaptability, efficiency, and resilience are crucial, the natural world offers a model that is both innovative and sustainable. As contemporary problems grow more intricate, traditional methods often prove inadequate. This book addresses that gap, offering a fresh perspective rooted in the wisdom of the natural ecosystem, providing practical frameworks for creative problem-solving.

The Case for Nature as the Ultimate Innovator

The natural world stands as the ultimate innovator, its strategies honed by unyielding cycles of trial and triumph. This book builds its case by illustrating how natural solutions are inherently sustainable, adaptable, and resilient—qualities desperately needed in today's rapidly evolving environment. By exploring how coral reefs maintain equilibrium amidst unpredictable conditions and how birds adapt to new challenges, the book highlights the brilliance of natural innovation. It's not just about mimicking these systems, but about understanding and adapting these principles to develop creative solutions that align with human needs.

The exploration of nature as a source of innovation is grounded in the author's extensive research and experience in biomimicry, ecological systems, and innovation management. This foundation ensures that the insights presented are not only scientifically rigorous but also deeply practical, making them accessible to professionals across various fields. The book posits that by embracing a cross-species approach to problem-solving, we can surpass the limitations of conventional thinking. This perspective allows us to view challenges from multiple angles, fostering more comprehensive and inventive solutions.

A Cross-Species Approach to Problem-Solving

Adopting a cross-species approach to problem-solving involves looking beyond our own species for inspiration, drawing from the vast array of life forms inhabiting our planet. This methodology breaks down silos and fosters a holistic understanding of creativity. By studying how diverse species have addressed universal challenges, the book reveals patterns and strategies that transcend specific scientific categories. For instance, ants demonstrate distributed efficiency while bees exemplify swarm intelligence, each offering insights into collective problem-solving and resource optimization.

The narrative is enriched with engaging anecdotes and real-life examples that demonstrate how these biological strategies can be translated into actionable frameworks. Readers are taken on a journey from the microcosm of cellular regeneration to the macrocosm of ecosystem stability, discovering along the way how these natural principles can be applied to human endeavors. This exploration not only deepens our understanding of the environment but also equips us with innovative tools to address challenges in business, technology, and personal development. The cross-species approach encourages readers to broaden their horizons and adopt a mindset that welcomes diversity and creativity.

How AI Unlocks Nature's Hidden Patterns

In the digital age, artificial intelligence emerges as a powerful tool to unveil the hidden patterns of the natural world. By analyzing vast amounts of biological data, AI can uncover strategies that were previously beyond our comprehension. The book explores how AI complements the study of natural systems, providing insights into efficiency, adaptation, and resilience that can be applied to modern challenges. With AI, we can simulate natural processes, identify optimal solutions, and predict how these strategies might perform in various contexts.

This section illuminates the symbiotic relationship between AI and the natural world, showcasing how technology can enhance our understanding and application of natural principles. The potential of AI to revolutionize our approach to innovation is immense, as it allows us to decode complex biological systems and apply their wisdom to real-world problems. The book illustrates this potential through case studies and examples of successful biomimicry, demonstrating how AI-driven insights can lead to groundbreaking innovations. Readers will come to appreciate the intricate dance between technology and the environment, and how leveraging this relationship can lead to sustainable solutions.

The introduction sets the stage for a book that is as insightful as it is practical, inviting readers to explore the universal principles of nature's creativity. It promises a wealth of knowledge and a fresh perspective on problem-solving that is both timely and transformative. As you turn the pages, prepare to be inspired by the ingenuity of the natural world and equipped with the tools to harness its wisdom in your personal and professional life.

Chapter One

Efficiency Maximizing Output With Minimal Resources

Deep within an age-old forest, where sunlight weaves through a tapestry of leaves, a diminutive hummingbird flits with grace, its wings a mere whisper of motion. This tiny wonder, with a heart racing over a thousand beats per minute, challenges our understanding of energy use. Each flicker of movement reveals a mastery of resourcefulness honed through countless generations. In nature's vast workshop, countless mechanisms have been refined, offering profound insights into achieving more with less. These natural marvels prompt us to reconsider efficiency in our own lives.

On this journey, we uncover the secrets of nature's exceptional resource management. From the agile flight of hummingbirds to the survival tactics of desert flora, we witness an unparalleled lesson in conservation. These life forms thrive in settings where every ounce of energy and every drop of water is treasured. Their survival techniques are not mere spectacles but vital blueprints for facing the modern world's sustainability challenges.

Beyond individual lessons, the forest reveals collective wisdom, illustrated by the industrious ant colonies. These tiny creatures, through decentralized teamwork, accomplish extraordinary feats without centralized oversight. Their cooperative endeavors suggest principles that could revolutionize business operations and technological design. By embracing these time-tested strategies, we explore new avenues for innovation and success, guided by the enduring wisdom of nature. As we delve deeper, the links between these natural phenomena and our own challenges become evident, paving the way for a transformative exploration of efficiency.

Energy Conservation in Biological Systems: From Humming birds to Cacti

Nature showcases a remarkable display of resourcefulness, offering an exquisite lesson in utilizing resources with precision and purpose. Across the expansive stage of the natural world, life forms have developed the art of thriving with minimal inputs, crafting survival strategies that range from the gentle flutters of a hummingbird to the steadfast endurance of a cactus. These clever adaptations illustrate how organisms flourish in varied and often challenging habitats, optimizing energy and resources while minimizing waste. This natural proficiency provides a wealth of inspiration for contemporary innovation, encouraging us to explore unconventional methods and draw wisdom from the subtle but powerful lessons of the environment.

Consider the hummingbird, a testament to metabolic precision, darting tirelessly as it meets its high energy needs with an eye for conservation. Or the cactus, excelling in water preservation, standing resolute in barren terrains with its clever modifications. Desert creatures exhibit adaptive cooling techniques, conserving energy amid severe heat, while succulents demonstrate impressive photosynthesis, thriving where others might falter. Each example opens a chapter from nature's guide on effectiveness, offering a blueprint that can inform our approaches to resource management. By delving into these biological strategies, we unlock the potential to transform our methods, creating systems that reflect nature's ingenuity.

Metabolic Efficiency in Hummingbirds: Balancing High Energy Demands

Hummingbirds exemplify nature's prowess in managing energy with remarkable efficiency. These diminutive birds have adapted to meet the substantial energy needs that come with their size. To sustain their rapid wingbeats and hovering capabilities, they consume sugar-rich nectar, converting it into energy with exceptional proficiency. This allows them to flap their wings up to eighty times per second and maintain a heart rate over 1,200 beats per minute during flight. Their energy processing prowess stems not only from their diet but also from specialized physiological features, such as an unusually large heart and an impressive ability to uptake and deliver oxygen.

A key aspect of a hummingbird's energy efficiency is its ability to switch between different metabolic states. While flying, they sustain a high metabolic rate, but at night, they can enter a state of torpor, reducing their energy use by up to 95%. This strategy balances high-energy activities with energy conservation. Such a dynamic approach to energy management can be applied to human contexts, like optimizing resource use in business or personal energy management.

Recent research has uncovered the genetic and molecular mechanisms behind these amazing capabilities. Scientists have identified specific enzymes and pathways that enable rapid energy conversion, offering potential insights for biotechnology and medicine. Imitating these processes could lead to more energy-efficient technologies or new methods for addressing metabolic disorders in humans. The hummingbird's adaptations provide a blueprint for exploring biological insights to tackle energy management and sustainability challenges.

The hummingbird's story challenges the traditional view of efficiency, not merely as output over input but as a balance of extremes. In human terms, this encourages a holistic view of efficiency, where peak performance is achieved through a strategic mix of exertion and rest. Studying how hummingbirds manage their energy demands offers a nuanced understanding that can transform productivity approaches, integrating rest and recuperation into high-performance environments.

Appreciating the hummingbird's energy dynamics encourages creative thinking about sustainability. If these birds can maintain such high efficiency within their environmental constraints, what lessons can we learn for our resource-intensive societies? The answers may involve reimagining how we use and conserve energy, crafting systems as adaptable and resilient as the hummingbird itself. Exploring these biological strategies opens the door to innovative solutions that harmonize human endeavors with the natural world.

Water Retention Strategies in Cacti: Surviving Arid Environments

Cacti, the steadfast guardians of barren terrains, reveal remarkable tactics for water preservation. These resilient plants have developed unique adaptations to flourish in harsh desert conditions where many others cannot survive. Central to their endurance is their ability to store water in their robust, fleshy tissues, functioning as a reservoir that sustains them through extended droughts. This feature ensures hydration long after the rains have ceased, serving as more than just a survival tactic—it's an evolution-refined adaptation that exemplifies resource management and offers insights for human ingenuity.

In addition to water storage, cacti possess various structural and functional traits to minimize water loss. Their spines, which might seem purely defensive, significantly reduce transpiration by shading and reducing airflow around the plant. The waxy cuticle covering their surface acts as a barrier against water loss, preserving vital moisture. Cacti breathe at night, when temperatures are cooler, through a process known as CAM photosynthesis. This allows them to reduce water loss during the day's heat, showcasing nature's innovative solutions.

Recent studies on cacti's water retention have revealed complex networks of signaling pathways that control water use efficiency. These pathways are responsive to environmental stressors, allowing the plant to adjust its water management strategies accordingly. This adaptability underscores the sophisticated biochemical processes at play, offering promising avenues for biomimetic applications in fields like agriculture and water management. By emulating these natural processes, we could develop more water-efficient crops or design systems that better manage water distribution in urban settings.

In a world facing water scarcity, cacti embody sustainability. Their resourceful use of water challenges us to reconsider our own habits, steering us toward more sustainable and resilient practices. Imagine city structures designed with materials inspired by cacti that capture and store rainwater, or farming systems that mimic their water-efficient metabolism to reduce irrigation demands. Such innovations could transform our relationship with water, turning scarcity into abundance by emulating nature's proven strategies.

Reflecting on the lessons from cacti encourages us to see challenges as opportunities for innovation. Just as cacti have transformed deserts into realms of possibility, we can reshape our environments by embracing nature's principles of efficiency and resilience. This perspective promotes a shift from scarcity to abundance, where natural constraints spark ingenious solutions. By studying the humble cactus, we learn to value every drop of water and view each challenge as a chance to innovate.

Adaptive Thermoregulation in Desert Animals: Minimizing Energy Loss

In the unforgiving desert climate, where temperatures fluctuate drastically between day and night, animals have evolved extraordinary methods to manage their body heat and conserve energy. These creatures excel in adaptation, using a mix of bodily and behavioral techniques to regulate their internal temperature and save energy. Fennec foxes, for example, possess large ears that act like natural cooling systems, releasing excess heat into the air. The proximity of blood vessels to the surface in their ears allows for effective heat dissipation. Camels, known for their endurance, can withstand significant body temperature changes, reducing the need for constant thermoregulation and conserving water.

Beyond physical traits, many desert animals adopt behaviors that boost their energy savings. Being active at night is a common tactic, enabling animals to avoid the intense heat of the day and forage in cooler conditions. This shift not only lessens the need for active cooling but also aligns energy use with more favorable temperatures, thus conserving energy. The Saharan silver ant takes this further by foraging during the hottest part of the day when predators are less active, utilizing its heat tolerance for an edge.

Recent research has unveiled intriguing insights into the genetic and molecular foundations of these adaptations. Studies on the Arabian oryx have identified specific genetic markers linked to extreme heat tolerance and efficient water use. Understanding these genetic codes opens doors for biotechnological innovations, potentially aiding fields like synthetic biology and sustainable farming. By decoding these natural templates, scientists can explore ways to improve crop resilience to climate change or develop materials that mimic these adaptive properties.

For innovators and problem-solvers, these natural strategies offer a wealth of inspiration. Businesses can draw parallels between desert animals' heat management tactics and the need to optimize energy use in buildings or data centers. Implementing systems that adjust to changing conditions, similar to these creatures' flexibility, can yield significant energy savings. Emulating the adaptability of desert wildlife can also inform the creation of responsive technologies, such as smart grids or adaptive cooling systems, which adjust dynamically to real-time demands.

These insights challenge us to rethink traditional approaches and consider how naturally evolved strategies might guide sustainable practices. As we face climate change and resource scarcity, the lessons from desert animals highlight the importance of designing systems that are not only efficient but also resilient and adaptable. How might we apply these concepts to develop products and services that thrive in changing environments? By observing and learning from nature's solutions, we can discover new pathways for innovation that are both effective and in harmony with our planet's ecosystems.

Photosynthetic Optimization in Extreme Conditions: Lessons from Succulents

Succulents are remarkable for their ability to flourish in some of the most challenging climates on Earth by fine-tuning their photosynthetic processes to maximize resource use. These resilient plants utilize a unique form of photosynthesis called Crassulacean Acid Metabolism (CAM), which enables them to conserve water while optimizing carbon intake. Unlike conventional photosynthesis, CAM plants open their stomata at night to absorb carbon dioxide, significantly reducing water loss during the hot daylight hours. This nighttime strategy for gas exchange allows succulents to sustain metabolic activity in arid regions, illustrating their exceptional adaptation to extreme conditions.

The evolutionary brilliance of succulents is not limited to their nighttime carbon capture. Their cellular structures are adept at storing substantial amounts of water, essential for maintaining photosynthesis during extended dry periods. Thick, waxy cuticles and specialized vacuoles help retain water and reflect sunlight, preventing overheating. Through precise management of their internal resources, succulents exemplify how living organisms can adjust to environmental changes, offering a model of efficient energy use that can be applied to various human activities.

New research delves into how succulents alter their photosynthetic systems at the molecular level in response to environmental pressures. Scientists have pinpointed certain proteins and enzymes that boost CAM photosynthesis efficiency, presenting potential pathways for genetic modification in agricultural crops. By leveraging these biological insights, researchers aim to develop plants capable of thriving with minimal water, addressing food security issues in regions with limited water supplies. This forward-thinking approach highlights the potential for translating natural solutions into sustainable farming practices.

Beyond agriculture, the principles of CAM photosynthesis are inspiring innovation in energy-efficient technology. Features derived from succulents' energy conservation abilities are influencing the development of solar panels and energy storage devices. By emulating the structure and function of succulent leaves, engineers are crafting materials that optimize solar energy capture while reducing thermal losses. These biomimetic advancements emphasize the extensive implications of understanding and applying nature's refined strategies to modern technological challenges.

For those aspiring to mirror the efficiency of succulents in their fields, the key lies in adapting precisely and flexibly to resource availability. This could involve crafting business processes that optimize resource distribution or creating products that perform effectively under diverse conditions. By examining the intricate mechanisms through which succulents enhance photosynthesis, innovators can derive insights into building systems that are both robust and efficient, promoting sustainable practices that echo the adaptability of these extraordinary plants.

Distributed Efficiency: Ant Colonies and Decentralized Networks

Ant colonies, alive with activity and purpose, offer a captivating glimpse into the strength of distributed productivity. These tiny natural architects excel at collaborating without a central command, thriving on a system where each individual understands its function through simple rules and direct interactions. This self-organized network is a testament to collective intelligence, where tasks flow smoothly and resources are skillfully managed. Observing this marvel, one can't help but admire how ants achieve such impressive coordination and adaptability. Their problem-solving approach, based on communication and teamwork, serves as an inspiring blueprint for improving human systems and networks.

The intricate dance of ants showcases the emergence of complex behaviors from basic principles. Each ant, guided by instinct and chemical cues, contributes to a broader system that flourishes through decentralization. This model of effectiveness, rooted in simplicity, underscores the potential for human networks to reach similar results by adopting decentralized frameworks. As we investigate ant-inspired algorithms to boost human network performance, we find an opportunity to rethink traditional organizational and communication methods. By applying these insights, we can create systems that are not only effective but also robust and flexible, much like the ant colonies that have prospered for millions of years.

Collective Intelligence and Task Allocation in Ant Colonies

Ant colonies demonstrate a unique form of collective intelligence, where each ant acts independently yet collectively achieves complex outcomes. This decentralized method of task distribution provides valuable insights for enhancing human networks. Ant colonies operate through a combination of instinctive behaviors and environmental signals, allowing them to allocate resources and labor efficiently to meet their needs. For example, ants communicate with pheromones to mark trails when foraging, guiding others to follow and reinforce successful routes. This method leads to effective resource gathering, as ants adjust their efforts based on the location and abundance of food. Such strategies can inspire business management systems where autonomy and local decision-making boost productivity and adaptability.

Ant colonies showcase how simple rules can lead to complex behaviors, highlighting the power of decentralized systems. Each ant follows basic protocols, yet together they achieve intricate results like building nests, maintaining cleanliness, and defending against threats. Studies reveal how ants use stigmergy—a type of indirect communication where actions leave traces in the environment, influencing subsequent actions by others. This creates a self-regulating system that adapts to changes without direct oversight. Applying these principles to human contexts could transform areas like logistics and urban planning, where adaptive, self-organizing systems are essential for managing complexity and ch ange.

Understanding ant communication networks involves recognizing the importance of redundancy and flexibility. Ant colonies show that having multiple individuals capable of performing various tasks ensures resilience amid disruptions. This flexibility is crucial in dynamic environments where quick responses to challenges are vital. Embracing these principles, organizations can design robust and agile teams, efficiently reallocating resources when unexpected situations arise. In crisis management, for instance, having personnel trained in multiple skills enables seamless role shifts, minimizing downtime and enhancing response effectiveness.

Research into biomimicry has led to ant-inspired algorithms improving network efficiency in fields like telecommunications and computing. These algorithms imitate the decentralized decision-making and path optimization seen in ant colonies. Ant colony optimization algorithms, for instance, have solved complex routing issues in telecommunication networks, ensuring data travels via the most effective routes. By integrating these biologically-inspired methods, industries achieve significant improvements in operational efficiency and resource use. Moreover, the adaptability of these algorithms allows customization for specific needs, offering a versatile tool for diverse applications.

The study of ant colonies and their inherent wisdom continues to inspire solutions to modern challenges. Observing how ants organize, communicate, and adapt offers principles to address inefficiencies in human systems. This leads to intriguing questions: How might decentralized strategies reshape collaboration in the digital age? What can we learn from ant colonies' resilience and adaptability to enhance our systems? Encouraging such reflections fosters a deeper understanding of nature-inspired strategies' potential applications. By embracing lessons from ant colonies, we can build more efficient, adaptive, and resilient networks, ready to thrive in an ever-changing world.

Emergence of Complex Behaviors Through Simple Rules

In the fascinating realm of ant colonies, intricate behaviors arise from simple rules, providing a masterclass in streamlined systems. Despite being individually straightforward creatures, ants collectively exhibit remarkable sophistication by following basic algorithms. These tiny insects utilize straightforward principles, such as pheromone trails for navigation and task distribution, which result in the creation of highly organized and adaptable structures. Recent research shows that ants adjust their roles dynamically to meet the colony's needs, displaying an exceptional level of self-organization. This decentralized decision-making process mirrors the principles seen in robust human systems like blockchain technology and distributed computing, where complexity emerges from simplicity without central oversight.

The elegance of these emergent behaviors lies in their adaptability and resilience. Ant colonies prosper in changing environments by employing redundancy and flexibility, enabling them to allocate resources efficiently and respond to external pressures. Studies highlight how ants can swiftly switch tasks based on real-time feedback, ensuring the colony's stability. This concept of emergence, when applied to human systems, suggests that organizations might achieve greater resilience by fostering environments where straightforward rules encourage autonomous decision-making and adaptability. The potential to create systems that mimic this natural efficiency opens new avenues for designing businesses that can evolve and thrive in ever-changing landscapes.

Ant-inspired algorithms have already been utilized in various sectors, spurring innovation in logistics, telecommunications, and problem-solving. The Ant Colony Optimization (ACO) algorithm exemplifies how nature's wisdom can address complex human challenges. By imitating how ants find the shortest paths to food sources, ACO has been employed to optimize network routing, reduce transportation costs, and enhance resource allocation. These applications illustrate how understanding and applying the principles of emergence can lead to tangible improvements in productivity and effectiveness across diverse industries.

To harness these insights, organizations can experiment with decentralizing decision-making processes and encouraging bottom-up innovation. By empowering individual team members to make decisions based on local information and simple guidelines, businesses can cultivate an environment where innovative solutions naturally arise. This approach not only enhances operational productivity but also fosters a culture of creativity and empowerment. Companies that have embraced such models report increased agility and employee satisfaction, illustrating the profound impact of adopting nature-inspired strategies.

Reflecting on the lessons from ant colonies prompts a thought-provoking question: How might other natural systems inform our understanding of complexity and efficiency? Encouraging curiosity and exploration of these biological models can lead to groundbreaking insights and transformative applications. By embracing the simplicity and elegance of nature's solutions, we can unlock new potential for innovation and growth, ultimately crafting human systems that mirror the intelligence found in the natural world.

Lessons from Decentralization in Ant Communication Networks

Ant colonies serve as a fascinating example of decentralized communication, demonstrating how complex networks can operate smoothly without a central leader. Ants use simple signals and pheromones to share crucial information, allowing them to coordinate sophisticated tasks like foraging and building nests. This decentralized system enables colonies to quickly adjust to changes in their environment and available resources. The way they maintain order and effectiveness without centralized control offers valuable insights for creating resilient human networks that function autonomously and can adapt to new challenges fluidly.

Central to ant communication is the concept of stigmergy, where ants leave traces in their environment to guide the actions of others. This form of indirect communication fosters a strong collective intelligence, helping colonies solve problems and allocate tasks efficiently. By studying how ants use pheromone trails to find optimal paths, researchers have developed algorithms like the Ant Colony Optimization (ACO) algorithm, which are applied to complex issues in logistics, telecommunications, and robotics. These nature-inspired algorithms highlight the potential of using biological principles to boost network performance.

In technology, decentralization offers benefits such as increased resilience and scalability. By applying ant communication strategies, engineers can design systems less prone to single points of failure and more capable of handling demand fluctuations or external disruptions. For instance, decentralized communication protocols in computer networks can manage data load more effectively, reducing congestion and improving overall efficiency. This method not only enhances network reliability but also supports the development of sustainable, energy-efficient systems by minimizing resource usage.

As our digital world continues to grow, the need for efficient and adaptable communication networks becomes crucial. By learning from ant colonies, we can discover innovative ways to manage information in distributed systems. This perspective encourages us to question traditional centralized models and embrace decentralized frameworks that promote flexibility and ingenuity. Through bio-inspired design, we can create communication networks that mirror nature's ability to balance efficiency and resilience, paving the way for more effective and sustainable technological solutions.

To put these lessons into practice, consider how decentralized principles can influence organizational structures or collaborative platforms. By empowering individuals within a network to make decisions using local information, organizations can boost their agility and responsiveness. Encouraging a culture of decentralized decision-making not only fosters innovation but also strengthens resilience, as teams can quickly adapt to changes and challenges. These insights invite readers to explore how adopting decentralized strategies can transform their systems, leading to more efficient and sustainable outcomes in both personal and professional arenas.

Applying Ant-Inspired Algorithms to Human Network Efficiency

Ant colonies serve as a powerful model of distributed effectiveness, demonstrating how decentralized networks can prosper through a system of collective wisdom. This intriguing phenomenon is gaining attention for its potential to transform human network performance. Ants employ straightforward yet effective algorithms to navigate intricate environments, optimize the distribution of resources, and secure their survival, offering a blueprint for creating resilient human systems. By examining these natural algorithms, we can uncover strategies to address inefficiencies in human networks, enhancing areas such as supply chain logistics and communication structures. This approach encourages us to reconsider centralized models, advocating for more flexible and robust systems.

A remarkable feature of ant colonies is their dynamic task allocation, which ensures that resources and labor are used efficiently without centralized control. This self-organizing behavior relies on local interactions and feedback loops, which can be mirrored in human network systems. By embracing decentralized decision-making principles, organizations can cultivate environments where individuals or nodes act on local information, resulting in more agile and adaptive networks. This shift can reduce bottlenecks and enhance the speed and precision of decision-making processes.

The emergence of complex behaviors from simple rules in ant colonies provides a compelling framework for developing human algorithms. In computational terms, this is akin to using heuristic methods that mimic ant behavior, such as ant colony optimization (ACO). ACO algorithms are gaining popularity for addressing complex optimization challenges, particularly in routing and scheduling. This technique leverages the stigmergic communication seen in ants, where indirect signals through environmental changes guide collective actions. By emulating this process, human networks can achieve greater effectiveness by utilizing indirect communication cues and adaptive learning mechanisms.

Beyond technical applications, ant-inspired algorithms also suggest a cultural shift towards valuing decentralized leadership and emergent strategies. This paradigm encourages organizations to foster environments where innovation emerges from the collective, rather than being dictated from the top down.

By promoting a culture that supports experimentation and iterative learning, organizations can unlock new possibilities for effectiveness and creativity. This approach aligns with the growing trend of agile methodologies, which emphasize flexibility and responsiveness over rigid hierarchical structures.

As we explore ant-inspired effectiveness, it is crucial to consider the ethical implications of adopting biologically inspired systems. While these models provide significant advantages, they also raise questions about autonomy and the balance between individual agency and collective benefit. Engaging in dialogue on these issues can lead to more thoughtful and responsible use of ant-inspired algorithms in human networks. By reflecting on these broader implications, we not only enhance our technical capabilities but also deepen our understanding of how natural systems can inform ethical and sustainable innovation.

Applying Nature's Efficiency Models to Business Operations

To begin, let's delve into how the intricate web of nature can illuminate pathways for optimizing business operations. Just as ecosystems flourish through cooperative interactions and adept resource management, businesses can adopt these principles to thrive in competitive arenas. Nature's unmatched proficiency provides a model for refining processes and enhancing productivity. By studying the efficient energy use in biological systems—such as the precise flight mechanics of hummingbirds or the water-saving tactics of cacti—we uncover valuable lessons in resource management and sustainability. These insights offer a refreshing perspective on minimizing waste and boosting productivity, essential for businesses striving to achieve excellence with limited resources.

As we delve deeper, the decentralized networks of ant colonies present a compelling model of distributed efficiency. Ants exhibit extraordinary problem-solving through collective intelligence, inspiring fresh approaches to teamwork and resource distribution within organizations. By mimicking these natural systems, businesses can streamline workflows and adapt effortlessly to challenges. The following sections will explore practical applications, from enhancing workflows through biomimetic principles to embracing circular economy models inspired by nature's regenerative processes. As we navigate these ideas, the potential to transform business operations into dynamic, efficient systems becomes not just feasible but an exciting opportunity.

Streamlining Workflow Through Biomimetic Principles

Drawing inspiration from nature can significantly enhance workflow efficiency by integrating biomimetic principles that reflect the streamlined processes found in biological systems. Nature often achieves extraordinary results with minimal resources, as seen in the efficient distribution of nutrients by phytoplankton through ocean currents. This example can guide businesses in developing flexible workflow systems that allocate resources precisely where needed, boosting productivity. Observing these natural dynamics enables us to design proactive workflow strategies that minimize waste and maximize output.

Incorporating biomimicry into workflow design involves understanding the self-organizing nature of ecosystems to maintain balance and output. Consider the synchronized movement of starlings in murmurations, which allows them to navigate complex environments without centralized control. Similarly, businesses can establish decentralized decision-making frameworks, empowering employees to make informed choices at every level. This not only cultivates innovation but also reduces bottlenecks, creating a more agile organizational structure. Such approaches promote autonomy and trust, essential components of a successful workplace.

Advancements in AI-driven analytics present new opportunities to emulate natural workflows. Machine learning can analyze extensive datasets to identify patterns akin to those in nature. For example, neural networks, modeled after the interconnectedness of the human brain, can optimize logistics and resource allocation in real-time. This technology allows businesses to adapt swiftly to changing conditions, much like a chameleon seamlessly blends with its surroundings. By leveraging these insights, organizations can foster continuous improvement and adaptability.

In terms of workflow optimization, the concept of modularity, drawn from biological ecosystems, offers a robust framework. Ecosystems thrive on interconnected yet independent modules, like the relationship between bees and flowering plants. Similarly, business workflows can be structured with autonomous modular components. This design ensures that issues in one area do not disrupt the entire system, reducing downtime and maintaining productivity. Implementing such systems requires understanding interdependencies and adopting a holistic view of workflow management.

To drive innovation, it's crucial to challenge traditional norms and invite diverse perspectives into workflow design. Imagine a team inspired by the collaborative hunting strategies of wolves, applying this to project management through cross-departmental collaboration. This approach can uncover hidden synergies and foster collective success. Encouraging teams to draw on natural principles when refining their work processes not only boosts efficiency but also nurtures curiosity and creativity. By continuously questioning and enhancing workflows, businesses can stay at the forefront of innovation, tapping into the immense wisdom offered by nature.

Leveraging Ecosystem Dynamics for Supply Chain Optimization

Nature's intricate systems reveal ecosystems as models of effectiveness, where every element contributes to sustaining balance and productivity. Businesses can learn from these dynamics to improve their supply chains, making them more robust and adaptable. In ecosystems, the interconnectedness of organisms facilitates a smooth exchange of resources, energy, and information. This concept can inspire companies to view their supply chains as networks instead of linear processes, promoting collaboration and resource-sharing to minimize waste and boost efficiency.

Recent studies highlight symbiosis in ecosystems, showing that mutually beneficial relationships enhance survival and resource use. In business, companies can form symbiotic partnerships with suppliers and distributors to efficiently and sustainably allocate resources. For instance, a firm might work with suppliers to establish a closed-loop system, where waste from one process serves as input for another. This approach not only reduces environmental impact but also cuts costs and strengthens the supply chain against disruptions.

The principle of biodiversity, fundamental to thriving ecosystems, offers insights for diversifying supply chains. Ecosystems with varied species are more resilient to change, and similarly, supply chains with diverse sourcing strategies can better navigate market shifts and unforeseen challenges. By diversifying suppliers, transportation methods, and distribution channels, businesses can mitigate risks and uncover innovation opportunities. Adopting this approach ensures supply chains remain robust, flexible, and capable of thriving in dynamic markets.

Incorporating feedback loops, a defining feature of natural ecosystems, can further enhance supply chain performance. Ecosystems constantly adjust based on environmental feedback, enabling swift responses to changes. Companies can implement similar systems using real-time data analytics and AI to monitor and refine supply chain operations, allowing for proactive decision-making and rapid resolution of potential bottlenecks or inefficiencies, akin to nature's adaptive responses.

To encourage businesses to apply these natural principles, consider envisioning a supply chain that mirrors a thriving ecosystem. How might current practices evolve when inspired by nature's effectiveness? By exploring such questions, leaders can pinpoint areas for improvement and innovation within their operations. Embracing an ecosystem mindset not only boosts supply chain efficiency but also cultivates a culture of continuous learning and adaptation, paving the way for sustainable growth and long-term success.

Implementing Circular Economy Models Inspired by Natural Systems

Nature's model of circular economy stands as a remarkable example of efficiency, transforming waste into valuable resources in a continuous cycle of renewal. This principle is vividly illustrated in ecosystems through nutrient cycles, such as carbon and nitrogen, which are endlessly recycled to sustain life. Businesses can learn from these natural systems by embracing circular economy practices that minimize waste while maximizing resource use. By rethinking product designs and processes to extend material life cycles, companies can cut costs, lessen environmental impact, and create value for stakeholders. This strategy not only supports sustainability goals but also sparks innovation, prompting the creation of new business models and technologies.

In pursuing circular economy strategies, organizations can look to nature's collaborative relationships for inspiration. Consider a forest: fallen leaves decompose to enrich the soil, which then nurtures tree growth. This mutualistic interaction can be replicated in industrial settings where businesses collaborate to exchange by-products and resources. Such industrial symbiosis, as exemplified by the Kalundborg Eco-industrial Park in Denmark, where companies share energy, water, and materials, can lead to cost savings and waste reduction. By adopting these principles, businesses can forge networks that boost efficiency and resilience, transforming potential waste into valuable inputs.

Advancements in biomimicry research have revealed innovative ways to integrate these natural cycles into business frameworks. The development of biodegradable materials inspired by leaf litter decomposition is gaining momentum. These materials emulate nature's ability to break down organic matter efficiently, offering sustainable alternatives to conventional plastics. Companies are exploring fungi-based packaging that decomposes quickly and enriches the soil. By adopting such innovations, businesses can reduce their environmental impact and attract eco-conscious consumers, staying competitive in a market that increasingly values sustainability.

Technology plays a crucial role in the success of a circular economy, facilitating these transitions. Artificial intelligence and machine learning can enhance resource management by predicting and analyzing waste patterns, akin to how ecosystems regulate nutrient flow. Data-driven insights enable companies to anticipate demand, minimize waste, and streamline operations. Blockchain technology provides transparency and traceability in supply chains, ensuring responsible sourcing and reuse of materials. By leveraging these cutting-edge technologies, businesses can refine their circular practices, ensuring efficiency and accountability throughout their operations.

Reflecting on nature's blueprint prompts us to rethink current linear consumption models and envision a future where circularity permeates every aspect of business. As industries evolve, the potential for circular economy models to drive innovation and sustainability becomes increasingly evident. What if businesses adopted the mindset of a forest, continuously regenerating and renewing? Such a transformation demands not only technological advancements but also a shift in corporate culture and consumer behavior. By embracing the ethos of circularity, companies can create systems that thrive in harmony with the natural world, ultimately leading to a more sustainable and prosperous future.

Enhancing Decision-Making with Nature-Inspired Algorithms

Decision-making is crucial for both biological and organizational success and can be significantly enhanced by algorithms inspired by natural systems. Consider the ant colony, where decentralized decision-making allows individual ants to follow simple rules while achieving complex goals collectively. This concept, known as swarm intelligence, can be leveraged in algorithmic design to optimize business decisions. By mimicking ants' resource allocation and adaptability to changing environments, companies can create more responsive and flexible decision-making frameworks. Algorithms inspired by nature's distributed networks can lead to more resilient and efficient business operations.

Recent advances in artificial intelligence have accelerated the development of these nature-inspired algorithms. Machine learning models can adopt principles from neural networks similar to those in human brains, learning and adapting from real-time data inputs. These algorithms offer a dynamic decision-making approach that mirrors the adaptability found in biological systems. By integrating feedback loops akin to those in natural ecosystems, businesses can develop decision-making processes that are both reactive and predictive, anticipating market changes before they fully occur.

Incorporating genetic algorithms, which replicate natural selection, into business strategies offers another promising avenue. These algorithms generate multiple potential solutions, refining them through processes akin to mutation and selection. This method enables organizations to discover optimal strategies that might otherwise remain hidden. For instance, logistics companies have used genetic algorithms to enhance route optimization, leading to reduced fuel consumption and improved delivery times. Such applications highlight the potential of nature-inspired algorithms to solve complex problems with elegant and efficient solutions.

Implementing these concepts requires a shift in organizational culture. Businesses must create an environment that encourages experimentation and embraces the iterative nature of these algorithms. By fostering a mindset that values adaptability and learning, companies can unlock the full potential of nature-inspired decision-making models. This approach aligns with emerging trends in organizational development that emphasize agility and resilience, essential attributes in today's ever-changing business landscape.

To spark thought and inspire action, consider a business facing sudden market disruption. How might a decision-making algorithm inspired by a flock of birds, which effortlessly changes direction in response to external stimuli, help the business pivot swiftly and effectively? Exploring such scenarios allows businesses to gain insights into the practical application of nature-inspired algorithms, ultimately enhancing their ability to navigate uncertainty and seize new opportunities. Encouraging decision-makers to adopt these frameworks can lead to more innovative and sustainable business practices, bridging the gap between nature's wisdom and human ingenuity.

As we wrap up our journey into productivity, the brilliance of nature's designs becomes evident. Observing how hummingbirds conserve energy and how cacti thrive in arid environments offers us valuable lessons on maximizing output with minimal resources. Ant colonies, with their cooperative structures, reveal insights into effective teamwork. When we apply these biological insights to business, we open doors to sustainable growth and groundbreaking ideas. Embracing principles like resource efficiency and decentralized systems not only boosts productivity but also fosters resilience and adaptability in our fast-evolving world. This blend of natural strategies inspires us to reflect on how we can conduct our activities with precision and grace. As we move on to the next topic, consider how these lessons might reshape daily routines and fuel innovative solutions. Perhaps the solutions to our complex problems lie in adopting the elegant simplicity seen in the natural world. Our exploration continues, inviting us to delve deeper, expand our thinking, and innovate with nature as our inspiration.

Chapter Two

Resilience Surviving And Thriving In Unpredictable Conditions

In the vast expanse of the Pacific Ocean, coral reefs flourish as vibrant symbols of nature's incredible ability to thrive despite adversity. These underwater marvels teem with life, showcasing an extraordinary capacity for endurance amid turbulent seas and shifting temperatures. Their narrative is one not merely of survival but of dynamic evolution, where challenges become stepping stones for growth. What if individuals and organizations could mirror this tenacity, navigating life's unpredictable currents with equal grace and strength? What could these ecosystems teach us about unlocking resilience in our own lives?

As we delve into this chapter, we uncover the profound wisdom inherent in nature's design. The resilience of coral reefs finds a parallel in the human nervous system's intricate web, where redundancy and flexibility ensure endurance. Neurons craft a complex, adaptive tapestry, responding to disruptions with remarkable efficiency. This natural symphony, harmonious yet complex, offers a blueprint for building systems that withstand shocks and stressors. These insights guide us as we explore how these principles can shape and empower human endeavors, from businesses to communities.

Nature's resilience, seen in these diverse forms, provides a guide for thriving amid uncertainty. By examining these natural phenomena, we gain valuable perspectives on cultivating resilience in our lives. This chapter invites you to envision resilience not just as enduring but as an active, adaptive force. Through the lens of nature's enduring innovations, we find inspiration to devise strategies that not only endure challenges but also transform them into opportunities for growth. As we proceed, we will draw from these lessons, forging connections between the natural world and the ever-changing landscape of human enterprise.

The Robustness of Coral Reefs and Ecosystem Stability

Venturing into the mesmerizing world of coral reefs, we uncover one of nature's most steadfast marvels. These vibrant underwater metropolises have flourished for thousands of years, adapting to the ever-changing tides of their environment. Often called the "rainforests of the sea," coral reefs harbor an astonishing array of life, serving as sanctuaries for countless marine species. Their continued existence depends on a finely tuned balance of relationships and an exceptional ability to endure and evolve under pressure. By delving into the resilience of coral reefs, we gain valuable insights into maintaining stability amidst uncertainty, offering lessons that extend beyond nature to inform our own paths to resilience.

Coral reefs possess an extraordinary capacity to absorb shocks and bounce back from disturbances, a trait essential to their survival. This fortitude is underpinned by a complex web of symbiotic relationships, where mutual dependencies not only ensure longevity but also bolster the ecosystem against external threats. Biodiversity acts as a crucial stabilizer, enhancing the reef's ability to recover from challenges. Yet, human activities pose serious risks, threatening the very existence of these ecosystems. Understanding the mechanisms that enable coral reefs to remain resilient can guide us in crafting robust strategies for both natural and human-made environments. As we explore these themes, we discover approaches that can strengthen our organizations and communities, drawing inspiration from the enduring vigor of coral reefs.

Resilience Mechanisms of Coral Reefs in Response to Environmental Stressors

Coral reefs, often likened to the sea's rainforests, showcase remarkable endurance amid environmental challenges. This endurance largely stems from their capacity to thrive in ever-changing, harsh conditions. A crucial factor in their resilience is rapid adaptation through genetic variety and phenotypic flexibility. The diverse coral species and their algal partners can swiftly adjust to shifts in temperature, acidity, and light, enabling these ecosystems to persist despite escalating climate change pressures. Recent research highlights how certain corals enhance heat tolerance by modifying their algal composition, exemplifying nature's adaptability.

Beyond genetic adaptation, coral reefs employ structural strategies to withstand environmental stress. Their intricate architecture not only offers habitat to a wide range of marine life but also protects against strong currents and waves. The tightly interwoven calcium carbonate structures form a dense matrix that absorbs and disperses energy, shielding the reef's integrity. This structural complexity fosters diverse microhabitats, bolstering the ecosystem's overall resilience. As scientists explore these natural strongholds, they gain insights into biomimetic applications for creating buildings and coastal structures capable of withstanding natural disasters.

Coral reefs' resilience is further enhanced by dynamic symbiotic relationships. The mutualistic interaction between corals and their algae, zooxanthellae, is vital to reef stability. These algae, residing within coral tissues, conduct photosynthesis and supply essential nutrients to their hosts, which in return provide protection and carbon dioxide. This exchange not only promotes reef growth but also aids in recovery from stress events. Understanding these interactions offers valuable lessons for developing sustainable agriculture practices that emphasize cooperative plant-microbe relationships to boost crop resilience.

Human activities undeniably impact coral reefs, yet strategies exist to strengthen their resilience against human-induced stressors. Initiatives like coral gardening and assisted evolution, where resilient coral strains are cultivated and reintroduced into vulnerable areas, show promise in enhancing reef recovery. Establishing marine protected areas also helps reduce local stressors such as overfishing and pollution, allowing reefs to regenerate naturally. These efforts highlight the importance of nurturing resilience through direct intervention and conservation strategies, providing a model for safeguarding other vulnerable ecosystems worldwide.

Coral reefs not only exemplify nature's resilience but also inspire reflections on applying these principles to human endeavors. Consider the potential of fostering diversity within teams to enhance organizational resilience or designing adaptive systems that can pivot in response to unexpected challenges. By studying how coral reefs survive and flourish, we gain not only an understanding of their complexity but also actionable insights that can be translated into innovative solutions across various fields. Such reflections encourage critical thinking about our interactions with natural systems and how best to align our practices with the wisdom found in the natural world.

Symbiotic Relationships and Their Role in Reef Stability

In the captivating underwater realm of coral reefs, symbiotic relationships form the foundation of ecological balance. These complex partnerships, developed over thousands of years, highlight nature's brilliance in fostering resilience in challenging conditions. Central to this dynamic is the mutualistic bond between corals and zooxanthellae, a type of photosynthetic algae. These tiny algae reside within coral polyps, performing photosynthesis to transform sunlight into energy, which in turn supports the coral's growth and vibrancy. In exchange, the coral offers protection and access to sunlight, crucial for the algae's survival. This symbiosis not only maintains the coral's vibrant hues but also boosts its ability to withstand environmental changes, offering a sophisticated model of interdependence that could inspire innovative solutions to cooperative challenges in human endeavors.

As climate change accelerates, coral reefs confront growing threats from rising sea temperatures, acidification, and pollution. Yet, the symbiotic ties within these environments provide valuable lessons in adaptive resilience. Research indicates that some zooxanthellae strains have a higher tolerance to heat, suggesting that fostering diverse algal partnerships may enhance coral survival in warming oceans. This idea of diversifying relationships to improve resilience presents an intriguing model for organizations navigating unpredictable markets. By nurturing a wide range of collaborative relationships, businesses can bolster their adaptability and strengthen themselves against unforeseen challenges, much like corals thrive through their varied symbioses.

Beyond the coral-zooxanthellae relationship, numerous other symbiotic interactions contribute to reef strength. Fish and invertebrates engage in mutualistic partnerships with corals, such as cleaning stations where smaller fish remove parasites from larger marine creatures. These exchanges not only ensure individual health but also bolster ecosystem stability. Drawing parallels, modern organizations can learn from such interspecies collaborations by promoting cross-departmental cooperation and building environments where diverse talents and skills are leveraged for mutual benefit. Encouraging symbiotic relationships within organizations can lead to more resilient and innovative solutions, mirroring the intricate balance that sustains coral ecosystems.

Exploring coral symbiosis encourages reflection on the potential of biomimicry to tackle current challenges. Imagine designing urban spaces or technological systems that mimic reef ecosystems, where diverse entities coexist peacefully, enhancing each other's functions. Emerging technologies, such as AI and machine learning, can help map these natural interactions, offering insights into creating resilient infrastructures. This perspective highlights the transformative potential of observing natural systems to inspire human innovation, pushing the boundaries of what is possible by integrating nature's time-tested strategies into modern design and development.

By delving into the complexities of coral reef symbiosis, we discover a rich tapestry of collaboration, adaptability, and resilience that transcends oceanic boundaries. These interactions not only stabilize marine ecosystems but also provide profound insights for human society. Emulating these natural partnerships allows us to cultivate environments where flexibility and cooperation are the pillars of resilience. This perspective challenges us to rethink traditional approaches and invites us to harness the wisdom of coral reefs, reshaping our understanding of resilience and innovation in a constantly evolving world.

Biodiversity as a Pillar for Ecosystem Robustness in Coral Reefs

Biodiversity is essential for the fortitude of coral reefs, forming a dynamic network of life that thrives in changing conditions. Each species within these ecosystems plays a distinct role, contributing to their strength. This variety ensures that if one species faces environmental challenges, others can compensate, preserving ecological balance. Such interdependence acts as a natural safeguard, maintaining the vitality and functionality of coral reefs. The interactions among diverse species enhance the reefs' ability to recover from disturbances and continue delivering vital services.

Recent progress in marine biology has uncovered detailed mechanisms through which biodiversity bolsters resilience. Researchers have pinpointed traits in various coral species, like thermal resilience and disease resistance, that help them thrive in different environments. This genetic variability provides a buffer against climate change impacts, offering hope for coral reefs' future. By understanding these adaptive traits, scientists can develop conservation strategies that enhance reef ecosystems' natural resilience. This highlights the importance of protecting genetic diversity as a means to counteract global warming and ocean acidification effects.

Incorporating indigenous knowledge and traditional ecological practices brings valuable insights into conservation efforts. Indigenous communities, who have lived alongside coral reefs for centuries, possess deep understanding of these ecosystems' natural rhythms. Their sustainable harvesting methods and cultural practices underscore the interconnectedness of biodiversity and resilience. By blending these time-honored approaches with modern scientific research, conservation efforts become more comprehensive and effective. This integration enriches our comprehension of the complex dynamics that sustain coral reef ecosystems and emphasizes the importance of preserving cultural and biological diversity.

Innovative technologies are significantly improving our understanding of biodiversity's role in reef resilience. Advanced monitoring tools, such as remote sensing and AI, enable scientists to gather detailed data on reef health and species interactions. These technologies provide insights into how biodiversity supports ecological stability. By leveraging data analytics, researchers can predict how reefs will respond to future environmental changes and identify key areas for conservation. This progressive approach aids in developing targeted strategies that enhance coral reefs' natural resilience, ensuring their survival in a rapidly changing world.

The lessons from coral reef biodiversity extend to broader applications in ecosystem management and resilience building. By fostering diversity in agricultural systems, urban planning, and organizational structures, we can mimic coral reefs' adaptive strategies. Encouraging a diversity of ideas, species, and resources enhances human systems' ability to withstand shocks and stresses. Embracing diverse perspectives in problem-solving can lead to more robust outcomes. By drawing inspiration from nature, we can create resilient systems that thrive amidst uncertainty, mirroring the enduring strength of coral reef ecosystems.

Human Impact and Strategies for Enhancing Coral Reef Resilience

Human activities have greatly affected coral reefs, but innovative strategies are emerging to boost their endurance. These ecosystems face threats from overfishing, pollution, and climate change, which disturb their fragile balance. Recent research highlights the potential of marine protected areas (MPAs) to counter these effects. By limiting activities such as fishing and tourism in specific zones, MPAs allow ecosystems to rejuvenate and flourish. Studies indicate that these protected regions can enhance biodiversity and biomass, strengthening the resilience of adjacent reefs. Expanding MPAs strategically and managing them effectively can enable humans to play a crucial role in preserving these essential ecosystems.

Another promising approach involves restoring and rehabilitating damaged reefs using innovative coral gardening techniques. These methods involve growing coral fragments in nurseries and replanting them in degraded areas. Advances have led to the development of super corals—genetically enhanced strains with greater tolerance to temperature changes and acidification. Although these engineered corals present a potential solution, they must be integrated thoughtfully within ecosystems to prevent unintended outcomes. By combining traditional conservation methods with modern biotechnology, we can rejuvenate reefs while respecting their complex dynamics.

The role of local communities in reef conservation is vital. Empowering indigenous and coastal communities through education and participation in conservation initiatives ensures efforts are culturally relevant and sustainable. Traditional ecological knowledge, passed down through generations, offers valuable insights into maintaining reef health. Collaborative projects that blend this knowledge with scientific research have led to innovative management practices. By building partnerships among scientists, policymakers, and communities, we create a comprehensive approach that fortifies coral reef resilience.

Technology offers groundbreaking tools for monitoring and managing reef ecosystems. Remote sensing and drone technology enable precise mapping and real-time monitoring of reef health over large areas. Machine learning algorithms are used to analyze these data sets, providing insights into stress patterns and predicting future changes. This data-driven approach equips conservationists with the information needed to devise timely and effective interventions. By embracing technology, we can improve our ability to protect these ecosystems amid growing challenges.

Imagining a future where coral reefs thrive requires a holistic understanding of their intricate dynamics and the proactive application of diverse solutions. Encouraging sustainable tourism, adopting eco-friendly practices, and enforcing regulations to reduce pollution are essential steps. Moreover, fostering global awareness about the importance of coral reefs can drive collective action. As individuals, policymakers, and corporations recognize the interconnectedness of human actions and reef health, we stand a better chance of preserving these vibrant ecosystems for future generations.

Redundancy and Flexibility in the Nervous System

Embark on a journey into one of nature's most fascinating phenomena: the nervous system's unique capacity to function and adapt amidst challenges. Envision a vast web of pathways, intricately linked yet ready to support or even replace one another when disruptions arise. This is the core of redundancy and flexibility within neural circuits—a remarkable display of resilience. In a world where change is constant, the design of the nervous system sheds light on navigating and thriving through life's uncertainties. As we delve into these complex biological processes, we uncover not just survival tactics but also strategies for thriving in unpredictable conditions. The nervous system's sturdiness offers a masterclass in preparing for the unforeseen, presenting a model for resilience that goes beyond biology.

Each neuron and synapse contributes to a grand symphony of adaptability and strength. The redundancy in neural circuits serves as a safety net against failure, ensuring that if one pathway stumbles, others stand ready to compensate. This is enhanced by the brain's incredible plasticity, enabling it to rewire and adjust to new circumstances. Distributed processing further enhances this flexibility, allowing the brain to tackle complex challenges with agility. These mechanisms, honed over millions of years of evolution, create a system that not only withstands disruptions but also evolves with them. As we explore these natural strategies, we gain inspiration for human endeavors, from building resilient organizations to fostering personal adaptability. The nervous system offers a rich tapestry of insights, providing a dynamic framework for navigating the unpredictable world.

Neural Circuit Redundancy as a Buffer Against Failure

The resilience of nature is embodied in the nervous system's ingenious use of neural circuit redundancy, which acts as a protective measure against potential failures. This design ensures that multiple neural pathways can perform similar functions, safeguarding critical processes even when parts of the system fail. Such redundancy serves as a biological safety net, allowing organisms to remain functional despite damage or loss. For example, stroke patients often experience undamaged brain areas compensating for impaired regions, showcasing the system's inherent strength. This adaptability is not merely a fallback but a dynamic feature highlighting the nervous system's evolutionary prowess.

Neural redundancy offers both stability and flexibility, essential in unpredictable environments. By having various neural routes to achieve the same goal, organisms can better manage sudden changes or disruptions, ensuring survival and success. This concept has influenced artificial intelligence, where redundant algorithms enhance system reliability and fault tolerance. By emulating the brain's design, engineers create systems that can self-correct and adapt swiftly.

Neuroscience research continues to uncover the complexities of redundancy, exploring its role in learning and memory. Studies show that redundant circuits boost the brain's plasticity, enabling it to remodel itself in response to new experiences and environments. This insight encourages reevaluating redundancy's application beyond biology. For instance, businesses can adopt redundancy by forming cross-functional teams capable of maintaining workflow during unexpected challenges. Organizations embracing such flexibility can better navigate the complexities of today's rapidly changing landscape.

The principles of neural redundancy extend to personal development, emphasizing the importance of cultivating diverse skills and pathways in life. Just as the brain uses multiple circuits to ensure continuity, individuals can benefit from developing a range of competencies to adapt to different circumstances. Encouraging a mindset that values diverse skills and perspectives enhances personal resilience, fostering creativity and innovation. This approach, inspired by the brain's architecture, provides a strategic advantage in an increasingly interconnected world.

By exploring the evolutionary mechanisms that have shaped neural redundancy, one gains a deeper understanding of its role in fortitude. This biological insight raises broader questions—how can we design systems, in both technology and society, that embody this principle? Integrating redundancy as a core design element can lead to more resilient infrastructures that withstand and adapt to unforeseen challenges. By looking to the natural world as a guide, we unlock the potential to create systems that mirror the robustness and adaptability found in nature's most intricate designs.

Plasticity and Adaptation in Neural Pathways

Neural pathways possess an extraordinary ability to adapt and transform, captivating both neuroscientists and innovators. This transformation is more than a biological curiosity; it's a crucial mechanism that lets organisms adeptly tackle environmental challenges. At its heart, neural plasticity is the brain's ability to reorganize by forming new connections, dynamically responding to stimuli. This adaptability acts as a safeguard against damage, allowing the nervous system to function even when certain pathways are compromised. Consequently, the brain's flexibility serves as an inspiring model for creating systems that thrive amidst uncertainty and change.

Pioneering research on neuroplasticity has shown how experiences, learning, and even injuries can reshape the brain's structure. Studies of stroke survivors reveal that targeted rehabilitation and cognitive exercises enable other brain regions to compensate for lost functions. This insight into the brain's transformative power holds significant potential for developing adaptive systems across various fields. In artificial intelligence, for instance, algorithms can be designed to mimic this plasticity, enabling machines to learn and adapt in real-time, akin to a human brain continuously refining its pathways in response to feedback.

Neural plasticity is further demonstrated by synaptic pruning, where redundant connections are eliminated to enhance network efficiency. This biological strategy offers lessons in optimization and resource allocation, applicable not only to biological systems but also to organizational structures and technological frameworks. By adopting this principle, businesses can streamline inefficient processes, fostering continuous improvement that's both effective and resilient. Applying this 'pruning' concept to problem-solving strategies enables the evolution of efficient methodologies that adapt to shifting circumstances.

In terms of resilience, neural plasticity highlights adaptability as vital for survival. Cultivating an environment that encourages flexibility and innovation allows organizations and individuals to better prepare for unforeseen challenges. This adaptability isn't just reactive but proactive, anticipating and mitigating potential disruptions. By fostering a mindset that values continuous learning, the principles of neural plasticity can enhance resilience across diverse fields, from education to technology, creating systems as robust and versatile as the neural networks they emulate.

Reflecting on neural plasticity's implications reveals that its lessons extend beyond neuroscience. These insights challenge us to rethink traditional problem-solving approaches, advocating for models that prioritize adaptability and learning. By drawing inspiration from the brain's inherent ability to evolve, we can craft innovative solutions that are not only resilient but also naturally aligned with sophisticated designs. Embracing this approach, we open the door to a new era of innovation that sees complexity and change as opportunities for growth and advancement.

Distributed Processing for Enhanced Brain Flexibility

The human brain's extraordinary capability to adapt and overcome challenges is deeply rooted in its distributed processing architecture. This decentralized setup enables various regions to collaborate, sharing tasks and information to bolster overall flexibility. Unlike systems that depend heavily on a single control point, the brain's design ensures that if one area is compromised, others can step in, maintaining functionality and endurance. This seamless interaction enhances both cognitive agility and the brain's ability to recover from injuries. Recent research in neuroinformatics highlights how this distributed nature optimizes processing speed and efficiency, enabling quick adjustments to constantly shifting environments.

Picture a vibrant city where each neighborhood has a distinct role but can cover for another when necessary. This city mirrors the brain's distributed processing system. Such redundancy ensures that vital functions persist even when parts of the system are under stress. This concept has inspired innovations in artificial intelligence and robotics, where systems are crafted to emulate this flexibility, enabling machines to adapt to unexpected situations without complete operational failure. These advancements point towards a future where technology mirrors the brain's robustness, creating systems less susceptible to breakdowns.

Delving deeper into this idea, distributed processing offers valuable insights for modern organizational challenges. Today's businesses can gain by decentralizing decision-making processes, empowering departments to operate independently while collaborating effectively. This strategy not only boosts resilience but also sparks innovation, as diverse teams bring unique perspectives to problem-solving. Applying distributed processing principles can transform rigid corporate structures into adaptive, innovative entities that thrive in unpredictable environments, much like the neural networks they emulate.

The concept of distributed processing also intersects with the emerging field of network neuroscience, which examines how the brain's network architecture influences cognition and behavior. Understanding these neural connections helps researchers uncover how distributed processing contributes to learning and memory consolidation. This knowledge is paving the way for new therapeutic strategies to treat neurological disorders, leveraging the brain's inherent adaptability. As science advances, the potential to harness distributed processing principles for enhancing human cognitive function becomes increasingly feasible.

To fully capitalize on the power of distributed processing, it's essential to consider applying these principles across various domains. Whether in engineering, education, or healthcare, the ability to distribute tasks and processes can lead to more resilient systems. By fostering environments where flexibility and redundancy are integral, individuals and organizations can better navigate complexity and uncertainty. As we continue to draw inspiration from nature's most sophisticated systems, the potential for groundbreaking advancements across multiple fields remains vast and promising.

Evolutionary Mechanisms of Nervous System Resilience

Exploring the evolutionary strategies that fortify the nervous system reveals a captivating array of biological brilliance. Over countless generations, natural selection has shaped neural designs capable of enduring disruptions and thriving under challenging conditions. A notable example is the concept of neural circuit redundancy, where multiple pathways fulfill similar roles. This redundancy serves as a protective measure, ensuring that if one pathway fails, others can step in to maintain function. Beyond being mere backups, these pathways allow the nervous system to distribute tasks and dynamically adjust to shifting circumstances, fostering strength against potential threats.

The extraordinary adaptability of neural pathways further illustrates evolutionary resilience. Neural plasticity—the brain's ability to reorganize by forming new connections—is fundamental to this adaptability. This dynamic trait is most visible in the process of learning and recovery from injuries, where the brain remodels itself to enhance performance or make up for lost functions. This plasticity not only highlights the nervous system's inherent flexibility but also its capacity for ongoing growth and evolution. Such adaptive traits can inspire innovative approaches in fields like artificial intelligence, where systems might evolve more naturally to tackle new challenges.

Distributed processing is another evolutionary wonder that boosts the nervous system's flexibility. Unlike a centralized control model, where a single point of failure can cripple the system, distributed processing enables parallel operations and decentralizes control, reducing susceptibility to breakdowns. This method resembles a network of nodes that independently process information, share insights, and collectively adjust to ensure optimal performance. In technological innovation, this principle can inspire decentralized organizational structures and collaborative networks that mirror the resilience found in biological systems.

The evolutionary journey of the nervous system is marked by a series of adaptations that have continuously enhanced its fortitude. For instance, the diversification of neurotransmitter systems offers a refined mechanism for adjusting responses to stimuli. By employing a variety of chemical messengers, the nervous system can tailor its reactions to specific environmental conditions, boosting its ability to handle diverse challenges. This evolutionary strategy underscores the significance of diversity and complexity in fostering resilience, a lesson applicable to crafting multifaceted solutions in complex human systems.

As we contemplate the evolutionary insights embedded within the nervous system, intriguing questions emerge: How can we emulate the brain's fortitude in our systems and structures? Can we create environments that encourage plasticity and redundancy, ensuring that our organizations and technologies remain adaptable and strong? By examining these evolutionary lessons, we gain valuable perspectives on designing systems that not only endure but also flourish amid uncertainty. The nervous system, with its intricate balance of redundancy, plasticity, and distributed processing, offers a model for creating resilient entities capable of navigating the unpredictable landscapes of both nature and human enterprise.

Designing Resilient Organizations: Lessons from Nature

Picture an organization that not only survives but flourishes in the midst of disorder, using unpredictability as a catalyst for growth. Nature, with its wealth of knowledge, offers a guide for building such resilience. Across its varied terrains, natural systems have evolved to withstand and adapt to the harshest conditions. When these principles are woven into organizational frameworks, they can create entities that not only withstand challenges but also transform through them. Just as coral reefs maintain ecological balance despite external disturbances, organizations can achieve fortitude by embracing strategies perfected by nature over eons. Delving into nature's resilient designs unveils a realm of opportunities for crafting organizations that are both robust and innovative.

The path to creating resilient organizations starts with embracing redundancy and diversity. Much like ecosystems that depend on a variety of species for equilibrium, organizations can bolster resilience by encouraging diversity in perspectives, skills, and resources. Next, adaptive structures inspired by ecosystem dynamics serve as the foundation for agile and responsive organizations. Nature's feedback loops, another marvel, enhance stability while fostering continuous learning and adjustment. By incorporating evolutionary principles, organizations can develop systems that grow stronger under pressure. These interconnected strategies lay the groundwork for organizations capable of navigating modern complexities with confidence and insight.

Embracing Redundancy and Diversity for Organizational Resilience

In the ever-changing landscape of today's world, organizational endurance is crucial, and nature provides valuable lessons for creating resilient frameworks. A key insight from natural ecosystems is the importance of redundancy. In biology, redundancy means having multiple pathways or components that perform similar tasks, ensuring that if one fails, others can fill the gap. The human brain, with its complex neural networks, exemplifies this by adapting to injuries while maintaining functionality. Organizations can adopt this principle by developing overlapping roles, cross-training employees, and setting up backup systems, making them better equipped to handle unexpected challenges.

Diversity, another vital element of ecological resilience, strengthens an organization's capacity to navigate change. Ecosystems rich in biodiversity are often more robust because various species can adapt to different stressors. This concept can be applied to the corporate world by fostering a workforce diverse in skills, backgrounds, and perspectives. A team with varied viewpoints can generate innovative solutions and adapt quickly. Organizations that embrace diversity can better respond to market or industry shifts by leveraging a wide range of experiences and ideas.

Research increasingly highlights the importance of diversity and redundancy for fostering resilient organizations. Studies indicate that companies with diverse teams and redundant systems outperform others in innovation and crisis management. Research in organizational behavior shows that heterogeneous groups excel in tackling complex problems. With a mix of skills and experiences, these teams can approach challenges from multiple angles, discovering solutions that might elude more uniform groups. The redundancy of knowledge within diverse teams ensures that crucial skills and information are shared across the organization.

Incorporating redundancy and diversity requires thoughtful strategy and foresight. Leaders should cultivate a culture that values these principles, encouraging an environment where employees feel empowered to share ideas and assume different roles as needed. This can be achieved through policies promoting continuous learning, flexible job roles, and inclusive recruitment practices.

It's also essential to implement feedback mechanisms that allow for ongoing evaluation and improvement of these strategies, similar to the natural feedback loops in ecosystems.

Consider a scenario where an organization faces a sudden technological disruption. An entity that has embraced redundancy and diversity will be more agile in adapting. Its cross-trained employees can transition into new roles, while its diverse team can devise innovative solutions. Reflecting on this, organizations should ask: Are we ready to pivot quickly if our current strategies falter? How can we build a workforce that mirrors the adaptability and resilience found in nature? By addressing these questions, businesses can transform lessons from nature into a strategy for enduring success.

Adaptive Structures Inspired by Ecosystem Dynamics

In the ever-changing realm of nature, ecosystems showcase an impressive ability to adapt, offering valuable lessons for building resilient organizations. These natural networks thrive on flexibility, thriving through decentralized interactions among diverse species. This design allows ecosystems to remain robust amidst unpredictability. Organizations can learn from this by nurturing diversity and interconnectedness within their structures, ensuring they stay strong when faced with challenges. This approach fosters innovative solutions and growth, akin to the adaptability seen in flourishing ecosystems.

Recent research on ecosystem resilience emphasizes the value of modular structures. In nature, modularity lets parts operate semi-independently while contributing to a unified whole. Organizations can mirror this by adopting modular designs, where teams work autonomously yet align with overarching goals. This enables swift responses to change without sacrificing stability. Such a framework enhances innovation and strengthens an organization's ability to withstand shocks, much like how coral reefs endure stress through their compartmentalized but interconnected nature.

Organizations can also draw inspiration from ecosystems' self-regulating mechanisms. Feedback loops are crucial for maintaining balance in nature, and organizations can implement similar processes to optimize operations. Real-time feedback allows for quick adjustments in response to both internal and external shifts, embedding continuous improvement into the organizational culture. This mirrors how ecosystems sustain equilibrium, constantly adapting to ensure resilience.

Adopting ecological dynamics requires a shift in perspective, encouraging organizations to view challenges as opportunities for growth. This mindset, akin to evolutionary adaptation, can lead to systems that are not only resilient but also antifragile, thriving amidst chaos. By embracing uncertainty, organizations can cultivate a proactive culture of resilience, drawing strength from challenges that might destabilize less adaptable entities.

Applying ecosystem principles to organizational design involves balancing diversity, autonomy, and interdependence. Organizations must create structures that are flexible yet coherent, diverse yet focused. By learning from nature's adaptive strategies, organizations can develop systems that not only endure change but also leverage it for new potential, positioning themselves as innovators and leaders in resilience. Nature offers a roadmap for organizations aiming to transcend traditional boundaries and redefine success in a constantly evolving world.

Leveraging Natural Feedback Loops to Enhance Stability

Feedback loops are crucial in maintaining the delicate balance within ecosystems, from lush forests to vast oceans. These natural cycles of input, processing, and output ensure homeostasis, offering valuable insights for organizations seeking to create steady and resilient structures. For example, predator-prey interactions demonstrate how feedback mechanisms regulate populations, preventing the dominance of one species over another. Analogously, companies can implement feedback systems to monitor and adjust resources, employee performance, and market strategies, promoting stability and adaptability.

Incorporating feedback loops in organizations not only stabilizes operations but also enhances flexibility in unpredictable scenarios. Consider the self-regulating nature of climate systems, like the ocean's role in carbon capture. These natural processes inspire businesses to establish systems that consistently gather feedback from customer interactions, market trends, and internal metrics. Utilizing advanced technologies such as AI and machine learning can process this information in real time, allowing businesses to swiftly respond to changes and make informed decisions that bolster endurance.

Beyond maintaining stability, feedback loops can ignite innovation and growth. In biology, genetic feedback loops drive evolution, enabling species to adapt over time. Organizations can emulate this by fostering a culture where feedback is actively sought and used to fuel innovation. Encouraging open communication and iterative development, where feedback is integrated into product and service design, can lead to continuous improvement. This proactive approach transforms feedback from a reactive measure into a strategic tool for growth.

Despite their benefits, feedback loops can have drawbacks. In nature, unchecked feedback can lead to disruptions like algal blooms. Similarly, organizations must be wary of echo chambers and confirmation biases, where feedback merely reinforces existing beliefs. By diversifying feedback sources and integrating independent perspectives, organizations can avoid these pitfalls, ensuring feedback remains constructive and promotes true adaptability.

To fully leverage feedback loops, organizations can take specific steps. First, establish transparent channels for collecting feedback across all levels, ensuring diverse insights. Use data analytics to interpret this information, revealing patterns and trends. Cultivate a culture of experimentation, where feedback is used to test and refine ideas, fostering continuous learning. By embracing these principles, organizations can evolve into dynamic systems capable of thriving amidst uncertainty and change, much like the resilient ecosystems they seek to emulate.

Building Antifragile Systems Through Evolutionary Principles

Living organisms have flourished for thousands of years by not merely surviving chaos but using it to evolve and thrive. This concept of antifragility seen in nature offers a fresh perspective for building organizations that prosper amid uncertainty. While traditional risk management focuses on harm reduction, nature shows us that successful systems harness volatility as a driver for growth. By viewing organizations as living entities rather than static structures, leaders can create environments where challenges and disruptions lead to learning, adaptation, and increased resilience.

The principles of evolutionary biology provide valuable insights for developing antifragile organizations. Evolution functions through countless trials, where diverse strategies are tested, and only the adaptable endure. Organizations can emulate this by cultivating a culture of experimentation and learning. Encouraging small-scale trials and viewing failures as opportunities for learning fosters an innovative ecosystem. This iterative method, similar to natural selection, ensures continuous improvement and adaptation to changing circumstances.

Antifragile systems also benefit from decentralized decision-making, reflecting the distributed intelligence found in nature. Consider the decentralized nature of ant colonies or the self-organized behavior of bird flocks; each member acts on local information, yet the group accomplishes complex objectives. Organizations can mirror this by empowering teams and individuals to make ground-level decisions, leveraging local insights and agility. Such decentralized structures not only enhance responsiveness but also tap into collective wisdom and creativity.

To further nurture antifragility, organizations can incorporate feedback mechanisms akin to nature's continuous feedback loops. In ecosystems, these loops maintain balance and foster growth, ensuring resilience against disruptions. By creating systems that capture real-time data and insights, organizations can dynamically adapt strategies, aligning with shifting external conditions. Feedback loops function as sensors, enabling timely responses to threats and opportunities, thus sustaining organizational vitality.

Envisioning organizations that not only withstand but thrive on volatility challenges traditional management philosophies. What if organizations grew stronger with each disruption? By adopting nature's evolutionary principles, embracing diversity, decentralization, and experimentation, organizations can turn challenges into opportunities for innovation and growth. This dynamic approach cultivates an environment where antifragility becomes a core philosophy, allowing organizations to become more robust, adaptive, and innovative in the face of uncertainty.

As we conclude our journey into the essence of resilience, we discover nature's remarkable teachings on enduring and flourishing amid uncertainty. From the resilience of coral reefs stabilizing ecosystems to the nervous system's creative use of redundancy and adaptability, nature reveals diverse strategies that promote longevity and flexibility. These lessons inform us in designing organizations capable of thriving through inevitable upheavals. By embracing these natural principles, both businesses and individuals can establish a dynamic foundation for resilience, crafting environments that not only withstand but also leverage change. This chapter's insights remind us that resilience involves more than enduring challenges; it involves transforming them into pathways for growth. As we continue our exploration of nature's innovative blueprint, reflect on how these lessons in resilience can be integrated into your life and work, encouraging you to consider: How can you utilize nature's resilience to better navigate your own challenges?

Chapter Three

Adaptation Evolving To Meet New Challenges

Imagine a world where the only certainty is change—a place where thriving demands not just strength, but a remarkable ability to adjust. Nature has perfected this art over billions of years. Visualize a minuscule bacterium flourishing in hostile environments where other life forms would perish, or a flock of birds crossing vast distances, altering their routes with stunning accuracy. These aren't just tales of survival; they showcase nature's unrivaled flair for transformation. As we delve into this exploration, consider how these evolutionary successes can guide and motivate our own strategies in the ever-evolving realms of business, technology, and personal development.

Thriving isn't merely about enduring; it's about flourishing amid unpredictability. Nature's knack for quickly crafting solutions in real-time highlights its genius. From the chameleon that shifts its hue based on environmental signals to the octopus that blends seamlessly into its surroundings, these adaptive methods reveal a deep intelligence beyond human inventions. How often have we faced market upheavals or technological shifts and longed for a piece of this natural adaptability? Tapping into such mechanisms offers vast potential for business creativity, paving the way for dynamic, flexible systems that respond effortlessly to fresh data and evolving demands.

This chapter weaves a narrative that connects the evolutionary flexibility seen in diverse species with the transformative power of adaptive business models. By translating nature's inherent versatility into practical frameworks, we open up new avenues for resilience and growth. As you journey through this examination of change and adaptation, you'll discover insights that challenge traditional thinking and encourage innovative solutions to contemporary challenges. In nature's grand experiment, adaptability is not a choice—it is an essential. Let's uncover how its lessons can enable us to advance and excel in our own pursuits.

Evolutionary Adaptability in Species: From Bacteria to Birds

Across the ages, the theme of adaptation has intrigued humanity, revealing nature's remarkable capacity to flourish amid ever-changing environments. From the tiny yet complex genetic shifts in bacteria to the expansive diversity of bird species, nature's adaptability showcases an array of strategies honed over millennia for survival and success. This ongoing dance with change is not confined to the annals of history but is an active process that continually unfolds, offering a wealth of inspiration for tackling today's challenges. The many forms of nature's adaptability highlight a fundamental truth: evolving and adjusting are vital for resilience and progress in our dynamic world.

In this journey of exploring evolutionary flexibility, we will first venture into the world of microbes, where bacteria rapidly change their genetic makeup to tackle environmental pressures. Next, we'll explore the phenomenon of adaptive radiation in birds, illustrating how they have diversified in response to ecological opportunities. Epigenetics adds another fascinating layer, showing how organisms can adapt without altering their DNA sequence. Finally, by comparing various species, we will uncover a spectrum of adaptive techniques, providing valuable insights for applying these natural principles to human endeavors. Together, these themes create a rich narrative of adaptation, encouraging readers to draw on nature's wisdom for crafting innovative solutions.

Microbial Mastery of Genetic Variation

Microbial organisms, often seen as basic life forms, reveal a rich landscape of genetic diversity that drives their impressive adaptability. Bacteria and archaea, among these microorganisms, possess a distinct genetic toolkit enabling them to flourish in varied and sometimes extreme habitats. This adaptability is a result of their rapid mutation and ability to exchange genetic material through processes like horizontal gene transfer, which helps them acquire beneficial traits from their environment. This genetic flexibility is not just a survival tactic but a sophisticated form of microscopic innovation. It challenges the traditional view of evolution as a slow, gradual process and instead showcases a dynamic system capable of quick adaptation to environmental shifts.

Consider antibiotic resistance, a phenomenon that highlights microbial expertise in genetic variation. Bacteria can become resistant to antibiotics through spontaneous mutations or by obtaining resistance genes from others. This quick adaptation to new threats not only underscores the tenacity of microbial life but also its potential to inspire innovative medical and biotechnological strategies. By examining these mechanisms, researchers can devise novel approaches to combat antibiotic resistance, such as developing drugs that target bacterial communication or using bacteriophages to target resistant populations. This microbial ingenuity encourages us to rethink solutions in healthcare and beyond, highlighting the need for adaptable, multi-faceted strategies.

In genetic variation, the CRISPR-Cas9 system emerges as a groundbreaking discovery. Originating from bacterial immune systems, this gene-editing technology exemplifies how insights from microbial genetics can drive innovation in genetic engineering. CRISPR allows precise modifications of genetic material, opening new frontiers in biotechnology, agriculture, and medicine. Its potential applications are vast, from creating disease-resistant crops to advancing gene therapies for genetic disorders. By drawing inspiration from microbial strategies, scientists are developing tools that can transform industries and improve human well-being, illustrating how biological systems can inspire technological revolutions.

Beyond practical applications, studying microbial genetic variation offers philosophical insights into innovation. Microorganisms show that innovation doesn't always require complex structures or large-scale systems; sometimes, the smallest entities display the greatest ingenuity. This perspective encourages valuing diversity and flexibility in our endeavors, recognizing that solutions may arise from unexpected sources. By adopting a mindset that embraces change and fosters experimentation, we can cultivate a culture of innovation akin to the adaptive success of microbial life.

Exploring microbial genetic variation prompts us to consider applying these principles to broader contexts, like business or personal growth. Just as bacteria adapt to survive and thrive, organizations and individuals can build resilience by embracing change and fostering environments that encourage experimentation and learning. This microbial perspective challenges our approach to problem-solving, urging strategies that prioritize flexibility, collaboration, and continuous adaptation in an ever-evolving world. Through this exploration, we gain a deeper appreciation for microbial life's sophistication and valuable insights into the art of innovation itself.

Adaptive Radiation in Avian Speciation

Birds provide a remarkable illustration of nature's adaptability through adaptive radiation, where a single species diversifies into numerous forms to occupy different ecological roles. Darwin's finches on the Galápagos Islands are a prime example. These birds evolved from a common ancestor, developing various beak shapes and sizes tailored to their specific diets and environmental needs. This diversification demonstrates nature's ingenuity, driven by the need to survive and flourish in diverse habitats. The finches' evolution is not just a historical tale but a vivid example of ongoing evolution, with environmental pressures sparking biological creativity.

Recent research has shed light on the intricate mechanisms behind adaptive radiation, highlighting advanced genetic and developmental pathways. Genomic sequencing has pinpointed the genes responsible for variations like beak shapes in Darwin's finches. These discoveries reveal the complex interaction between genetic potential and environmental cues. The swift evolution of new traits in response to ecological opportunities showcases nature's problem-solving prowess. Understanding these genetic frameworks offers insights into how life on Earth continuously evolves, providing a valuable model for human innovation in the face of rapid change.

Beyond finches, Hawaiian honeycreepers present another fascinating case of adaptive radiation, diversifying from a single ancestor in an isolated environment with ample ecological roles. These birds have evolved specialized traits, including varied beak forms and feeding behaviors, allowing them to exploit diverse food sources. This rapid diversification underscores adaptive radiation's potential to generate biodiversity and fill ecological gaps. Such natural processes can inspire resilient strategies in human contexts, promoting adaptability in business models or technological advancement.

Lessons from avian adaptive radiation extend beyond ecological narratives, offering a blueprint for strategic flexibility. In business, organizations can draw parallels by encouraging diverse strategies and rapid idea development. Just as birds adapt to new niches, companies can succeed by identifying and responding to emerging market opportunities. This requires openness to experimentation and the ability to pivot swiftly in changing circumstances. By embracing nature's adaptive methods, businesses can boost their resilience and growth potential.

Exploring adaptive radiation's broader implications reveals that nature's solutions are not just biological curiosities but profound sources of innovation. Readers are encouraged to reflect on their own adaptability, considering how they might apply these principles to personal or organizational challenges. What untapped opportunities exist in their lives or industries, and how might they evolve to seize them? By applying the lessons of adaptive radiation, individuals and organizations can adopt a future-oriented approach, ready to navigate the complexities of an ever-changing world.

The Role of Epigenetics in Evolutionary Flexibility

Epigenetics, exploring inheritable shifts in gene activity without DNA sequence changes, is pivotal in how species adapt evolutionarily. This agile system enables organisms to react promptly to environmental changes, bypassing the lengthy genetic mutation process. Modifications like DNA methylation and histone changes serve as switches, activating or deactivating genes, thus adapting an organism's traits to its surroundings. This adaptability is vital for thriving in ever-changing ecosystems, offering a rapid-response capability that complements genetic evolution.

Consider the peppered moth during England's Industrial Revolution. The increase in soot-darkened landscapes caused a shift from light to dark-colored moths. While typically viewed as a natural selection example illustrating genetic evolution, recent studies suggest epigenetic mechanisms might have also facilitated this swift adaptation. By altering gene expression in response to environmental cues, epigenetics can propel changes across generations, helping species address swiftly evolving challenges. This insight not only deepens our understanding of evolutionary biology but also provides a model for businesses to adapt rapidly to market changes with precision.

In agriculture, epigenetic knowledge is spurring innovations to boost crop resilience. Researchers are investigating how epigenetic changes can create plant varieties resistant to drought, pests, and diseases. For instance, introducing specific epigenetic markers in crops has increased their tolerance to extreme weather, a critical development amid climate change. By emulating nature's adaptive capabilities, agronomists are fostering more robust and sustainable agricultural systems. These advances highlight epigenetics' potential to drive breakthroughs beyond biology, inspiring adaptable strategies in diverse sectors like technology and finance.

This expanding field of epigenetics also prompts reflection on inheritance and identity. Unlike the static nature of genetic code, epigenetic patterns are flexible, influenced by lifestyle, diet, and social interactions. This discovery challenges traditional views on heredity, suggesting adaptability seeds are not only planted at conception but also cultivated throughout life. It raises intriguing questions about human agency in shaping biological and cultural destinies. As we unravel these intricate inheritance layers, we unlock new possibilities for personal growth and societal innovation.

For those aiming to apply epigenetic principles practically, the key is creating environments that nurture adaptability. Businesses can foster a learning culture, enabling teams to pivot quickly in response to new information or market shifts. Similarly, individuals can harness epigenetics' adaptive potential by adopting lifestyle changes promoting well-being and resilience. Lessons from nature's epigenetic strategies offer a compelling framework for tackling modern challenges, envisioning a future where adaptability is not just biologically essential but also a strategic edge.

Comparative Analysis of Adaptive Strategies Across Taxa

Exploring adaptive strategies across diverse life forms reveals a vibrant array of evolutionary creativity. Each organism, from the tiniest bacterium to the most majestic bird, has developed unique methods to adapt over countless generations. At the microbial level, bacteria exhibit exceptional flexibility by engaging in horizontal gene transfer, which enables them to acquire new genetic traits and quickly respond to environmental changes. This process resembles an open-source system in nature, where genetic information circulates freely to tackle new challenges. In contrast, complex organisms often depend on genetic recombination and mutations through generations, offering a slower but equally effective adaptation mechanism.

Birds provide a fascinating glimpse into adaptive evolution through their diverse species. The phenomenon of adaptive radiation, as seen in Darwin's finches, demonstrates how a single ancestral species can evolve into multiple forms to exploit different ecological niches. This highlights the role of resource availability and environmental conditions in shaping biodiversity. Additionally, many bird species show phenotypic plasticity, adjusting physical traits like beak shape or plumage in response to immediate environmental shifts. This ability to modify characteristics without altering genetic makeup underscores a flexible survival strategy, balancing genetic determinism with environmental influence.

Epigenetics adds another dimension to adaptability by examining how organisms can regulate gene expression in reaction to external factors without changing their DNA sequence. Mechanisms like DNA methylation allow species to respond swiftly to environmental signals, sometimes within a single generation. These temporary yet potent changes can be inherited by offspring, representing a sophisticated adaptation tool. Such mechanisms reveal nature's complexity and offer insights into how humans might leverage similar processes for advancements in health or technology.

Comparing adaptive strategies uncovers not only the diverse mechanisms across species but also shared themes that transcend individual boundaries. Whether through genetic mutations, phenotypic flexibility, or epigenetic changes, the themes of creativity, endurance, and resourcefulness echo throughout the natural world. Examining these strategies provides a deeper understanding of life's success across various environments, offering a wealth of solutions for contemporary human challenges. Recognizing these parallels encourages an interdisciplinary approach, drawing from biological principles to inspire innovation in diverse fields like engineering and urban planning.

As readers delve into these adaptive strategies, they are prompted to consider their applications beyond biology. How might businesses mimic microbial adaptability in fast-changing markets? Could urban planners draw lessons from avian speciation to build more resilient cities? By exploring these questions, this journey not only enhances our appreciation of nature's wisdom but also challenges us to apply these lessons creatively and proactively. In doing so, we cultivate a mindset attuned to adaptation, equipping ourselves to navigate the ever-evolving landscapes of the modern world with agility and insight.

Rapid Prototyping: How Nature Adjusts in Real-Time

Nature's unparalleled ability to innovate rests on its remarkable capacity for swift adaptation—a dynamic interplay of trial, error, and instant recalibration that unfolds across diverse ecosystems and species. This natural process exemplifies the power of flexibility, demonstrating how life forms, from the tiniest microbes to intricate animal communities, navigate the ever-shifting landscapes of their environments. Faced with challenges, organisms in nature don't merely react; they evolve, fine-tuning their approaches through an ongoing interaction with their surroundings. This agility is a testament to resilience, offering a wealth of insights for those keen to harness nature's time-tested methods to tackle modern issues.

In this journey, we delve into the extraordinary mechanisms driving these rapid transformations. Nature's feedback systems offer a constant flow of information, enabling quick recalibrations in real time. Genetic mutations serve as a potent mechanism, allowing life forms to pivot and flourish amidst abrupt changes. Epigenetic shifts further illustrate environmental flexibility, showing how external factors can influence gene expression without altering the DNA itself. Additionally, the fluid dynamics within symbiotic relationships and ecosystems underscore the interconnectedness of life, where collaboration fuels swift change. By exploring these processes, we unveil a blueprint for agile innovation, relevant to business, technology, and personal growth alike.

Nature's Feedback Loops and Real-Time Adjustments

Nature's feedback loops demonstrate an extraordinary capacity to adjust dynamically, weaving a complex web of interconnected processes. These loops are crucial for preserving ecological balance, enabling organisms to rapidly adapt to environmental shifts. The predator-prey relationship typifies this concept, as changes in prey numbers naturally lead to corresponding fluctuations in predator populations, achieving equilibrium. In coral reefs, studies have shown that coral polyps sense slight variations in water temperature and acidity, prompting physiological changes that enhance their survival in challenging conditions. This self-regulation secures resilience and offers a model for innovative solutions in human systems.

Advancements in computational biology reveal how these feedback systems can propel technological and industrial innovation. Engineers are integrating feedback loop principles into autonomous vehicle design, allowing for real-time adjustments to traffic and road conditions. Mimicking the self-correcting traits of biological systems, these vehicles aim for improved safety and efficiency. Additionally, smart energy grids utilize similar concepts to optimize electricity distribution in response to real-time demand changes. These applications highlight the transformative potential of feedback loops in addressing complex global challenges.

A deeper comprehension of these natural processes can reshape our approach to personal development and decision-making. Embracing the iterative nature of feedback loops encourages individuals to develop adaptability and resilience in everyday life. For instance, mindfulness practice involves continuous self-evaluation and adjustment to sustain mental health, mirroring nature's feedback mechanisms and offering a framework for personal growth. By adopting a mindset of continuous improvement, akin to nature's iterative processes, individuals can experience significant transformations in both personal and professional spheres.

Exploring feedback loops requires openness to various interpretations and applications. While often associated with stability, some researchers suggest these systems can spur innovation by allowing exploration of new possibilities. By challenging existing norms and fostering experimentation, feedback loops can lead to breakthroughs across multiple fields. This perspective invites consideration of how we can leverage these self-regulating mechanisms to foster creativity and progress, rather than merely maintaining the status quo.

To apply the insights from nature's feedback loops, consider practical steps for integration into organizational strategies or personal routines. Establish systems for regular feedback collection and analysis, facilitating prompt responses to emerging challenges. In business environments, this might involve implementing agile methodologies for rapid pivots based on customer feedback or market trends. On a personal level, cultivating a habit of regular self-reflection and adaptation can enhance problem-solving skills and resilience. By internalizing these principles, both individuals and organizations can thrive in dynamic environments, drawing inspiration from nature's remarkable adaptability.

Genetic Mutations as a Rapid Response Mechanism

Genetic mutations serve as nature's rapid adaptation tools, enabling organisms to swiftly adjust to environmental challenges. These changes in DNA, while often random, can prove advantageous by bestowing new traits that improve survival or reproduction. In the microbial realm, bacteria exemplify this by evolving resistance to antibiotics, highlighting their evolutionary agility. As antibiotics impose selective pressure, only bacteria with beneficial mutations endure and proliferate, showcasing a dynamic evolutionary process. This ability to quickly shift genetically underscores nature's resilience, offering insights into engineering adaptive systems in technology and business.

Recent genetic research indicates that mutations arise not solely by chance but can be influenced by environmental factors. Certain plants, for example, have adapted to harsh climates by acquiring mutations that alter their metabolic pathways, enabling survival in arid or saline environments. This adaptability mirrors the way organisms can fine-tune their genetic makeup for optimal survival. Understanding these processes can inspire businesses to adopt flexible strategies that allow quick adjustments to market changes or consumer demands, ensuring competitiveness and longevity.

The role of genetic mutations extends beyond survival to include diversity and innovation. Mutations contribute to genetic variation, fueling natural selection and the development of new traits and species. This continuous cycle of adaptation and invention parallels the iterative process of product development in technology sectors, where rapid prototyping and feedback loops drive innovative solutions. By emulating nature, companies can cultivate a culture of experimentation, fostering adaptive thinking and continuous learning, crucial in a world of constant change.

Furthermore, the study of genetic mutations reveals that some organisms can exhibit foresight in their evolutionary strategies. Certain species have mechanisms that increase mutation rates under stress, accelerating adaptation when necessary. This strategic increase in genetic variability serves as a model for businesses aiming to enhance resilience in uncertain environments. By investing in innovation and adaptability during stable times, organizations can build reserves of potential solutions for future challenges, mirroring nature's foresight.

To translate genetic mutation principles into actionable insights, one could embrace strategic experimentation and calculated risk-taking. Encouraging a culture of constant, incremental change can lead to significant breakthroughs. Organizations might create cross-functional teams to bring diverse perspectives to problem-solving, fostering a rich environment for innovation. Aligning these practices with a clear vision allows businesses to harness adaptability, enabling not just survival but thriving in an ever-evolving landscape.

Epigenetic Changes and Environmental Adaptability

Epigenetic transformations open up a captivating dimension in understanding adaptability, showcasing how life forms can adjust to environmental changes without modifying their genetic blueprint. Unlike genetic mutations, which permanently alter DNA sequences, epigenetic shifts are reversible and occur swiftly, serving as a rapid adaptation mechanism. This ability for immediate adjustment enables organisms to fine-tune their physiology and behavior in response to environmental variations, such as climate change, resource availability, or predator presence. Acting as a biological archive, epigenetics allows organisms to transmit acquired traits to their descendants, adding a sophisticated layer to traditional evolutionary processes.

Recent studies emphasize the significance of epigenetic mechanisms across various species, from flora to fauna, highlighting their broad relevance. Research on plants illustrates how epigenetic adjustments enable them to adapt to diverse sunlight exposure or soil nutrient levels, boosting their survival and reproduction. In animals, epigenetic shifts have been documented in reaction to stressors like food shortages or habitat changes, influencing everything from metabolism to social interactions, thereby providing tools for navigating complex environments. The emerging field of social epigenetics further explores how social contexts and relationships shape epigenetic patterns, illustrating the intricate dynamics between organisms and their environments.

Insights from epigenetics hold profound implications for human progress, especially in areas like personalized medicine, agriculture, and environmental stewardship. Unraveling how epigenetic mechanisms function could lead to breakthroughs in developing crops more resilient to climate fluctuations or tailoring medical treatments to align with individual epigenetic profiles. By emulating nature's dynamic adaptability, businesses can create more flexible organizational structures and strategies that swiftly respond to market shifts, enhancing competitiveness and sustainability. This approach encourages a shift from rigid, uniform models to more adaptive, personalized solutions reflecting the complexities of modern challenges.

A deeper understanding of epigenetic adaptability invites reflection on humanity's broader relationship with the environment. It challenges us to consider how our actions impact not only our immediate surroundings but also the epigenetic legacy of future generations. Recognizing the interconnectedness of life and the capacity for rapid adaptation fosters a more harmonious coexistence with nature. This perspective encourages innovative thinking that prioritizes long-term resilience and sustainability over immediate gains, a crucial mindset in an era of ecological uncertainty and global change.

As we explore the potential applications of epigenetic insights, critical questions arise: How can we ethically harness these mechanisms to benefit society without causing unintended consequences? What role should epigenetics play in shaping public policy or education? These questions invite ongoing dialogue and research, pushing the boundaries of our understanding of adaptability and prompting the integration of scientific knowledge with ethical considerations. By embracing the lessons of epigenetic adaptability, we can develop strategies that address current challenges and anticipate future ones, ensuring a more resilient and adaptable world.

Symbiotic Relationships and Dynamic Ecosystem Shifts

Nature's complex web of interdependent relationships provides a fascinating model for understanding how ecosystems adapt to change. These partnerships, which often involve mutual benefits, illustrate how species work together to survive in shifting environments. Interactions such as mutualism and parasitism contribute to the resilience and adaptability of ecosystems. For example, the relationship between mycorrhizal fungi and plant roots is a classic example of mutualism, where fungi facilitate nutrient absorption for plants, receiving carbohydrates in return. This symbiosis allows both partners to flourish in nutrient-poor soils, highlighting nature's ability to adjust through cooperative partnerships.

Recent ecological research sheds light on the complexity and adaptability of these symbiotic networks. These relationships are dynamic, evolving in response to environmental pressures. A striking example is the interaction between coral reefs and their algal partners. As ocean temperatures rise, some coral species have been observed to switch their algal symbionts to more heat-tolerant varieties. This flexibility demonstrates the crucial role of adaptation and diversification in maintaining ecological balance in the face of climate change. Such insights can inspire innovative approaches in human systems, suggesting new ways to build adaptable frameworks within organizations through diverse partnerships.

The idea of dynamic ecosystem shifts can be applied to modern challenges, especially in business and technology. By mimicking nature's symbiotic strategies, organizations can create agile approaches to navigate market changes and technological upheavals. Companies that cultivate strong partnerships, similar to nature's symbiotic relationships, can harness complementary strengths and resources, enhancing their adaptability and resilience. For instance, technology firms partnering with startups can boost their innovation capacity by integrating groundbreaking ideas while offering stability and resources to their partners. This approach fosters a dynamic exchange of value, enabling all parties to evolve with changing market demands.

Understanding nature's symbiotic dynamics encourages us to explore individual and collective adaptability. Recognizing the importance of interconnectedness and collaboration, people and communities can create environments where diverse perspectives and skills converge to tackle complex problems. Consider urban ecosystems, where biodiversity and human activity intersect. By promoting green infrastructure and urban gardening, cities can create habitats that support a wide range of species, enhancing both ecological resilience and human well-being. These initiatives show how natural symbiosis principles can inform sustainable urban planning and community development.

Engaging with symbiotic relationships invites reflection on future applications and paradigms. What if businesses and communities prioritized symbiotic collaborations as a core growth strategy? Could educational systems incorporate lessons from nature's resilience to create adaptive learning environments? These questions challenge traditional thinking and encourage exploring symbiosis as a tool for innovation. By adopting a mindset that values interdependence and adaptive partnerships, we can discover new ways to address the complex challenges of the modern world, drawing inspiration from nature's enduring strategies.

Adaptive Business Models: Applying Nature's Flexibility to Market Changes

Imagine waking up one morning to discover that the business world has shifted dramatically, mirroring the unpredictable intricacies of natural ecosystems. In this ever-changing landscape, companies no longer strictly adhere to rigid plans. Instead, they draw inspiration from the natural world, embracing its adaptive qualities to navigate a fluctuating market. Just as a forest thrives through the diversity and interaction of its plants and animals, businesses can build resilience by reflecting the interconnectedness and variety found in nature. By cultivating a culture that appreciates diversity—not just among people but also in ideas and methods—organizations can establish a strong foundation to withstand market uncertainties and unexpected challenges. This approach mirrors nature's ability to adapt and flourish, turning potential threats into opportunities for growth.

As we delve into the harmony between nature's adaptability and business agility, consider how natural feedback loops can guide responsive decision-making. These loops, similar to the reflexes of a living organism, enable businesses to adjust swiftly and accurately. Furthermore, the symbiotic relationships observed in nature offer valuable insights into collaboration and innovation, providing a model for partnerships that foster mutual success. By incorporating these evolutionary strategies, businesses can achieve sustainable growth, much like species that adapt to thrive in their environments. Seen through this lens, adaptive business models become dynamic entities, constantly evolving to meet the demands of an ever-changing market.

Emulating Ecosystem Diversity for Business Resilience

In nature, the richness of ecosystems contributes significantly to their strength and resilience, offering a blueprint that businesses can follow to navigate volatile markets. An ecosystem's diversity prevents reliance on a single species, instead thriving through a network of interactions where various organisms play distinct roles. Businesses can draw parallels by fostering organizational diversity, where a mix of skills, viewpoints, and backgrounds creates a more adaptable enterprise. Companies that embrace a range of ideas and strategies can better handle market shifts, much like diverse ecosystems withstand environmental changes. By building a workforce and leadership team that embodies a wide spectrum of experiences and insights, businesses can enhance problem-solving and innovation.

Recent studies highlight the advantages of diversity in the business world, showing that teams with varied perspectives are more likely to generate new ideas and solutions. For example, research from the Harvard Business Review indicates that diverse companies are significantly more likely to tap into new markets. This mirrors how diverse ecosystems explore new niches and opportunities. By cultivating an environment where every voice is valued, companies can leverage the collective intelligence of their teams, leading to innovative products and services tailored to a broad customer base. This approach also helps businesses anticipate and adapt to shifts in consumer preferences, regulations, and technology, gaining a competitive edge.

To put ecosystem-inspired diversity into practice, businesses can implement strategies like cross-functional teams, rotational leadership roles, and collaborative platforms that promote knowledge sharing. These approaches reflect the interactions in ecosystems where different species contribute unique roles, maintaining balance and productivity. Establishing flexible structures that encourage the exchange of ideas and expertise fosters an environment where adaptability thrives. Additionally, companies can seek partnerships with external organizations, such as startups and academic institutions, to bring in fresh perspectives and expertise, akin to ecosystems benefiting from neighboring habitats.

Looking at nature's adaptability, businesses can model their strategies on the dynamic behavior of ecosystems. Recognizing that market conditions are always changing, forward-thinking companies build resilience by fostering a culture that values continual learning and experimentation. This involves investing in training programs that enhance workforce skills, promoting a growth mindset, and empowering employees to take calculated risks. This not only enhances the company's ability to adapt but also creates an environment where innovation is a constant, ensuring the organization remains competitive.

Reflecting on the lessons of ecosystem diversity, businesses should evaluate their structural and strategic composition. Are they genuinely fostering a diverse and inclusive environment? Are they agile enough to handle unexpected challenges? By addressing these questions and embracing the principles of diversity and adaptability, organizations can position themselves to thrive amid uncertainty, much like ecosystems that have endured over time. Adopting nature's wisdom holistically not only strengthens business resilience but also aligns corporate practices with a sustainable and innovative future.

Harnessing Natural Feedback Loops for Agile Decision-Making

In today's business landscape, valuable insights can be drawn from the feedback loops present in nature, which have evolved to help organisms flourish in ever-changing environments. By examining how plants and animals continually assess and adapt to their surroundings, companies can develop systems that respond swiftly to market shifts. Consider how octopuses use chromatophores in their skin to instantly change appearance based on environmental feedback. This biological phenomenon exemplifies the power of real-time data processing and adaptive response, a concept that businesses can implement. Companies can leverage digital analytics and machine learning to achieve similar agility, enabling them to modify strategies and operations according to consumer behaviors and market dynamics.

Advanced data analytics and artificial intelligence offer businesses unparalleled opportunities to harness feedback loops similar to those found in nature. These technologies allow organizations to collect vast amounts of data, process it swiftly, and extract actionable insights, mimicking the neural networks in animal brains. For instance, a retailer could use AI to scrutinize buying trends, adjust inventory, and customize marketing strategies, creating a dynamic system that adapts to customer needs in real time. This approach boosts efficiency and customer satisfaction while fostering a culture of continuous improvement and innovation.

Feedback loops extend beyond data collection and action; they encompass learning and evolution. In nature, feedback and adaptation drive evolutionary progress, enabling species to refine survival strategies over generations. In business, this can be reflected through iterative product development, where customer feedback is continuously integrated to refine offerings. This method, often employed in agile software development, ensures that products evolve with consumer expectations and technological advancements, maintaining relevance and competitiveness in a rapidly changing market.

To nurture a feedback loop-driven culture, organizations must empower teams to experiment and learn from outcomes, both successful and unsuccessful. Creating an environment where employees feel safe to innovate and adapt based on feedback is essential. This openness mirrors the adaptive processes seen in ecosystems, where diversity and experimentation lead to resilience and innovation. By fostering a culture that values flexible thinking and adaptability, businesses can not only survive but thrive in the face of volatility and change.

Critically engaging with feedback loops also involves recognizing potential challenges. While rapid adaptation offers significant benefits, it can lead to a reactive rather than strategic mindset. Organizations must find a balance, ensuring that feedback-driven decisions align with long-term goals and values. This balance can be achieved by establishing clear frameworks and guidelines that prioritize strategic objectives while remaining open to necessary adjustments. By doing so, businesses can draw on the wisdom of nature's feedback loops, creating systems that are both agile and aligned with their overarching mission.

Leveraging Symbiotic Relationships to Drive Innovation

In the natural world, symbiotic relationships showcase how mutual interaction can fuel innovation and resilience. Examples like fungi with plants or birds with large mammals are testaments to evolutionary brilliance, where partnerships magnify each participant's strengths, leading to outcomes that surpass individual capabilities. Businesses can draw from these natural alliances to inspire innovation and adaptability. By mimicking these cooperative strategies, companies can foster environments where collaboration flourishes, spurring groundbreaking advancements and lasting growth. This requires a shift from traditional competition to valuing synergistic partnerships, both within teams and with external entities.

By mirroring the delicate balance of mutualism seen in ecosystems, businesses can build networks that enhance creativity by leveraging diverse resources and viewpoints. Take the acacia tree and ants: the tree offers food and shelter, while the ants provide protection. Companies can emulate this by forming strategic alliances that capitalize on each partner's strengths. For example, tech firms collaborating with academic institutions can fast-track research and development by merging industry know-how with academic insights. This synergy not only boosts creativity but also spreads risk, as shared resources and expertise create a robust system capable of adapting to market changes.

Another lesson from symbiotic relationships is the power of natural feedback loops, which ensure that interactions remain mutually beneficial by making real-time adjustments to maintain balance. Businesses can adopt similar mechanisms to enhance agility and responsiveness. Through iterative processes that continuously assess and refine strategies based on actual data, companies can stay attuned to market dynamics and customer needs. Agile frameworks, inspired by these feedback systems, facilitate rapid prototyping and development, enabling businesses to pivot effectively in response to emerging trends and challenges. This approach not only encourages innovation but also nurtures a culture of ongoing learning and improvement.

Symbiosis also highlights the importance of trust and reciprocity in fostering innovation. In nature, these relationships rely on a delicate balance of give and take, where each party depends on the other's reliability and contribution. For companies, establishing trust-based networks is crucial for creating environments where innovative ideas can thrive. Open communication, shared goals, and a dedication to mutual benefit create fertile ground for creativity and experimentation. Organizations that prioritize building trust with partners, employees, and stakeholders are more likely to develop resilient, innovative solutions that meet the complexities of today's marketplace.

To incorporate the principles of symbiosis into business practice, organizations should identify potential partners whose strengths complement their own. This involves looking beyond traditional competitors to consider unconventional allies who offer fresh perspectives and capabilities. Encouraging cross-disciplinary collaborations and fostering an inclusive culture that values diverse viewpoints can lead to innovative breakthroughs. Additionally, establishing systems that facilitate open dialogue and feedback ensures these partnerships remain dynamic and beneficial. By embracing symbiotic strategies seen in nature, businesses can unlock new avenues for growth and innovation, creating ecosystems that thrive amid modern uncertainties.

Integrating Evolutionary Strategies for Sustainable Growth

Embracing evolutionary strategies for sustainable growth requires businesses to learn from nature's remarkable ability to adapt and persist in changing environments. Central to this concept is the idea of ongoing improvement, much like the evolutionary processes seen in various species. These organisms have fine-tuned their survival skills by constantly adjusting to their surroundings. Businesses can replicate this by nurturing a culture of continuous innovation, where growth is part of an ongoing journey rather than a fixed goal. With an evolutionary mindset, companies build resilience to market changes and prepare for unexpected challenges, requiring agility and a willingness to rethink conventional business models, enabling them to pivot in response to both opportunities and threats.

Nature's mechanisms stress the significance of genetic diversity, ensuring species can adapt to new environments. In business, this translates to fostering a diverse ecosystem of ideas, perspectives, and talents. Encouraging cross-disciplinary collaboration and valuing diverse viewpoints can ignite innovation and uncover novel solutions to complex problems. This diversity counters stagnation, promoting a vibrant environment where creativity thrives. Diverse teams in strategic decision-making not only produce stronger solutions but also enhance the organization's ability to anticipate and respond to varied market scenarios.

Incorporating feedback loops into business strategies mirrors nature's ecosystems, which rely on feedback networks to maintain balance and adapt. Structured feedback mechanisms help companies refine strategies continuously, allowing real-time assessment and adjustment that inform decision-making and support agile responses to market shifts. Businesses prioritizing feedback from customers, employees, and other stakeholders can refine their offerings and processes to align with evolving needs and preferences. Such adaptability is essential for long-term growth and can be cultivated through a culture that encourages experimentation and views failures as learning opportunities.

Symbiotic relationships in nature provide a model for sustainable business growth. Observing how species cooperate for mutual benefit, companies can identify opportunities for strategic partnerships that drive shared success. Through alliances, joint ventures, or innovative collaborations, businesses can enhance their capabilities by leveraging partners' strengths. These partnerships lead to resource sharing, knowledge exchange, and co-innovation, resulting in more sustainable outcomes for all parties involved. By adopting a cooperative mindset, organizations can create ecosystems that support collective growth and resilience in the face of challenges.

For sustainable growth, businesses must adopt a long-term perspective similar to nature's evolutionary timeline, setting strategic goals that balance immediate needs with future aspirations. This ensures short-term gains don't compromise long-term viability. Companies can learn from nature's cyclical patterns, recognizing that growth often involves cycles of expansion, contraction, and renewal. By planning for these cycles and building flexibility into operations, organizations can navigate modern market complexities confidently. Encouraging an adaptive and forward-thinking mindset empowers businesses to thrive in an ever-evolving landscape.

Nature's ability to adjust and thrive amidst evolving circumstances showcases a profound blend of resilience and ingenuity, a theme that echoes throughout the living world. From the nimble bacteria to the soaring birds, life on Earth exemplifies an extraordinary capacity to flourish in shifting environments. This evolutionary prowess offers valuable lessons for modern-day progress, emphasizing the importance of adaptability. By studying how nature swiftly crafts solutions and responds to challenges, we gain crucial insights into developing flexible business models capable of navigating unpredictable markets with ease. Embracing change and evolving is not just a survival tactic but a pathway to success in our rapidly changing world. As we draw inspiration from nature's brilliance, we are encouraged to consider how these principles can be woven into our personal and professional endeavors. How can we leverage nature's flexibility to reach new levels of creativity and progress? As we ponder these questions, our journey continues, urging us to stay curious, adaptive, and inspired by the relentless creativity of the natural world.

Chapter Four

Collaboration Harnessing Collective Intelligence

Amidst a vibrant forest where sunlight gently weaves through a tapestry of leaves, a fascinating partnership unfolds between two unlikely allies: the ant and the acacia tree. This duo, each with its own unique traits, demonstrates the remarkable power of cooperative relationships. The tree provides sustenance and a home, while the ants offer protection against herbivores and rival plants. This age-old symbiosis is not merely a chance occurrence but a testament to the strength of working together. Such alliances are abundant in the natural world, showcasing a complex network of cooperation that can inspire us as we navigate innovation in our own lives.

As we delve into the essence of teamwork, we discover that nature's design is both elegantly simple and extraordinarily complex. From the seamless choreography of bird flocks to the intricate societies of bees, nature illustrates how collective wisdom often surpasses individual capabilities. This chapter reveals the mysteries of group intelligence, where the whole truly exceeds the sum of its parts, and explores how these concepts are already shaping advanced AI technologies. Insights drawn from these natural marvels illuminate new avenues for enhancing human collaboration, offering strategies to unlock hidden potential within our communities and organizations.

By observing the myriad ways creatures collaborate, we can revolutionize our approach to solving intricate problems. Nature shows us that by embracing diversity and nurturing teamwork, we can achieve resilience and adaptability in the face of uncertainty. This chapter invites you to explore the symphony of shared effort, urging a shift in mindset toward valuing interconnectedness and common goals. As we investigate these natural strategies for success, consider how they might enrich your own pursuits, advancing not only personal achievements but also the collective progress of humanity.

Symbiotic Relationships in Nature

The intricate dance of partnerships in the natural world unveils a profound web of interdependence that sustains life on our planet. This dynamic interaction among living beings, whether through cooperative efforts or subtle competition, is more than a fascinating biological phenomenon; it is a fundamental force maintaining Earth's ecological harmony. As we delve into the various forms of these alliances—from vibrant collaborations that enhance ecosystem resilience to the competitive interactions that drive evolutionary progress—the insights gleaned become increasingly pertinent. In a world where teamwork is essential, learning from nature's age-old strategies can illuminate new approaches to improving human systems, whether in business or science.

Central to these natural interactions is a complex exchange where mutual support becomes a stabilizing force, ensuring the survival and flourishing of entire ecosystems. Yet, the narrative isn't solely about harmony. Parasitic encounters, often viewed as conflicts, play a key role in fostering evolutionary creativity and strength. Meanwhile, less apparent commensal relationships significantly contribute to biodiversity, underscoring the variety of life's connections. As we untangle the complexity and coevolution inherent in these interactions, the parallels to human collaboration become vividly apparent. Nature's design for collective wisdom offers a rich source of inspiration for rethinking how we work together, overcoming individual limitations to achieve shared goals.

Mutualism as a Driver of Ecosystem Stability

Mutualism forms a crucial part of ecological balance, illustrating the intricate interdependencies that sustain life on Earth. These relationships in nature highlight how organisms cooperate for mutual benefits, promoting ecological stability. Consider the relationship between bees and flowering plants: bees gather nectar and pollen for sustenance, while aiding in plant pollination and promoting genetic diversity. This interaction not only supports the survival of both species but enriches ecosystems by enhancing biodiversity. Such interactions suggest potential frameworks for human collaboration, demonstrating how mutualism can boost resilience and productivity across various fields.

Research into mutualistic networks uncovers a complex web that can inspire innovation. Studies reveal that these networks stabilize ecosystems by providing multiple pathways for energy and nutrients, allowing adaptation to disturbances without collapse. The partnership between mycorrhizal fungi and plants, where fungi boost nutrient uptake in exchange for carbohydrates, exemplifies a dynamic model of resource sharing. This interconnected approach offers insights into designing robust supply chains and collaborative business models capable of weathering disruptions. By imitating nature's strategies, organizations can create sustainable and adaptable operations.

Mutualism extends beyond resource exchange, offering insights into cooperation and competition. In many ecosystems, these relationships develop amidst competition, leading to adaptations that optimize mutual benefits. The cleaner fish and client fish relationship is an example, with cleaner fish removing parasites from their hosts and receiving nourishment in return. This interaction not only benefits the individuals involved but also improves the health of the entire reef community. Such biological models inspire innovative strategies in conflict resolution and team dynamics, where cooperation amidst competition enhances group performance and well-being.

Emerging research challenges traditional views by revealing the fluidity and adaptability of mutualistic partnerships. These relationships evolve in response to environmental changes, showing remarkable flexibility. Climate shifts or resource changes can alter the dynamics of these interactions, prompting species to adjust their roles. This adaptability serves as a model for businesses and organizations navigating a changing landscape. By fostering dynamic partnerships, entities can better handle uncertainties and seize new opportunities, mirroring nature's resilient systems.

While mutualism offers a robust framework for collaboration, its intricacies warrant further exploration. Consider how its principles could guide technological innovation, where AI and human intelligence can form synergistic systems. By combining their strengths, we can develop solutions beyond the reach of either alone. Imagining a future where technology and humanity thrive together in mutualistic harmony challenges us to rethink progress. By learning from nature's strategies, we unlock the potential to create more harmonious, sustainable, and innovative systems that reflect the balance found in the natural world.

Parasitic Interactions and Their Role in Evolution

Parasitic interactions, often viewed negatively, play a complex and essential role in the evolution of life. These interactions are not just harmful; they can stimulate remarkable evolutionary developments and adaptations. Parasites, from tiny bacteria to intricate multicellular organisms, impose selective pressures on their hosts, leading to a continuous cycle of adaptations that enhance genetic diversity and drive evolutionary progress, enriching the stability and variety of ecosystems.

Consider the interaction between the cuckoo bird and its unsuspecting avian hosts. Cuckoos trick other bird species into raising their offspring by laying eggs in their nests, which often comes at a cost to the host's own young. In response, host birds have developed sophisticated defenses, such as identifying and discarding foreign eggs. This ongoing evolutionary contest has not only refined the cuckoo's deception but also advanced the host's recognition skills, illustrating a dynamic interplay that elevates both sides to higher levels of complexity.

Recent research has uncovered deeper insights into the molecular foundations of parasitism, showing how parasites can alter the genetic makeup of their hosts. Studies in genomics and epigenetics reveal that parasitic interactions can awaken dormant genes or suppress others, resulting in new traits and adaptations. This genetic dance highlights the subtle yet powerful ways parasites drive evolutionary innovation, urging hosts to develop unique defenses and strategies that might not have surfaced in an environment devoid of parasites.

Beyond biology, lessons from parasitic interactions can inspire human endeavors, particularly in promoting resilience and adaptability. Businesses, for instance, can learn from these dynamics by recognizing and exploiting their own 'parasitic' challenges, like market upheavals or competitive pressures, to fuel innovation and growth. By viewing obstacles as opportunities for adaptation and development, organizations can foster a culture of resilience, turning potential weaknesses into strengths.

Reflect on the broader implications of these interactions: How can we apply the insights gained to cultivate beneficial collaborations in our own lives? By appreciating the evolutionary advantages of parasitism, we can leverage these lessons to create partnerships and strategies that benefit all parties, whether in business or personal growth. Embracing the complexity of parasitic interactions opens the door to harnessing their hidden wisdom, transforming challenges into catalysts for innovation and progress.

Commensal Relationships and Their Impact on Biodiversity

In the natural world, commensal relationships weave a rich tapestry of interactions where one organism reaps benefits while the other remains unaffected. These seemingly straightforward connections play a crucial role in sustaining and boosting biodiversity. Take the cattle egret and the grazing animals it follows: as these animals traverse the grasslands, they disturb insects, offering the egrets an easy meal. The grazers remain unharmed, illustrating a dynamic interaction that aids the ecosystem by managing insect populations without impacting the grazers. This balance underscores how commensalism contributes to ecological harmony and stability, supporting a diverse array of species within a shared habitat.

Recent studies on commensal relationships uncover their significant influence on ecosystem functionality and resilience. Research indicates that organisms engaged in these interactions often display high adaptability, which can enhance genetic diversity within populations. For example, some bird species nest in trees that offer protection and a strategic viewpoint without affecting the trees. This interaction enables birds to flourish in various habitats, fostering a more resilient and diverse avian community. Such adaptability is vital amid environmental changes, positioning commensal relationships as a key factor in species survival and evolution.

Emerging trends in biomimicry aim to draw inspiration from these natural models of commensalism to fuel human innovation. Companies are exploring how businesses might coexist in mutually beneficial ways. Urban planners, for instance, are considering designs for cities where infrastructure works harmoniously with natural environments, like buildings that provide habitats for urban wildlife. This approach not only boosts urban biodiversity but also promotes sustainable development practices aligned with natural symbiotic principles.

The complexity of commensal relationships often extends beyond immediate interactions, affecting broader ecological networks. These connections can yield indirect benefits for other species, creating a ripple effect across ecosystems. Consider epiphytic plants that grow on larger trees: while they gain physical support, they also offer habitat and food for various insects and small animals, which in turn attract predators, enriching the entire food web. Such intricate networks highlight life's interconnectedness, where even seemingly one-sided relationships enhance a thriving, dynamic environment.

Integrating the wisdom of commensalism into human practices encourages a shift toward more collaborative and sustainable approaches. By acknowledging and emulating these natural interactions, individuals and organizations can create settings where mutual benefit and non-detrimental coexistence are prioritized. This opens up critical reflection on designing social, economic, and ecological systems, prompting questions like: How can we establish business models that prosper without exploitation? Which urban designs can enrich human life while safeguarding natural ecosystems? By looking to nature as a guide, we can pave innovative paths that align with commensalism's principles, ultimately leading to resilient and harmonious communities.

Complexity and Coevolution in Symbiotic Partnerships

Symbiotic partnerships in the natural world reveal an intricate web of complexity and coevolution, demonstrating how diverse organisms evolve together to form networks of mutual advantage. These relationships are shaped by a dynamic exchange of evolutionary pressures, where each participant adjusts its strategies to maximize gains while reducing weaknesses. Mycorrhizal networks between fungi and plants illustrate this complexity; fungi provide vital nutrients to plants, which, in turn, supply carbohydrates, creating an interdependent system that boosts ecosystem productivity. This sophisticated interplay of adaptation and counter-adaptation results in a symbiotic balance, where the distribution of benefits and costs is continuously adjusted, prompting partners to refine their roles and interactions over time.

Recent studies uncover the molecular intricacies that underpin these partnerships, showing how genetic modifications can significantly alter symbiotic dynamics. For instance, research on the gut microbiomes of herbivores, like cows, illustrates how bacterial communities evolve alongside their hosts to enhance digestion and nutrient uptake. These microbial groups are not static; they adapt to dietary changes, environmental influences, and even shifts in the host's physiology. This coevolutionary process exemplifies how symbiotic relationships are dynamic interactions that evolve to improve the survival and reproductive success of each participant.

Such insights into natural symbioses provide valuable frameworks for human endeavors. Modern business ecosystems can learn from these natural partnerships, fostering inter-organizational collaborations that are resilient and adaptive. Companies, akin to symbiotic organisms, can evolve together by sharing resources, aligning objectives, and innovating collectively to strengthen their competitive position in volatile markets. The automotive industry, for instance, is witnessing a surge of collaborative innovation, with car manufacturers teaming up with tech companies to integrate autonomous driving technologies, reflecting the complex mutualisms observed in nature.

The complexity of coevolutionary relationships also presents exciting opportunities for technological progress. Artificial intelligence and machine learning models can be crafted to mimic the adaptive nature of symbiotic partnerships, leading to systems that learn and evolve in response to external stimuli. These models could transform fields like healthcare, where personalized medicine can be customized to the unique symbiotic interactions within an individual's microbiome, offering treatments that are both more effective and less invasive.

Consider the potential of applying these principles to team dynamics and organizational behavior. By understanding the symbiotic nature of successful partnerships, leaders can create environments that encourage collaboration, adaptability, and shared growth. Imagine a workplace where teams function like the synchronized movements of a school of fish, each member contributing to a collective wisdom that exceeds the sum of its parts. This vision challenges traditional hierarchies and invites exploration of decentralized teamwork models, where flexibility and coevolution drive innovation and success.

Swarm Intelligence: From Bees to AI Algorithms

Imagine a meadow teeming with life, where bees dart purposefully, each one instinctively tuned to its role within the hive. At first glance, it might seem chaotic, but beneath this lively dance lies an intricate network of communication and collaboration. This marvel, known as swarm intelligence, showcases nature's knack for tackling intricate challenges through straightforward rules and communal effort. Creatures like bees and ants harness this collective wisdom, using decentralized control and simple interactions to accomplish extraordinary tasks. These natural phenomena reveal how individual actions, driven by shared objectives and limited information, can give rise to intelligent group dynamics. It's a concept that fascinates scientists and engineers alike, offering a template for breakthroughs in areas as varied as robotics, logistics, and artificial intelligence.

In the technological sphere, the essence of swarm behavior is being transformed into robust algorithms that confront problems resistant to conventional methods. Consider the bees' communication strategies, which have inspired algorithms optimizing network flow and resource distribution. As we delve into the synergy between natural swarm conduct and technological progress, the possibilities appear limitless, from enhancing data management to crafting autonomous systems. However, like any scientific frontier, these innovations come with their own hurdles. Deciphering the nuances of biological teamwork and translating them into practical technological applications requires continual exploration and adaptation. This journey into swarm intelligence challenges us to rethink system design, urging us to leverage the power of collective effort to navigate the complexities of today's world.

Understanding the Principles of Swarm Behavior in Nature

Swarm behavior in the natural world presents an intriguing example of how cooperation and efficiency can lead to results far beyond the capacity of individuals. This phenomenon relies on decentralized decision-making and self-organization. Unlike hierarchically structured systems, natural swarms such as bird flocks or fish schools reveal how intricate patterns arise from simple individual rules. Each participant reacts to local cues, creating a cohesive and adaptable group movement. This concept of emergent order is vital for understanding how diverse entities collaborate to tackle challenges, optimize resources, and reach common objectives.

The intelligence of bees exemplifies swarm behavior, notably through their waggle dance—a sophisticated method of conveying details about resource locations. This dance informs hive members about the direction and distance to nectar sources, highlighting the efficiency of swarm intelligence. Bees manage to share critical information swiftly and effectively without a central command. The waggle dance demonstrates how straightforward behavioral rules can lead to a complex system where collective wisdom exceeds individual abilities. Observing these natural processes offers insights that can enhance algorithmic efficiency in artificial systems.

Recently, scientists have leveraged these natural principles to create algorithms mimicking swarm behavior, leading to innovative applications in technology. Swarm-based algorithms are increasingly utilized in robotics, where autonomous drones cooperate to execute complex tasks like search and rescue operations. This method allows for adaptive problem-solving, as each drone can independently respond to environmental changes and contribute to the mission. Another promising application is optimizing traffic flow in smart cities, where swarm algorithms dynamically reroute vehicles using real-time data, helping to manage congestion. These technological advancements highlight the potential of swarm intelligence to transform various fields, from logistics to urban development.

Despite the vast benefits of swarm intelligence, fully integrating these concepts into AI systems presents challenges. One major obstacle is developing algorithms that balance individual autonomy with group cohesion, crucial to avoiding overly centralized inflexibility or decentralized disorganization. Researchers are also working on enhancing the adaptability of swarm-based systems to function efficiently in unpredictable environments. Ethical considerations, particularly regarding the transparency and accountability of autonomous decision-making in swarm systems, are also being explored.

As we consider the future impact of swarm intelligence in AI, essential questions arise regarding societal implications and ethical guidelines. How can we ensure that swarm-based AI systems benefit humanity without compromising individual freedoms? What steps can we take to foster trust in these autonomous systems, often operating beyond direct human supervision? Reflecting on these questions lays the groundwork for a future where swarm intelligence not only propels technological advancement but also aligns with human values. Continued research in this area promises to reveal new aspects of collective intelligence, offering valuable insights applicable across various domains.

Translating Bee Communication into Algorithmic Efficiency

Bees, renowned for their complex methods of communication and teamwork, offer an inspiring model for enhancing algorithmic effectiveness. Their unique waggle dance serves not just as a communication tool but as an advanced system for efficient information exchange, crucial for maximizing resource acquisition. By delving into this behavior, scientists have crafted algorithms that emulate these natural patterns, tackling intricate challenges in computer science and operations research. Dubbed "bee-inspired," these algorithms reveal the potential of drawing from nature to advance technological processes, driving forward innovations in data handling and optimization.

A notable example of such innovation is the Bee Algorithm, developed to solve optimization challenges that often stump conventional methods. Mimicking bee foraging behaviors, this algorithm adeptly navigates various potential solutions, similar to bees seeking out the most promising flowers. This collaborative approach enables the algorithm to assess multiple variables at once, enhancing both the speed and precision in achieving optimal outcomes. Sectors such as logistics and network design have reaped the benefits of these algorithms, which provide greater efficiency and adaptability than traditional techniques. The triumph of bee-inspired algorithms underscores the merit of translating natural processes into digital innovations.

Beyond technical implementations, the principles of bee communication can revolutionize human organizational frameworks. Just as bees utilize a decentralized system for coordination, businesses can adopt similar strategies to create more agile and responsive teams. Encouraging autonomy and strong communication within teams can lead to more creative and effective problem-solving. This shift emphasizes empowering individuals in organizations, recognizing that collective wisdom often outperforms hierarchical mandates. As companies adapt to ever-evolving landscapes, insights from bee communication can guide them towards more dynamic and resilient team structures.

Recent research has also explored embedding bee-like communication strategies into artificial intelligence systems, especially those involving multi-agent coordination. By replicating the decentralized yet highly efficient communication found in bee colonies, AI systems can achieve greater flexibility and scalability. This method proves particularly valuable in fields like robotics and autonomous vehicles, where agent coordination and communication are paramount. Ongoing developments highlight the transformative potential of applying biological insights to tech innovations, paving the way for more advanced AI solutions.

While leveraging bee communication principles for algorithmic efficiency holds promise, it also presents challenges and opportunities for further exploration. Researchers must carefully model biological behaviors and translate them into digital frameworks. The ethical considerations of automating decision-making inspired by nature also require careful thought. As this field evolves, it invites continuous dialogue and collaboration across disciplines, ensuring that the integration of natural insights into technology remains both responsible and revolutionary. By engaging with these challenges, innovators can continue to harness nature's intelligence, crafting solutions as elegant and effective as those in the natural world.

Applications of Swarm Intelligence in Modern Technology

Swarm intelligence, inspired by the collective behaviors seen in nature, has significantly influenced modern technology. By examining the seamless operations of creatures like bees and ants, researchers have developed innovative algorithms that address complex challenges. These solutions draw from the decentralized decision-making and cooperative interactions characteristic of natural swarms, leading to algorithms that solve intricate problems without needing a central control. They excel due to the interactions and feedback among individual components, reflecting the adaptability and efficiency of natural systems. This method has been especially transformative in enhancing routing and scheduling tasks, providing robust and adaptable solutions in dynamic environments.

A notable application of swarm intelligence is in robotics, specifically swarm robotics, which involves numerous simple robots working together to perform tasks beyond the capability of a single unit. Mimicking ant colonies or bee swarms, these robots undertake tasks such as search-and-rescue missions, environmental monitoring, and even complex construction activities. Their decentralized structure allows them to function effectively even when individual units fail, demonstrating resilience and fault tolerance. This has led to innovative initiatives like autonomous drone swarms for agricultural monitoring, where their collective intelligence ensures thorough data collection and analysis.

In telecommunications, swarm intelligence boosts network efficiency and reliability. Drawing parallels with the intricate paths of foraging ants, communication networks benefit from algorithms inspired by these natural systems. These algorithms dynamically adapt to traffic fluctuations, optimize data flow, and enhance connectivity, ensuring efficient network operations. By continuously learning from network conditions and adjusting in real-time, these systems reduce congestion and increase throughput, showcasing the potential of swarm intelligence to revolutionize data management and transmission, creating more resilient and adaptable communication infrastructures.

Swarm intelligence also influences financial markets, enhancing trading strategies by applying collective behavior principles. Algorithms analyze market trends and make predictions with increased accuracy by gathering information from diverse sources, similar to a swarm collecting resources. This approach not only improves decision-making but also reduces risk by providing a comprehensive market view. As financial systems grow more complex, the role of swarm intelligence in fostering stability and insight becomes increasingly crucial.

Looking forward, the future of swarm intelligence in artificial intelligence systems holds great promise. Current research explores integrating swarm principles with machine learning to create hybrid systems that combine the strengths of both fields. This fusion could lead to AI systems that are not only intelligent but also adaptable and capable of self-organization. By fostering collaboration between swarm intelligence and other advanced technologies, researchers are venturing into new areas of AI development. This exploration encourages readers to consider how these advancements might redefine technology, motivating them to apply these insights to real-world challenges and envision the future potential of collective intelligence in innovation.

Challenges and Future Directions in Swarm-Based AI Systems

Exploring the realm of AI systems inspired by swarms reveals an intriguing blend of natural phenomena and technological advancement. A significant hurdle is replicating the effortless coordination seen in natural swarms, such as ants and bees, which operate without centralized oversight. Crafting algorithms that mirror this decentralized harmony demands a profound grasp of local interactions that culminate in cohesive global actions. Researchers are delving into advanced simulations and machine learning to model these interactions, aiming to build AI systems capable of adapting to changing environments, much like their natural inspirations. This endeavor not only boosts algorithmic effectiveness but also lays the groundwork for creating robust, scalable AI solutions.

Recent strides in swarm robotics underscore the transformative potential of these systems in sectors like logistics, environmental monitoring, and disaster management. By harnessing swarm intelligence, robotic systems can function autonomously, adjust to fluctuating conditions, and tackle intricate tasks collectively. Yet, deploying these systems presents challenges, such as ensuring reliable communication among agents and managing the computational demands of real-time decision-making. Researchers are confronting these issues by developing innovative communication protocols and refining computational methods, thereby enhancing the feasibility of swarm-based technologies.

In algorithm development, translating the natural efficiency of bee communication into digital systems offers unique prospects and hurdles. For example, the bee's waggle dance, which effectively communicates resource locations, inspires algorithms for optimizing network routing and data processing. However, adapting this biological communication to digital frameworks involves overcoming scalability and data security challenges. Innovative strategies, including blockchain technology, are being explored to secure decentralized communication channels, addressing these issues while preserving system integrity and efficiency.

As swarm-based AI systems evolve, their potential applications extend into emerging realms like smart cities and autonomous transportation. These systems promise to elevate urban infrastructure by optimizing traffic flow, energy use, and public safety through intelligent decision-making. Integrating swarm intelligence into such complex environments requires tackling ethical issues and ensuring accountability in AI-driven decisions. Interdisciplinary research and collaboration are essential to establish frameworks that balance innovation with ethical responsibility.

To drive these advancements, a cross-disciplinary approach is crucial, drawing insights from biology, computer science, and social sciences. By examining swarm behavior across diverse ecosystems and integrating these insights into AI development, the path forward becomes clearer. This holistic approach not only deepens our understanding of swarm intelligence but also empowers innovators to create AI systems that resonate with nature's harmony and efficiency. Engaging with these concepts encourages reflection on the potential of collaboration, both human and artificial, to address pressing challenges.

Translating Biological Cooperation into Team Dynamics

Picture waking up to discover that your workplace is now the vast and intricate tapestry of the natural world. In this dynamic environment, every creature, from the smallest ant to the grandest tree, participates in a seamless ballet of mutual benefit and cooperation. For billions of years, nature has thrived on collaboration, a guiding principle that has fostered its resilience and adaptability. From the life-sustaining partnerships found in symbiotic relationships to the collective wisdom seen in swarming behaviors, nature offers profound lessons in teamwork that hold the potential to revolutionize our approach to collaboration. Nestled at the crossroads of biology and human ambition lies a wealth of insights ready to be integrated into our teams and organizations. By embracing these natural principles, we not only illuminate our collaborative efforts but also unlock new dimensions of shared intelligence in our modern world.

Consider how nature's intricate strategies for working together can be mirrored in our interactions. As we delve into the lessons of symbiosis, we begin to understand how interdependence can drive both productivity and creativity. The concept of swarm intelligence challenges us to rethink our methods of decision-making and problem-solving, fostering environments where every contribution, regardless of size, is recognized. Adaptive partnerships, mirroring those found in nature, promote resilience and flexibility within our teams, empowering us to navigate the complexities of a constantly shifting landscape. Network theory, a concept as ancient as the ecosystems it reflects, provides a blueprint for addressing intricate challenges through interconnected thinking. By drawing on these natural models, we embark on a journey to harness the power of cooperation found in the natural world, paving the way for more dynamic and effective team dynamics.

Lessons from Symbiotic Relationships in Nature

The complex interplay of cooperative relationships in the natural world provides a wealth of insights for enhancing modern team dynamics. Observing the mutualism between the clownfish and sea anemone, for instance, reveals how collaboration can yield greater rewards than solo efforts. The clownfish gains protection from predators, while the anemone benefits from nutrients in the fish's waste. This partnership illustrates how diverse entities can find common ground and prosper together. In team settings, such relationships inspire a shift from competition to cooperation, harnessing diverse talents and perspectives to achieve a shared vision. By fostering an environment where individual strengths complement one another, organizations can cultivate a culture that mirrors the interdependence observed in nature.

Further exploration of cooperative relationships uncovers mechanisms that can enhance team cohesion and productivity. Research into mycorrhizal networks—fungal systems connecting plant roots—demonstrates a sophisticated form of communication and resource sharing. These networks enable plants to access nutrients and environmental information, acting as a support system that ensures collective resilience. Translating this concept into human collaboration, teams benefit from structured communication channels that facilitate the flow of information and resources. Implementing systems that promote openness and trust empowers team members to anticipate challenges and adapt proactively, akin to how plants utilize their fungal partners for survival and growth.

To draw actionable insights for teamwork, consider the principles of reciprocity and resource allocation observed in cooperative partnerships. Just as cleaner fish and larger marine species engage in mutually beneficial exchanges, effective teams operate on equitable contributions and rewards. Encouraging team members to recognize and value each other's input fosters a more engaged and motivated workforce. Organizations can implement policies that reward collaboration and shared success instead of individual achievements, aligning incentives with the team's collective well-being. This approach nurtures an environment where cooperation is prioritized, and the advantages of working together become evident.

Beyond tangible collaboration aspects, the psychological dimensions of cooperative relationships hold valuable lessons. Studies on social cooperation in animals, such as the intricate partnerships between ants and aphids, show that emotional bonds and trust are critical for sustained cooperation. These findings emphasize the importance of fostering emotional intelligence within teams, where empathy and understanding are essential for maintaining harmony and resolving conflicts. By promoting an ethos of mutual respect and support, teams can create a safe space for innovation and risk-taking, elements essential for thriving in today's rapidly changing environment.

Considering how to apply nature's lessons to human collaboration, envision a business team tackling a complex project. Drawing parallels with cooperative relationships, the team could strategize by identifying complementary skills among its members and establishing clear communication pathways. Prioritizing resource sharing and mutual support enhances the team's collective insight and adaptability. Such a strategy not only mirrors nature's efficiency but also sets the stage for a dynamic and resilient team culture. By internalizing these principles, organizations can transform their approach to collaboration, turning natural wisdom into practical strategies for success.

Applying Swarm Intelligence to Enhance Team Performance

Swarm intelligence, inspired by the collective actions of social insects such as bees and ants, provides a fascinating model for boosting team efficiency. These insects demonstrate how decentralized systems solve intricate problems using simple rules and interactions. In an organizational setting, this approach encourages teams to function with minimal hierarchical control, allowing members to make independent decisions based on local insights. This results in a more agile and adaptable team that can swiftly react to changes. Studies indicate that teams adopting swarm-like decision-making not only enhance efficiency but also drive innovation by tapping into diverse perspectives.

A key element in integrating swarm intelligence into team dynamics is the focus on real-time communication and feedback. Similar to how bees use dances and pheromones to convey information about food locations, modern teams can leverage digital tools for continuous communication and data sharing. This ranges from basic messaging platforms to advanced collaborative software that incorporates AI to analyze patterns and provide insights. Such systems keep team members informed, enable quick adaptation to new challenges, and maintain alignment towards common goals. Establishing a culture where information circulates freely and feedback is actively utilized enhances collective problem-solving capabilities.

Swarm intelligence also highlights the importance of diversity within teams. In nature, varying actions and roles within a swarm allow the group to adapt to diverse environmental challenges. Similarly, teams that embrace a broad spectrum of skills, experiences, and viewpoints are better positioned to tackle complex issues. Promoting diversity involves not only assembling varied team compositions but also nurturing an inclusive environment where different perspectives are valued. This diversity-driven synergy can lead to stronger solutions and groundbreaking innovations that a homogenous team might miss. Leaders play a crucial role in recognizing and harnessing these differences, ensuring each team member feels valued and empowered to contribute uniquely.

Incorporating swarm intelligence into team dynamics also requires balancing autonomy with alignment. While individual team members should have the freedom to make decisions, there must be a shared vision and common objectives guiding these actions. This balance can be achieved through clear communication of goals and establishing guiding principles for decision-making. By providing a structured framework within which individuals can operate independently, teams can achieve the nimbleness of a swarm while staying aligned with broader organizational aims. This not only boosts performance but also fosters a sense of ownership and accountability among team members.

To fully harness swarm intelligence, teams can engage in scenario-based exercises that simulate real-world challenges and demand collective problem-solving. These exercises help teams develop the reflexes needed to function like a swarm, enhancing their ability to respond to unexpected situations with agility and creativity. By iterating on these scenarios, teams can identify and refine effective strategies across various contexts, building resilience and adaptability over time. Encouraging a mindset that views challenges as opportunities for learning and growth further ingrains the principles of swarm intelligence, preparing teams to excel in an ever-evolving landscape.

Building Resilient Teams Through Adaptive Collaboration

Fostering resilient teams through flexible cooperation involves learning from nature's ability to adapt to changing conditions. Take coral reefs, for instance. These ecosystems flourish through intricate partnerships among marine species, showcasing resilience by collectively adjusting to environmental pressures. This natural blueprint can guide organizations in nurturing adaptability within teams. By cultivating a culture that encourages members to shift strategies as challenges arise, organizations can develop robust teams equipped to thrive amidst uncertainty.

Research in organizational behavior underscores the role of psychological safety in team resilience, a concept seen in natural ecosystems. When team members feel secure in voicing ideas and concerns without fear of criticism, they collaborate more effectively, leading to innovative solutions akin to nature's cooperative systems. Openness nurtures collective wisdom, valuing diverse perspectives, much like ecosystems that thrive through mutual support. Leaders can facilitate this by modeling transparency and building trust, laying the groundwork for adaptive responses.

Network theory underscores the strength of interconnected systems, illustrated by a forest where trees exchange resources through an underground fungal network. This demonstrates the power of shared knowledge. Organizations can mirror this interconnectedness by ensuring information flows freely, breaking down silos to enable cross-functional teamwork. This fosters resilience by drawing from diverse expertise, much like nutrients flowing through an ecosystem.

Continuous learning and feedback loops are vital for adaptive cooperation, similar to how ant colonies adjust their foraging strategies based on environmental cues. Teams prioritizing iterative approaches by reflecting on processes can adjust strategies in real time, maintaining performance and innovation. This iterative process thrives on learning from both successes and setbacks. Leaders can support this by embedding regular feedback mechanisms that encourage growth.

Imagining scenarios where adaptive cooperation is essential can highlight its value. In fast-moving industries like technology, where market demands shift quickly, teams adept at adjusting strategies will have a competitive advantage. Encouraging scenario planning and role-playing exercises can enhance teams' ability to respond to unforeseen challenges, much like birds altering their flight path in response to threats. By simulating high-pressure situations and fostering creative problem-solving, teams build resilience and adaptability, preparing them for future uncertainties.

Leveraging Network Theory for Complex Problem Solving

Network theory serves as a potent framework for dissecting and enhancing complex systems, offering valuable insights into improving collective problem-solving. By studying the interconnectedness within natural ecosystems, we uncover strategies applicable to human organizations. In nature, networks channel resources, information, and energy, allowing organisms to adapt and prosper in challenging environments. Similarly, by understanding and refining networks in human systems, we can achieve more effective cooperation and innovation. Research indicates that decentralized networks, similar to those in

ant colonies, can improve decision-making speed and accuracy within corporate teams. By adopting a network-oriented approach, organizations can
create an environment where knowledge and resources flow seamlessly, enabling teams to address challenges more efficiently.

Drawing from the resilience of biological networks, we can explore concepts like redundancy and robustness, which are intrinsic to natural systems.
These features ensure functionality even when certain connections fail. In
team dynamics, this translates to structures where multiple members have
overlapping skills or information. Such redundancy not only cushions the
impact of individual setbacks but also fosters diverse viewpoints, leading to
innovative solutions. Recent studies in organizational behavior suggest that
teams with built-in redundancies are more resilient during unexpected challenges, much like robust ecosystems that endure environmental changes.

Network theory also highlights the significance of weak ties—connections that might not be immediately influential but become crucial in unforeseen situations. These ties often link separate groups, facilitating the
flow of new ideas and driving innovation. Encouraging such connections
in professional settings can lead to breakthroughs by introducing fresh
perspectives and expertise. This concept complements the growing trend of
cross-disciplinary collaborations, where insights from varied fields converge
to tackle complex issues. Organizations that nurture open communication
and interconnectedness are better equipped to leverage the creative potential of their diverse teams.

As organizations tackle increasingly intricate problems, network theory
provides a strategic framework for enhancing team dynamics and collaboration. By mapping and analyzing the intricate web of interactions within
a team, leaders can pinpoint key influencers and potential bottlenecks,
optimizing the flow of information and resources. Advanced tools like social
network analysis now allow organizations to visualize and interpret these
interactions, offering actionable insights to boost team performance. This
approach not only strengthens collaboration but also fosters an adaptive
culture capable of navigating the ever-evolving challenges of today.

Reflecting on the blend of network theory and team dynamics challenges
us to rethink how we organize and manage human endeavors. By adopting
a network mindset, individuals and organizations can unlock the hidden
potential within teams, promoting a more creative and resilient approach to
problem-solving. As we continue to draw from nature's wisdom, integrating
these concepts into our professional practices promises to transform how
we address the complex challenges of our era. Thoughtful reflection on
these ideas can lead to actionable strategies that enhance both individual
and collective capabilities, driving a more innovative and adaptable society.

In exploring the theme of cooperation, we have delved into the fascinating dynamics of nature's collective wisdom, shedding light on the profound teachings embedded in mutualistic partnerships and group behaviors. These natural occurrences highlight the strength of unity and a common goal, offering valuable insights for enhancing human collaboration and organizational effectiveness. Observing how creatures such as bees and ants execute complex tasks through straightforward guidelines provides us with practical lessons for refining our decision-making and nurturing environments where teamwork excels. This chapter has illuminated the transformative potential of applying biological cooperation to strategies for innovation and solving problems. By integrating these principles into our daily and professional activities, we create pathways for more robust and adaptable systems. By embracing nature's cooperative wisdom, we not only deepen our comprehension of teamwork but also advance toward a future where human efforts harmonize with the sustainable and efficient processes of the natural world. As we progress, let's consider how principles of cooperation can inspire solutions to the challenges we encounter, inviting us to contemplate our role within the broader tapestry of life.

Chapter Five

Optimization Finding Perfect Balance

Imagine yourself in a verdant woodland, where each leaf and branch whispers tales of harmony honed over countless generations. In this serene setting, amid the gentle rustle of trees and the quiet buzz of life, nature showcases its remarkable talent for balance. It's an intricate dance of resourcefulness, where nothing is wasted, and everything has its place, ensuring both survival and growth. This delicate equilibrium prompts us to ask: How does the natural world achieve such a feat? In our era, where sustainability is a pressing goal and human innovation often seeks to achieve more with less, this forest stands as a sage guide, beckoning us to heed its lessons.

With this natural tableau as our guide, we embark on a quest to unravel the principles of refinement woven into the fabric of the world around us. Nature's creations—from the spirals found in seashells to the branching patterns of trees—often mirror the mathematical grace of the Fibonacci series. These designs are far from random; they are the blueprints of the environment for achieving both efficiency and beauty. As we delve into these patterns, we uncover the crucial role of response mechanisms in maintaining natural systems, ensuring that equilibrium is not just achieved but also preserved. These insights provide a compass, equipping us with the means to bring precision into our own innovations, from product development to process optimization.

As we delve further, the wisdom gleaned from nature's workshop guides us in rethinking our approach to design and creativity. The pursuit of improvement becomes a journey into understanding the intricate balance between precision and flexibility, a journey with significant implications for shaping our world. By embracing these environmental principles, we unlock the potential to not only boost our efficiency but also to create systems that are robust, sustainable, and in tune with the natural world's rhythm. Through this exploration, we discover inspiration and practical guidance, bridging the ancient with the contemporary, empowering us to craft solutions as graceful and effective as those found within the heart of the forest.

The Fibonacci Sequence in Nature's Designs

Imagine a world where the secrets of nature fuel our innovative spirit. Central to this realm is the Fibonacci sequence, a captivating mathematical pattern that finds expression in the spirals of shells, the graceful unfurling of fern fronds, and the intricate branching of trees. This sequence is not a mere cosmic fluke; it embodies a universal order that underpins balance and efficiency in the natural world. Each number in the Fibonacci series is the sum of the two preceding ones, transcending its mathematical roots to become a guiding principle for natural architecture. Through this sequence, nature achieves optimal growth and form, crafting patterns that are both visually appealing and functionally sound. This harmonious interplay inspires us, offering insights to tackle complex human challenges.

As we delve into this concept, we see the Fibonacci sequence shaping plant growth, where leaves, petals, and seeds align with precision to harness light and space. These principles extend to the animal kingdom, influencing proportions and patterns that contribute to the fluid elegance of creatures in motion. Beyond individual life forms, Fibonacci dynamics permeate ecosystems, fostering stability and resilience through a balanced distribution of resources and energy. Exploring further, the sequence's influence becomes apparent in biomimicry, where designers and innovators draw from these natural patterns to create products and systems that enhance functionality and sustainability. The journey through the Fibonacci sequence reveals a collaboration between numbers and nature, offering a blueprint for innovation that aligns our endeavors with the enduring wisdom of the natural world.

Patterns of Growth in Plants and Shells

Nature's complex designs often hint at a hidden order that aligns seamlessly with mathematical precision, illustrated vividly by the Fibonacci sequence. In this sequence, each number is the sum of the two preceding ones, and it appears in various natural patterns, showcasing an inherent harmony that optimizes growth and form. In the plant kingdom, the arrangement of leaves, petals, and seeds frequently follows Fibonacci numbers, enhancing sunlight exposure and spatial efficiency. The spiral formations in sunflowers, pinecones, and pineapples are more than just visually stunning; they are strategic configurations that ensure optimal packing and growth. Similarly, seashells demonstrate logarithmic spirals, a result of the Fibonacci sequence, allowing for proportional expansion as the organism matures, maintaining structural stability and balance.

The principles of Fibonacci extend beyond mere observation and form a basis for understanding resilience and resource management in biological systems. Cutting-edge biomimicry research examines these patterns to inspire innovations in architecture and engineering. Architects, for example, are adopting Fibonacci-based designs to create structures that are both aesthetically pleasing and structurally sound, drawing from the spiral arrangements found in mollusk shells and plant growth. This approach not only boosts visual appeal but also enhances energy efficiency and stability, reflecting nature's affinity for balance and refinement.

In the animal world, Fibonacci patterns surface in the proportions and structures of various species, affecting their movements and interactions with their surroundings. The spiral shapes of ram horns or the scale patterns on a pangolin are examples of nature's ability to blend functionality with aesthetics. These patterns are not random but represent evolutionary adaptations that provide advantages in aerodynamics, predator evasion, or resource acquisition. By examining these natural models, scientists and designers can create advanced materials and technologies that mimic such efficiency, leading to breakthroughs in fields like robotics and aerodynamics.

When exploring ecosystems, the Fibonacci sequence offers insights into the organization and interdependence of species. The arrangement of branches and leaves adheres to these patterns, optimizing light capture and nutrient distribution within intricate forest structures. Understanding these dynamics allows ecologists to better grasp how ecosystems maintain balance and resilience under external pressures. This knowledge can guide conservation strategies, helping to design interventions that support biodiversity and ecological health by emulating these naturally refined structures.

Drawing inspiration from Fibonacci's legacy, practical applications in biomimicry continue to evolve. From developing sustainable farming practices inspired by plant spirals to designing aerodynamic vehicles modeled after animal morphologies, the potential is immense. By embracing these natural principles, innovators can create solutions that not only address immediate challenges but also contribute to a sustainable future. Encouraging readers to consider how these ancient numerical patterns can be utilized in modern contexts, this exploration of Fibonacci's influence highlights the endless possibilities provided by nature's blueprint.

Mathematical Harmony in Animal Morphology

Nature's artistry is beautifully showcased through the mathematical elegance seen in animal shapes, where the Fibonacci sequence plays a crucial part. This series of numbers, where each term is the sum of the two before it, appears in the spiral formations and proportions of various creatures. Consider the nautilus shell, whose spirals follow the Fibonacci sequence, forming a logarithmic spiral that ensures both strength and efficient growth. This sequence is not just visually appealing; it embodies a fundamental principle of natural balance and proportion, guiding the development of many life forms.

Modern scientific investigations explore how these mathematical patterns enhance functionality and survival. In animal morphology, the golden ratio, closely linked to the Fibonacci sequence, often appears in anatomical structures. The spiral horns of a ram and the arrangement of scales on a pine cone serve as prime examples. These features not only please the eye but also provide mechanical advantages and efficient growth patterns. Such natural designs offer valuable insights for fields like robotics and architecture, where efficiency and resilience are crucial.

Recent studies suggest that this sequence affects not only physical form but also behaviors. Birds often utilize Fibonacci principles in their flight formations, optimizing energy use and boosting group cohesion. This knowledge inspires innovation in swarm robotics, where machines mimic these formations for improved coordination and resource management. Using Fibonacci principles in technology and design shows how nature's strategies can guide the creation of systems that require harmony and precision.

For those looking to apply these insights, the key lies in recognizing the inherent balance in Fibonacci-inspired designs. Engineers and designers can leverage these principles to create systems and products that are efficient, sustainable, and adaptable. By integrating mathematical harmony into technological creations, one can achieve solutions that are innovative and aligned with natural laws.

Consider the potential of adopting a Fibonacci-inspired approach in problem-solving. What new opportunities might arise if businesses embraced these principles to streamline operations or design products? This perspective encourages critical thinking, challenging the reader to move beyond traditional methods and explore the potential of nature's mathematical harmony as a blueprint for future innovations. Through this lens, the Fibonacci sequence transcends its numerical origins, becoming a vital tool in achieving balance and excellence across various fields.

Fibonacci Dynamics in Ecosystem Structures

Nature's ecosystems flourish through complex patterns that often reflect the Fibonacci sequence, a series where each number is the sum of the two preceding ones. This sequence is visible in various natural phenomena, such as the spirals of hurricanes, tree branches, and the arrangement of leaves around a stem. These patterns are strategic, optimizing space, energy, and resources within ecosystems. For instance, spiral leaf arrangements maximize sunlight exposure, boosting photosynthesis and growth. By studying these patterns, we can learn to create balance in complex systems, from ecological networks to urban planning.

The Fibonacci sequence also influences animal habitat architecture. Honeycomb structures crafted by bees showcase efficiency and strength. Each hexagonal cell uses minimal material while maximizing storage, embodying Fibonacci principles in hive construction. This natural engineering inspires innovations in structural design, emphasizing the harmony between form and function. Researchers are exploring biomimetic applications, aiming to develop materials and structures that replicate these efficiencies, potentially revolutionizing sustainable design.

Entire ecosystems display Fibonacci-inspired dynamics. Coral reefs, for example, exhibit fractal patterns that enhance resilience. These formations support diverse marine life by increasing habitat complexity and resource distribution. Their fractal design facilitates self-repair and adaptation, allowing ecosystems to endure environmental changes. By deciphering these natural blueprints, scientists and engineers can create resilient systems in other fields, such as adaptable telecommunications networks or disaster-resistant architectural designs.

Recent research has explored how Fibonacci principles affect predator-prey relationships and resource allocation in ecosystems. This highlights the need for balance, applicable to agriculture aiming to increase yield without exhausting resources. By adopting these natural strategies, sustainable farming can grow, promoting biodiversity and soil health. Integrating Fibonacci-inspired techniques in agriculture can lead to innovative solutions that ensure food security while maintaining ecological balance.

Fibonacci dynamics also extend to the digital world. Algorithms based on these patterns optimize data storage and retrieval. By structuring data like natural systems, computational models achieve greater efficiency and speed, advancing artificial intelligence and machine learning. This blend of natural and artificial systems fosters a symbiotic relationship between technology and nature, driving innovations that benefit both fields. As we unlock the secrets in nature's designs, we pave the way for sustainable and efficient solutions across various sectors.

Advanced Applications of Fibonacci in Biomimicry

Nature's creativity, as exemplified by the Fibonacci series, serves as a remarkable model for innovation, especially in biomimicry. This mathematical pattern, a symbol of natural symmetry, has spurred groundbreaking advancements in design and technology. In modern architecture, the spiraling forms of shells have inspired the creation of energy-efficient buildings that emulate the natural circulation of air and water, enhancing thermal control. Likewise, the leaf arrangement around a stem, designed for maximum sunlight exposure, has been adapted into solar panel designs that improve energy capture. These instances highlight how Fibonacci-inspired designs can surpass conventional methods, promoting innovation that aligns with ecological values.

In robotics, Fibonacci dynamics provide a framework for developing more agile and adaptive machines. Engineers have examined the movement patterns of animals, such as the spiral swimming of the nautilus or the coiling of a chameleon's tail, to create robots with superior balance and efficiency. This application has resulted in machines capable of effortlessly navigating complex terrains, offering solutions in sectors from search and rescue missions to space exploration. This fusion of biological insight and technological progress highlights the transformative potential of Fibonacci-based biomimicry, expanding the limits of machine capabilities.

The influence of the Fibonacci sequence reaches the microscopic level, where researchers investigate its role in cellular organization and function. Recent findings show that the arrangement of proteins and cellular components often follows Fibonacci patterns, optimizing biological processes. By emulating these configurations, scientists are developing new materials and pharmaceuticals with enhanced features, like greater strength or improved drug delivery. This intersection of biology and materials science showcases cutting-edge applications of Fibonacci principles, offering a glimpse into a future fueled by nature-inspired innovations.

In sustainability, Fibonacci-inspired models are used to create systems balancing efficiency with ecological harmony. Urban planners, for example, incorporate spiral patterns into city layouts to optimize resource distribution and transportation networks, reducing energy use and environmental impact. These designs are informed by the self-organizing principles of natural ecosystems, where resources are allocated to support resilience and adaptability. By adopting these natural patterns, we can develop human systems that not only fulfill our needs but also protect the environments we rely on.

To fully leverage Fibonacci-based biomimicry, it's crucial to cultivate a mindset that values curiosity and innovation. Consider how integrating these principles could enhance your work or projects. Could the spiral growth of a plant inspire a new product development approach or streamline workflows? What if the harmony observed in animal morphology guided the creation of more efficient machines or structures? By exploring these possibilities, we can unlock the transformative power of nature's most elegant designs, advancing solutions that are both sustainable and ingenious.

The Role of Feedback Loops in Natural Systems

In this exploration, we delve into the complex interplay of feedback mechanisms that shape the natural world, driving the elegance and efficiency of life on Earth. These mechanisms are the unseen maestros of nature's symphony, maintaining harmony and balance in ecosystems and organisms alike. Whether they are encouraging growth or imposing limits, feedback processes are the strands that weave stability with transformation. Within the vast narrative of evolution, they are the unsung champions, fostering the adaptation and resilience of species over countless generations. By orchestrating the flow of energy, resources, and information, these processes ensure that systems remain vibrant and finely balanced. From the homeostasis of a single cell to the equilibrium of entire ecosystems, feedback mechanisms reveal the deep wisdom inherent in nature's design.

As we journey deeper into this subject, we uncover how these natural systems offer valuable insights for human innovation and development. Positive and negative feedback processes are not just scientific curiosities; they are foundational principles that can be harnessed to optimize operations, enhance stability, and catalyze change in human endeavors. From the intricate relationships among species in a forest to the adaptive strategies that enable life to flourish in varied habitats, feedback mechanisms exemplify how interconnectedness and adaptability are vital for survival and success. By unraveling the intricacies of these processes, we gain knowledge to craft systems—whether in business, technology, or personal growth—that are not only efficient but also adaptable and resilient. Our exploration of feedback mechanisms in ecosystem stability, evolutionary adaptation, and advanced computational models promises a journey into the core of nature's wisdom, offering innovative pathways that are both robust and inspiring.

Understanding Positive and Negative Feedback Mechanisms

Feedback loops are crucial components in the intricate web of natural systems, acting as regulators that help maintain balance. These loops, categorized as either amplifying or stabilizing, manage diverse processes from cellular activities to ecosystem dynamics. Amplifying loops, such as those seen during childbirth with the hormone oxytocin, drive processes forward and can lead to rapid changes. Stabilizing loops, on the other hand, work to restore balance, as seen in the regulation of blood sugar levels through the interplay of insulin and glucagon. By understanding these loops, we gain insight into the delicate balance between change and stability that underpins survival and adaptation.

Recent biological research has revealed deeper roles for these loops, emphasizing their importance in resilience and adaptability. For example, studies on coral reefs show how interactions between algae and coral can either bolster an ecosystem's resilience or lead to its collapse under stress. These discoveries highlight the role of feedback loops not only in maintaining stability but also in shaping ecological and evolutionary pathways. By studying these natural patterns, innovators can derive insights for creating systems that are both robust and adaptable, capable of thriving amid uncertainties.

Applying the principles of feedback loops to human activities encourages a new approach to problem-solving and design. In sustainable agriculture, for instance, feedback-informed practices are revolutionizing crop management. By using data from soil sensors and satellite imagery, farmers can develop adaptive systems that optimize resource use, enhancing yields while reducing environmental impact. This mirrors nature's efficiency, using feedback to refine processes and achieve optimal outcomes. Such applications demonstrate the potential of feedback loops to drive innovation across various fields, from urban planning to healthcare.

Beyond their practical uses, feedback loops offer profound insights into change and development. They serve as reminders that progress often arises from cycles of action and reflection, where feedback informs adaptation and improvement. In personal growth, this perspective can be transformative. By becoming aware of our own feedback mechanisms—through self-reflection or external input—we can foster growth and resilience, turning challenges into opportunities for learning and evolution.

Reflecting further, one might consider the implications of feedback loops in artificial intelligence and machine learning. As these technologies increasingly mimic biological processes, integrating feedback mechanisms could enhance their ability to learn and adapt on their own. This poses intriguing questions about the future of human-machine interaction and the potential to create intelligent systems that evolve in sync with their environments. As we continue to explore the mysteries of feedback loops, the possibilities for innovation and discovery remain vast, a testament to the profound wisdom inherent in nature's designs.

Feedback Loops in Ecosystem Stability and Change

Feedback loops weave sophisticated communication pathways within ecosystems, governing the intricate dance between stability and change. These loops, classified as positive or negative, ensure ecosystems retain balance while allowing for dynamic transformations. Negative feedback loops serve as equilibrium maintainers, correcting deviations within systems. A classic example is the predator-prey cycle: as prey numbers rise, predator populations grow, eventually reducing the prey count and reinstating balance. In contrast, positive feedback loops can instigate change leading to new equilibriums, like how nutrient influxes cause algal blooms in water bodies, fundamentally altering ecosystem structure. Grasping these mechanisms provides crucial insights into ecosystem responses to various pressures, offering guidelines for crafting resilient human systems.

Recent ecological research has highlighted the pivotal role of feedback loops in fostering ecosystem resilience. Scientists have discovered how these loops help ecosystems withstand disruptions such as climate changes or human activities by absorbing impacts and reorganizing structures. For instance, the resilience of coral reefs amidst bleaching events is partly due to feedback mechanisms in symbiotic relationships between coral and algae. As stressors escalate, feedback drives the system toward balance, sometimes favoring more resilient species. This knowledge pushes us to reconsider traditional conservation strategies, emphasizing the preservation of feedback systems that sustain entire ecosystems.

Applying these natural principles to human-made systems is gaining momentum, particularly in designing sustainable urban areas. By emulating ecological feedback loops, cities can boost adaptability and sustainability. Urban planners are integrating green infrastructure that mimics natural processes, such as using vegetated surfaces for stormwater management, creating a feedback cycle of water absorption and purification. This not only reduces flooding risks but also enhances urban microclimates, showcasing how feedback loops can transform urban environments into self-regulating ecosystems.

Advancements in computational models have opened new avenues for simulating feedback loops in ecosystems, providing deeper insights into their functions and effects. These models, leveraging advanced algorithms and machine learning, can forecast ecosystem responses to various scenarios like climate change or habitat fragmentation. By merging data on species interactions, environmental conditions, and human impacts, researchers can identify potential tipping points and develop strategies to prevent ecological collapse. The implications for conservation and environmental management are significant, enabling more informed decisions aligned with natural rhythms and feedback patterns.

Exploring feedback loops in ecosystems prompts broader reflections on our role within these systems. How can we, as part of the biosphere, positively influence these loops without overstepping natural limits? By embracing a mindset sensitive to nature's feedback systems, we can cultivate a symbiotic relationship with our environment, where human actions enhance ecological health rather than diminish it. This shift demands not only technological advancements but also a cultural reorientation toward viewing ecosystems as partners in our shared quest for sustainability. Such an approach empowers us to draw on nature's wisdom in crafting solutions that are innovative and deeply aligned with the planet's life-sustaining processes.

The Role of Feedback in Evolutionary Adaptation

Feedback serves as a fundamental catalyst in the evolutionary process, ensuring organisms are intricately aligned with their surroundings. This system of response plays a pivotal role in evolution, where advantageous traits are magnified through positive responses, and detrimental ones are minimized through negative reactions. Such mechanisms allow species to adeptly navigate survival's complexities. As environments change, these systems facilitate gradual genetic refinement, enabling species to flourish or adjust to new challenges. From an evolutionary biology perspective, this continuous exchange between organisms and their environments fosters a symbiotic relationship that promotes adaptation, highlighting the essential role of feedback in evolution and providing insights beyond just biological realms.

A compelling illustration of feedback in evolutionary adaptation is seen in the dynamics between predators and prey. Here, response mechanisms maintain the equilibrium between predators and their prey. An increase in prey leads to a rise in predator numbers, which subsequently reduces the prey population, creating a cycle that stabilizes both groups over time. This balance prevents any species from dominating the ecosystem, showcasing a sophisticated form of natural regulation. Such interactions illustrate how feedback not only drives adaptation but also encourages biodiversity by maintaining ecological balance. Observing these natural phenomena offers insights into biological self-regulation and serves as a template for managing complex systems in diverse areas.

In genetic evolution, feedback guides adaptation by affecting gene expression and mutation rates. When environmental conditions favor certain traits, positive responses can enhance the spread of beneficial genes, while negative reactions can suppress the expression of less favorable traits, optimizing an organism's genetic structure to meet current environmental demands. These genetic feedback patterns are observed across numerous species, from bacteria developing antibiotic resistance to plants adjusting to climate change. The precision of these mechanisms demonstrates nature's optimization capabilities, offering a model for developing adaptive technologies that respond to changing conditions in real-time.

Advancements in computational biology allow researchers to model these systems with remarkable accuracy. By simulating evolutionary processes, scientists can explore the potential outcomes of various feedback scenarios, deepening the understanding of natural selection and adaptation. These models have practical applications in designing adaptive algorithms for artificial intelligence, enabling systems to learn and evolve based on environmental responses. The intersection of biology and technology through these models opens new pathways for innovation, providing tools to tackle complex challenges in fields such as medicine and environmental management.

Engaging with feedback within evolutionary adaptation prompts intriguing questions about the future of innovation. How might we leverage these mechanisms to create self-improving systems in technology and industry? What can we learn from nature's millennia of adaptation to enhance our resilience and adaptability? By translating these natural principles into actionable strategies, we can develop systems that are both efficient and sustainable, reflecting the wisdom inherent in evolution. Through this exploration, readers are encouraged to consider how feedback can inform the design of systems that are as adaptable and resilient as the natural world.

Advanced Computational Models of Biological Feedback Systems

Biological systems rely heavily on feedback loops, which are vital for maintaining stability and adaptability in life. These loops, whether reinforcing or balancing, control the complex interactions within organisms and ecosystems, ensuring they remain stable while adapting to environmental changes. With advancements in computational models, scientists can now replicate these natural feedback processes, offering valuable insights and applications across various fields, from ecology to artificial intelligence. By simulating the intricate cause-and-effect dynamics found in nature, these models pave the way for innovation, showcasing the immense potential of drawing inspiration from nature's strategies.

Advanced algorithms and simulations allow researchers to study biological feedback systems with exceptional accuracy. Inspired by ecosystems' self-regulating features, scientists create virtual environments to observe and manipulate these feedback processes. For instance, predator-prey relationships, governed by these loops, form the basis for predictive models that improve our understanding of population changes and resource management. These simulations not only clarify natural processes but also inspire strategies for sustainable development and conservation.

Feedback mechanisms in biology also play a crucial role in evolutionary adaptation, acting as catalysts for change and refinement. Incorporating feedback into computational models enables researchers to simulate evolutionary processes, exploring how organisms adapt to changing environments over time. These models are pivotal in developing genetic algorithms that mimic natural selection to tackle complex optimization challenges. By leveraging feedback mechanisms, genetic algorithms iteratively evolve solutions, refining them in response to simulated environmental pressures, much like their biological counterparts.

Beyond ecological and evolutionary contexts, feedback principles resonate in modern technology. Adaptive control systems, for example, mimic natural feedback processes to maintain balance in dynamic settings. These systems learn and adjust in real-time, optimizing performance in areas like autonomous vehicles and smart energy grids. By embedding feedback mechanisms, engineers create systems that not only react to changes but also anticipate them, ensuring robustness and efficiency in a constantly evolving landscape.

Exploring the potential applications of these insights reveals that understanding and imitating biological feedback systems could revolutionize our approach to innovation. Imagine scenarios where feedback-driven models inform decision-making in business and technology. By adopting a mindset attuned to the iterative and adaptive nature of feedback mechanisms, individuals and organizations can cultivate resilience and agility, turning challenges into opportunities for growth. Aligning with nature's age-old wisdom offers a compelling future vision where humanity collaborates with the natural world in a harmonious dance of progress.

Applying Precision and Optimization in Product Design

Nature has perfected the art of creating designs that are both efficient and sustainable, serving as a beacon for modern innovators who strive to integrate form with function. By examining the graceful curves of shells or the intricate patterns of honeycombs, designers can gain insights into crafting products that achieve their goals with minimal waste and significant impact. This journey uncovers a wealth of strategies where the beauty of nature's solutions can be emulated in human creations, ensuring that each component has a purpose and contributes to a larger vision.

As we delve into the intersection of nature and technology, advanced tools play a crucial role. Artificial intelligence acts as a valuable partner, turning vast data into actionable insights, refining the design process, and allowing for precision in creating products that resonate with nature's principles. Evolutionary algorithms replicate the adaptive techniques of the natural world, steering the continuous development of inventive designs that can adapt and improve over time. Combined with systems thinking, these methods offer a comprehensive approach to product design, where every part and its connection to the whole are taken into account. With this perspective, the quest for improvement becomes a journey towards creating products that are not only effective but also sustainable and in harmony with the environment.

Harnessing Biomimicry for Sustainable Design Solutions

Biomimicry acts as a connector between the timeless wisdom found in nature and the forefront of modern design, offering solutions that are both sustainable and technologically sophisticated. This discipline encourages the study of how natural organisms tackle intricate problems, using these insights to guide product development. For example, the lotus leaf's micro-textured surface, which naturally repels water and dirt, has inspired the creation of self-cleaning materials. These innovations not only extend the life of products but also minimize the need for chemical cleaning agents, promoting a more sustainable future. By embracing nature's efficient, resource-conserving strategies, designers can create products that are both functional and environmentally harmonious.

Exploring biomimicry uncovers numerous applications across diverse industries, from architecture to electronics. The study of termite mounds, for instance, has led to advancements in passive cooling systems for buildings, which utilize the natural ventilation techniques of termites to maintain steady internal temperatures. This energy-efficient approach reduces carbon footprints, demonstrating biomimicry's potential to drive eco-friendly innovation. Similarly, the streamlined bodies of fish have informed the design of advanced aquatic vehicles, enhancing speed and energy efficiency. These instances highlight biomimicry's capacity to transform product design by elegantly merging form with function.

Integrating biomimicry into design demands a shift in perspective, urging designers to adopt an ecological viewpoint. This approach uncovers innovative solutions that traditional methods might overlook. Supported by a growing body of research into nature's systemic patterns, this shift is exemplified by the decentralized communication in ant colonies, which has inspired algorithms that improve logistics and supply chains. By fostering a curious and exploratory mindset, designers can expand the boundaries of possibility, creating products that are both groundbreaking and ecologically sound.

To effectively utilize biomimicry for sustainable design, interdisciplinary collaboration is essential. By bringing together biologists, engineers, and designers, a richer understanding of the natural principles that underpin robust systems emerges. This collaborative approach enhances the creativity and depth of design solutions and ensures products are developed with a comprehensive view of their environmental impact. Encouraging cross-disciplinary dialogue and knowledge exchange can accelerate biomimicry adoption, leading to rapid advances in sustainable design and manufacturing.

As we continue to unlock the potential of biomimicry, staying open to nature's diverse possibilities is crucial. By challenging conventional design paradigms and embracing natural complexity, we can create products that are technically superior and aligned with ecological principles. This approach not only addresses immediate design challenges but also aligns with long-term sustainability goals. Encouraging designers to ask insightful questions and consider how nature's strategies can be adapted to human needs fosters a culture of innovation that is both responsible and forward-looking. By drawing inspiration from nature's oldest systems, we pave the way for a future where human creativity and natural intelligence coexist harmoniously.

Integrating AI-Driven Data Analysis in Design Processes

In product design, AI-driven data analysis offers remarkable advantages by enabling designers to achieve unprecedented precision and refinement. Through advanced algorithms, AI examines extensive datasets to uncover hidden trends and relationships that might otherwise go unnoticed. This function not only speeds up the design process but also improves the quality and performance of the final product. For example, AI can rapidly simulate numerous design iterations, pinpointing the most effective configurations to meet specific performance goals. This iterative process nurtures an innovative design environment, resulting in products that are both visually appealing and functionally superior.

A notable example of AI's transformative role in product design is in the automotive sector. By analyzing data from millions of vehicles, AI can forecast the effects of design changes on fuel efficiency and safety, allowing manufacturers to produce vehicles that are environmentally friendly and robust. This data-centric approach enables designers to make informed decisions, reducing dependency on traditional trial-and-error methods. Furthermore, AI insights allow for the personalization of products to cater to consumer needs, boosting satisfaction and market competitiveness. The capability to tailor products based on data-driven insights marks a significant shift in design philosophy, focusing on adaptability and precision.

The merging of AI and design also paves the way for sustainable innovation. By leveraging AI's predictive power, designers can foresee the environmental impact of their products throughout their lifecycle. This foresight optimizes materials and processes, reducing waste and minimizing carbon footprints. For instance, AI can assess the durability and recyclability of materials, suggesting alternatives that meet sustainability objectives without sacrificing performance. This convergence of technology and environmental responsibility highlights an evolving design trend—creating products that fulfill their purpose while promoting a sustainable future.

AI's influence in product design extends beyond mere enhancement; it encourages a culture of experimentation and creativity. Designers can use AI to explore unconventional concepts and test their feasibility in virtual environments before creating physical prototypes. This ability fosters risk-taking and the exploration of innovative ideas that might otherwise be overlooked due to cost or practicality concerns. By lowering barriers to innovation, AI empowers designers to push boundaries and develop groundbreaking products that redefine industry standards. This dynamic interaction between AI and human creativity initiates a new era in design where limitations are continually redefined.

The ethical implications of AI in product design require careful attention. As AI increasingly influences design decisions, it is vital to ensure these tools are used responsibly and transparently. Designers must be aware of potential biases in AI algorithms and strive to create products that are inclusive and fair. Promoting an ethical framework in AI-driven design processes safeguards against unintended consequences and enhances the societal value of products. By addressing these ethical considerations, designers can fully leverage AI's potential while upholding principles of fairness and accountability, contributing to a more equitable and innovative design landscape.

Leveraging Evolutionary Algorithms for Product Innovation

In the sphere of product development, evolutionary algorithms illuminate the pathway to innovation by emulating natural selection and adaptation, crafting groundbreaking design solutions. These algorithms replicate evolutionary principles like variation, selection, and inheritance, driving the creation of optimized products through continuous refinement. By mirroring nature's strategies, developers can explore a wide range of design possibilities, zeroing in on those that exemplify efficiency and functionality. Their impact spans various industries, from aerospace, where they contribute to the development of lightweight yet durable components, to consumer electronics, where they help achieve a balance between aesthetics and performance.

A remarkable feature of evolutionary algorithms is their capacity to discover novel solutions by exploring uncharted design spaces. Unlike traditional optimization methods limited by human biases or set parameters, these algorithms navigate a plethora of possibilities, sometimes identifying unexpected yet highly effective configurations. This ability is particularly valuable in complex systems with many interdependent variables, where human intuition may fall short. This results in a design process that is not only more innovative but also closely aligned with the complex balance observed in natural ecosystems.

Incorporating evolutionary algorithms into product design requires a blend of human creativity and computational prowess. Designers need to define success criteria and establish parameters for optimal performance, allowing the algorithmic process to explore and iterate. This collaborative effort ensures that the final product benefits from both computational efficiency and human insight. The interaction between human and machine fosters a dynamic environment where creativity is enhanced, leading to solutions that might otherwise remain undiscovered.

Recent advancements in computational resources and machine learning have significantly bolstered the capabilities of evolutionary algorithms, making them more accessible and powerful. These advancements facilitate the rapid processing of complex data and the ability to model intricate relationships within a design. Consequently, product developers can tackle challenges once deemed insurmountable, pushing the boundaries of possibility. The ongoing evolution of these technologies ensures that product innovation remains in constant flux, with each new breakthrough paving the way for further possibilities.

Considering the potential of evolutionary algorithms in product innovation, it is important to reflect on their broader implications. How can these algorithms be leveraged not only to create superior products but also to address societal issues like sustainability and resource conservation? By adopting a holistic approach that includes both technical and ethical considerations, innovators can ensure that this technology benefits the greater good. Engaging with these questions encourages a deeper exploration of how evolutionary algorithms can be integrated into broader design philosophies, ultimately shaping a future where technology and the natural world work in harmony.

Advanced Systems Thinking for Holistic Product Optimization

In the world of comprehensive product enhancement, employing advanced systems thinking is crucial. This approach integrates various components into seamless and effective designs, drawing inspiration from the interconnectedness seen in natural ecosystems. Here, each element is vital for maintaining balance and functionality. By studying how natural systems operate cohesively, designers can create products that maximize resource efficiency, reduce waste, and boost performance. Consider the mutual relationships in coral reefs, where species coexist and support each other, ensuring the ecosystem's survival. Similarly, product design can benefit from a systems approach that considers environmental impact, user experience, and economic sustainability, leading to efficient and enduring solutions.

A prime example of systems thinking applied to product enhancement is the creation of closed-loop systems, which emulate nature's cyclical processes. In these systems, materials are reused continually, reducing the demand for new resources and minimizing ecological impact. Companies like Interface, a pioneer in sustainable manufacturing, have implemented closed-loop models successfully, transforming waste into new products. This not only aligns with ecological principles but also provides a competitive advantage by lowering costs and attracting environmentally aware consumers. Viewing products as part of a larger ecosystem allows designers to uncover innovation opportunities that traditional linear models might miss, promoting a culture of continuous improvement and adaptability.

Incorporating advanced systems thinking also involves utilizing cutting-edge technologies, such as artificial intelligence and machine learning, to analyze complex interactions throughout a product's lifecycle. These technologies can reveal patterns and insights that might otherwise remain hidden, enabling designers to optimize products with exceptional precision. AI-driven simulations can forecast a product's performance under various conditions, allowing for adjustments before physical prototypes are built. This accelerates the design process and enhances the final product's reliability and efficiency. The fusion of digital tools with systems thinking creates a powerful synergy, broadening the horizons for transformative and practical innovation.

Advanced systems thinking prompts a shift from focusing on individual components to considering the entire system. This perspective encourages designers to question the conventional boundaries of their projects, exploring how each element interacts and contributes to overall goals. By adopting this holistic view, designers can develop solutions that are innovative and resilient in changing conditions. For instance, the automotive industry is moving towards designing vehicles as part of an integrated transportation network, where optimization extends beyond fuel efficiency to include connectivity, user experience, and environmental impact. This comprehensive approach ensures that products remain relevant and effective over time, adapting to evolving societal and planetary needs.

To fully leverage the potential of systems thinking in product enhancement, cultivating a mindset of curiosity and openness to new ideas is essential. This involves challenging established norms and exploring diverse perspectives, akin to how nature evolves through variation and selection. Designers and innovators are encouraged to pose thought-provoking questions, such as how a product might function in a future dominated by renewable energy or how it could contribute to a circular economy. By fostering a culture of inquiry and experimentation, organizations can unlock new avenues for innovation and sustainability. Advanced systems thinking thus provides a robust framework for navigating modern design complexities, empowering creators to develop products that harmonize with the intricate web of life on Earth.

Nature offers a masterclass in balance and precision, where survival hinges on the delicate dance of efficiency and harmony. The Fibonacci sequence, a testament to mathematical grace, unveils the intricate patterns that form the backbone of countless natural designs, shedding light on how we might bring this harmony into our own creations. Feedback loops, nature's tool for maintaining balance, emphasize the necessity of ongoing reflection and adaptation both in ecosystems and in our human-made systems. By weaving these natural principles into product design, we open doors to innovations that champion sustainability and efficiency. This journey into optimization not only highlights its role in nature's grand design but also challenges us to rethink our approach to problem-solving. As we delve deeper into nature's vast laboratory, consider how these lessons might reshape your perspective on tackling challenges. What other marvels of the natural world are poised to inspire our next leaps forward? Seen through this lens, the future brims with possibility, urging us to stay curious and attuned to the insights nature provides.

Chapter Six

Self Organization Order Without Central Control

As the sun dips below the horizon in a vibrant city, streetlights flicker on, casting a warm glow on the unfolding spectacle above. A flock of starlings rises into the twilight, creating mesmerizing patterns in the sky. This stunning display, known as a murmuration, is a marvel of nature's spontaneous choreography, where order materializes without any single leader. Watching this seamless dance invites us to consider how such intricate harmony can emerge from simplicity, urging us to explore similar dynamics in our own pursuits, sparking creativity and fostering systems that thrive on shared coordination.

This principle of autonomous coordination is not confined to the skies; it resonates throughout the natural world. From the tiny interactions within cells to the vast migrations of animal groups, nature showcases systems that function with breathtaking efficiency and resilience, often without hierarchical oversight. These systems excel in adaptability and optimization, frequently surpassing human-engineered solutions. By delving into the mechanics of these natural wonders, we gain insights that could transform how we design our organizations, communities, and technologies.

In this chapter, we will uncover nature's blueprint for achieving order without central control. We will explore the principles of decentralized order through the wonders of biology and translate these ideas into practical strategies applicable to various aspects of human life. Nature's proven systems offer a new model for progress—one that values collaboration, adaptability, and emerging harmony. By aligning with these natural processes, we become better equipped to navigate the complexities of modern life with grace and efficiency.

Flocking Behavior in Birds and Self-Organized Systems

In the vast expanse of the sky, flocks of birds perform a captivating dance, crafting intricate patterns that captivate the eye. This mesmerizing spectacle is a testament to the power of autonomous coordination, where each bird, acting on simple instincts and cues from nearby companions, contributes to a stunning display of synchronicity. Despite the absence of a leader, these flocks exemplify decentralized order, illustrating how complex behaviors naturally emerge from local interactions. This phenomenon, intriguing to both scientists and innovators, demonstrates that order and adaptability can arise without centralized control, offering insights with far-reaching implications beyond the avian realm.

Delving into the dynamics and patterns that characterize these flocking behaviors, we encounter mathematical models that encapsulate the essence of such systems. These models not only enhance our appreciation for nature's brilliance but also inspire inventive algorithms that drive technological progress. By exploring the principles of distributed decision-making, we gain valuable insights applicable to various complex systems, from ecological networks to organizational structures. This journey into the world of emergent systems promises to reveal nature's lessons, providing transformative insights that fuel human creativity and advancement.

Patterns and Dynamics of Avian Flocking

In nature, the flocking of birds stands out as a prime example of autonomous coordination, where each bird follows simple rules to create intricate and coordinated movements without a central leader. This phenomenon goes beyond mere spectacle, revealing a complex system of communication and coordination crucial for survival and efficiency. Birds in a flock respond to their neighbors' positions and speeds, maintaining unity while avoiding collisions and rapidly adapting to environmental shifts. Species like starlings and sandpipers showcase this spontaneous behavior, highlighting the efficiency of decentralized decision-making in achieving optimal outcomes. Recent research underscores the precision with which birds adjust their paths, offering deep insights into the mechanics of emergent systems.

Mathematical models of flocking provide valuable frameworks for understanding self-organization in diverse contexts. The Boids model, for instance, uses algorithms to simulate flocking dynamics, focusing on alignment, separation, and cohesion. These models demonstrate that complex group behaviors can emerge from simple local interactions, a principle applicable beyond ornithology. Researchers have applied these insights to fields like robotics and computer science, developing algorithms that mimic flocking to enhance coordination in autonomous vehicles and wireless sensor networks. This cross-disciplinary application of bird-inspired models highlights the universal nature of self-organizing principles, showcasing their potential to transform technological systems.

Flocking behavior inspires innovative solutions, especially in swarm robotics. By mimicking the decentralized control seen in bird flocks, engineers have developed robotic systems that solve problems efficiently and flexibly. These robots, like birds, operate without central commands, relying on simple peer-to-peer interactions to accomplish complex tasks. This method has advanced areas such as environmental monitoring, where swarm robots adaptively cover vast regions, and logistics, where they streamline warehouse operations. Insights from avian flocking continue to expand technological possibilities, challenging traditional notions of control and coordination.

The implications of decentralized order extend beyond technology, influencing how we view and manage complex systems in various fields. In ecosystems, autonomous coordination fosters resilience and adaptability, allowing species to thrive in changing environments. In human organizations, adopting similar principles can create more dynamic and responsive structures. By decentralizing decision-making and empowering individuals, businesses can boost innovation and agility, mirroring natural systems' adaptive strategies. This shift encourages moving away from hierarchical models, fostering a culture of collaboration and emergent problem-solving.

Reflecting on the grace of avian flocking prompts us to reconsider traditional organizational and management approaches. How can our systems benefit from the fluidity and adaptability seen in nature? What lessons can we learn from the seamless coordination of birds to enhance human collaboration? By exploring these questions, we can discover new pathways for innovation, drawing directly from nature's enduring wisdom. Embracing the principles of autonomous systems holds the promise of transforming not only our technologies but also the frameworks we use to navigate the complexities of our world.

Mathematical Models of Self-Organization in Nature

In nature, self-organization is evident through complex patterns and behaviors that develop without a central guiding force. Mathematical models have become crucial in deciphering these phenomena, revealing the fundamental rules that govern systems as varied as ant colonies, neural networks, and weather patterns. These models offer frameworks to abstract complex biological interactions into measurable parameters, enabling researchers to simulate and predict behaviors in natural and synthetic settings. For instance, the Vicsek model—a significant mathematical construct—illustrates how simple local rules can lead to the coordinated movement of bird flocks. By assigning each agent a velocity and direction based on the average direction of nearby agents, the model encapsulates flocking behavior's essence, showcasing the strength of decentralized order.

Advanced computational techniques have refined these models further, allowing for more precise simulations that consider additional factors like environmental influences and inter-agent communication. The exploration of agent-based models (ABMs) has deepened our understanding of autonomous coordination, providing insights into how straightforward, rule-based interactions can result in complex, adaptive system-wide behaviors. These models extend beyond theoretical studies; they hold practical significance in designing autonomous systems in fields like technology and robotics. By mimicking the decentralized decision-making processes seen in nature, engineers can develop robust, scalable systems capable of adapting to unforeseen challenges, akin to a flock of birds reacting to a predator.

The expanding field of swarm intelligence heavily relies on these mathematical models, pushing the limits of what's achievable in autonomous, multi-agent systems. Innovations such as drone swarms, which can collectively execute tasks like mapping or search-and-rescue missions, draw their strategies from the principles of decentralized order. The algorithms guiding these swarms are inspired by natural models, enabling the drones to function without a central command, thus enhancing flexibility and resilience. This mirrors the natural world's efficiency, where organisms like bees or ants optimize resource use through collective behavior, ensuring survival in various environments.

In business and organizational strategy, these mathematical insights have significant implications. By embracing self-organizing principles, companies can enhance innovation and adaptability. This shift encourages a move away from rigid hierarchies towards more agile, responsive structures, where decision-making is distributed among individuals or teams. Such an environment fosters creativity and problem-solving, empowering employees to act autonomously, similar to agents in an emergent system. Applying these principles can lead to increased efficiency, as teams self-regulate and collaborate dynamically to tackle challenges, echoing the adaptive strategies observed in nature.

As we delve deeper into mathematical models of autonomous coordination, critical questions arise: How can these models be refined to incorporate more complex interactions and variables? What ethical considerations must be addressed when implementing autonomous systems inspired by nature? By tackling these questions, innovators and researchers can expand the boundaries of what's possible, utilizing natural principles to address contemporary challenges. The lessons derived from these models not only enhance our understanding of natural systems but also offer a blueprint for creating more resilient, adaptable, and intelligent human systems.

Insights from Flocking Algorithms for Technological Innovation

Birds soaring in unison, moving with extraordinary precision, exemplify nature's remarkable coordination. This phenomenon, known as flocking behavior, fascinates scientists and technologists alike, inspiring the creation of algorithms that replicate these natural mechanics. The essence of such self-regulating systems is their ability to function without centralized control, achieving impressive synchronization and flexibility. By analyzing these patterns, researchers have developed flocking algorithms that become powerful tools for technological advancement. These algorithms, based on the principles of alignment, cohesion, and separation, offer a foundation for designing systems that are robust, efficient, and adaptable.

In computer science and robotics, flocking algorithms have sparked progress in autonomous vehicle navigation and swarm robotics. For instance, the concepts borrowed from bird flocking allow drones to maneuver through complex environments together, improving their capabilities in operations like search and rescue or environmental monitoring. These systems feature agents that communicate locally and adjust their actions based on neighboring agents, mirroring the decentralized decision-making seen in bird flocks. This method not only enhances system resilience but also lightens the computational burden on each agent, promoting efficient function in dynamic settings.

Beyond the realm of robotics, the insights gained from flocking algorithms have influenced data networking. Similar to how birds communicate directional changes, data packets in decentralized networks can be rerouted on the fly, optimizing traffic flow and boosting network reliability. This self-organizing strategy is increasingly relevant as bandwidth demands rise and network topologies grow more intricate. Implementing these algorithms in network protocols promises to improve the efficiency and scalability of communication systems, ensuring smooth data transmission even in changing conditions.

The potential of flocking algorithms extends further into organizational management and business structures. Companies are exploring models that move away from traditional hierarchies in favor of more fluid, self-organized teams. By creating an atmosphere where employees can autonomously align their actions with broad objectives, businesses can foster creativity and agility.

This strategy not only mirrors the adaptability of bird flocks but also equips organizations to respond swiftly to market shifts and innovation opportunities. Encouraging distributed decision-making empowers individuals while maintaining collective coherence, driving both personal and organizational growth.

As we look to the future of technological innovation, we must consider: How can we further leverage the principles of self-organization to tackle the growing complexity of modern systems? Exploring flocking algorithms invites us to rethink the way we design, manage, and optimize both natural and artificial systems. By embracing the elegance of self-organization, we can unlock new levels of efficiency and resilience, guiding us toward a future where technology seamlessly integrates with the intricate dynamics of the natural world.

Implications of Decentralized Control in Complex Systems

Decentralized control in complex systems reveals a fascinating interplay where order naturally emerges from disorder. This concept is beautifully demonstrated by the intricate dynamics of bird flocks. These gatherings of birds show a delicate balance between independence and collaboration. Each bird follows simple rules, yet the group forms complex and harmonious patterns without a central leader. This phenomenon challenges the conventional belief that top-down control is necessary for organized behavior. The beauty of these systems lies in their resilience and adaptability. By examining these natural patterns, researchers gain insights into creating artificial systems that mirror this self-organizing efficiency, offering new avenues for innovation across various fields.

In technology, decentralized control underpins advancements such as swarm robotics and distributed networks. Here, individual units use local information to work together towards a shared goal without centralized direction. This method boosts resilience, allowing systems to adjust to new conditions and recover from disruptions with minimal external help. Swarm robotics, for instance, takes cues from the self-organized behavior of bird flocks, enabling robots to collaborate on tasks like search and rescue or environmental monitoring. These innovations demonstrate the potential of decentralized control to transform the design and implementation of complex technological solutions.

Beyond technology, the application of decentralized control is reshaping business structures. Traditional hierarchies are being replaced by more fluid and dynamic models. Companies are experimenting with organizational frameworks that empower employees to make decisions independently, fostering innovation and flexibility. By distributing control and encouraging self-organization, businesses can respond swiftly to market changes and customer demands. This approach not only boosts efficiency but also increases employee engagement, as individuals experience a greater sense of ownership and responsibility. The insights from nature's decentralized systems offer a blueprint for organizations aiming to succeed in a fast-changing environment.

A deeper exploration of decentralized control invites a reevaluation of how we perceive complexity. Instead of viewing complex systems as puzzles needing intricate solutions, nature shows us that simplicity can lead to sophistication. In self-organized systems, each participant follows straightforward rules, yet the collective result is an intricate and effective structure. This insight challenges conventional wisdom and encourages exploration of how simple, scalable strategies can address complex human challenges. Embracing this perspective opens doors to innovative approaches that leverage decentralized control in surprising ways.

As we ponder the potential of decentralized systems, intriguing questions emerge: How can we use the principles of self-organization to tackle global issues like climate change or resource distribution? What role does decentralized control play in enhancing resilience in social systems, and how can these principles be woven into policy-making? These questions prompt critical thinking about the possibilities and limits of decentralized control, encouraging a deeper exploration of its implications across various domains. By learning from nature, we gain not only a deeper appreciation for the intricacies of complex systems but also a powerful toolkit for crafting innovative solutions in an interconnected world.

The Cellular Automaton: How Cells Organize and Regenerate

Imagine a morning where our bustling cities operate with the seamless efficiency of a finely tuned orchestra, each part moving in harmony without a central conductor. This vision of autonomous coordination, where order naturally arises from chaos, is a fascinating phenomenon vividly showcased in the microscopic realm of cellular automata. In nature, cells transcend their roles as mere structural units; they are vibrant, dynamic entities adept at organizing, communicating, and regenerating with astonishing accuracy. Their capacity for autonomous coordination and repair transcends mere biological intrigue, offering a masterclass in resilience and adaptability. As we delve into this cellular symphony, we uncover the principles guiding their intricate choreography, revealing a world where each cell inherently knows its purpose and function.

This cellular dance offers profound insights for human innovation, suggesting new paradigms for designing our systems and structures. By exploring the mechanisms of regeneration and the dynamic patterns emerging from cellular interactions, we can reimagine our problem-solving approaches and organizational designs. These insights extend beyond biology, challenging us to rethink how businesses and communities might embrace this natural wisdom. As we embark on this journey, the lessons of cellular coordination present a compelling vision of decentralized order, inviting us to draw inspiration from the microscopic to the macro and apply these insights to our own complex systems.

Principles of Cellular Coordination and Communication

In life's intricate web, cells engage in sophisticated communication and coordination, executing complex tasks without a centralized authority. This self-governing phenomenon, known as autonomous coordination, is crucial for cellular operations, allowing systems to sustain harmony and resilience. At the core of this cellular dance lies an intricate exchange of signals. Cells employ chemical and electrical cues, akin to a biological Morse code, to transmit information. These signals direct cellular processes like growth, differentiation, and apoptosis, ensuring each cell plays its part in the organism's health. Recent breakthroughs in cellular biology have shed light on these communication pathways, revealing a dynamic interplay that adapts to both internal and external stimuli.

A particularly fascinating aspect of cellular coordination is quorum sensing, a mechanism that enables cells to sense their population density and modify their behavior accordingly. This process is like a biological voting system, where the 'votes' are chemical signals exchanged among cells. In bacteria, quorum sensing regulates behaviors like biofilm formation and pathogenicity, highlighting its vital role in survival and adaptation. This concept has inspired novel approaches in biotechnology, such as designing synthetic systems that mimic these natural processes to achieve outcomes like targeted drug delivery and environmental monitoring.

Delving deeper into cellular communication, gap junctions and receptor-ligand interactions become essential. These structures and processes enable direct intercellular communication, allowing cells to synchronize their activities. Gap junctions create channels between neighboring cells, facilitating the transfer of ions and small molecules, crucial for maintaining tissue balance. Meanwhile, receptor-ligand interactions involve the binding of molecules to specific receptors, triggering a cascade of intracellular events. These mechanisms exemplify nature's ingenuity in fostering coordinated responses without centralized control, offering a blueprint for designing decentralized networks in technology and business.

The implications of autonomous coordination extend far beyond biology, providing fertile ground for innovation in various human endeavors. By emulating the decentralized communication strategies of cells, businesses and organizations can achieve greater adaptability and resilience. The rise of flat organizational structures and distributed networks in the corporate world mirrors the cellular paradigm, promoting autonomy and rapid decision-making. This approach fosters an environment where teams can self-organize, respond to challenges fluidly, and seize emergent opportunities. Such adaptive strategies are becoming increasingly valuable in today's fast-paced and unpredictable landscape.

As we explore the intricacies of cellular communication, it becomes clear that nature's autonomous systems offer profound insights into the essence of innovation. By understanding and applying these principles, we can transcend traditional boundaries, crafting solutions that are not only efficient but also inherently sustainable. The dance of cellular communication and organization challenges us to rethink our approaches to problem-solving, urging us to embrace complexity and harness it to drive meaningful change. In doing so, we unlock the potential to create systems that are both robust and harmonious, reflecting the elegance of nature's own designs.

Mechanisms of Cellular Regeneration and Repair

The natural world is a testament to the remarkable ability of living systems to regenerate and repair themselves—a sophisticated process honed by evolution. At the core of this phenomenon is a complex web of signals that allows cells to identify damage and activate precise repair mechanisms. For example, when the skin incurs an injury, cells quickly spring into action to mend the wound. This response is orchestrated by growth factors and signaling pathways that guide cells in their movement, division, and specialization. Such self-healing demonstrates an intricate understanding of resource optimization, as cells efficiently restore function without centralized control, much like musicians in an orchestra who create harmony without a conductor.

Cutting-edge research into cellular regeneration reveals the pivotal role of stem cells, which serve as the body's fundamental building blocks, capable of transforming into various cell types required for repair. Nestled within tissues, these adaptable cells remain dormant until injury signals awaken them. Upon activation, they multiply and evolve into specialized cells that seamlessly integrate into existing structures. This versatility offers a blueprint for breakthroughs in medicine and bioengineering, where scientists strive to harness stem cells for innovative therapies. By replicating nature's strategies, researchers hope to develop treatments that activate the body's inherent repair abilities, providing new hope for conditions once deemed beyond cure.

The concept of emergent behavior in cellular systems highlights the elegance of self-organization seen in how cells communicate through chemical and mechanical signals to synchronize their actions. This interaction fosters the development of complex structures and functions, such as liver tissue regeneration or bone repair. This phenomenon captivates various fields, inspiring novel problem-solving approaches that prioritize cooperation and flexibility over rigid hierarchies. By adopting principles of emergent behavior, organizations can stimulate creativity similar to cellular processes, promoting decentralized decision-making and adaptive responses to changing environments.

The lessons of cellular self-organization extend beyond biology, offering valuable insights for human innovation. In business, applying self-organizing principles can lead to more resilient and agile structures. Empowering teams to function independently enhances adaptability to shifting markets and customer demands. The cellular model encourages a move from top-down management to a network of interconnected units working collaboratively, akin to cells in tissue. This shift can boost efficiency and innovation, as employees are motivated to take initiative and capitalize on their unique talents within a supportive framework.

To apply these insights practically, consider how cellular regeneration mechanisms can guide strategies for organizational renewal. Just as cells use feedback loops to regulate their repair processes, organizations can establish systems for continuous evaluation and adaptation. This involves nurturing a culture of ongoing learning and improvement, where feedback is valued and informs decision-making. Encouraging experimentation and risk-taking, akin to the trial-and-error processes in cellular repair, can further enhance an organization's capacity to innovate and thrive in a constantly changing landscape. By drawing inspiration from the cellular world, we can uncover new pathways for growth and transformation in our pursuits.

Patterns of Emergent Behavior in Cellular Systems

In cellular systems, the phenomenon of autonomous coordination is captivating. It showcases how intricate behaviors emerge from basic rules and interactions between individual units, all without a central command. Within these systems, cells exchange information and synchronize through chemical messages, mechanical forces, and electrical signals, weaving complex patterns and functionalities. This collective behavior is not orchestrated by a singular authority but emerges from the actions of numerous cells, each responding to its immediate environment. A prime example is the development of a multicellular organism, where cells diversify and arrange into tissues and organs, steered by genetic instructions and environmental influences. This process resembles a symphony, with each musician contributing to a harmonious and purposeful ensemble.

The regenerative prowess of cellular systems further underscores the potential of autonomous coordination. When an organism sustains an injury, nearby cells swiftly communicate and reorganize to mend the damage. This intricate process, driven by feedback loops, encompasses cell proliferation, their migration to the wound, and differentiation into requisite cell types. Research into salamanders, renowned for their limb regeneration abilities, has shed light on some conserved molecular pathways, offering insights into enhancing regenerative medicine for humans. By deciphering and leveraging these natural processes, scientists are pioneering therapies that could transform healing and tissue regeneration.

Self-organized interactions are also vital in immune responses. The immune system's capacity to detect and neutralize pathogens hinges on the coordinated actions of diverse cell types. Lymphocytes, macrophages, and dendritic cells collaborate through intricate signaling networks to mount a robust defense. This decentralized strategy allows rapid adaptation to new threats, illustrating a resilient system. Advances in systems biology and computational modeling have deepened our understanding of these interactions, highlighting how subtle molecular changes can significantly affect immune function. Such insights pave the way for novel immunotherapies that harness the body's natural defenses with precision.

In the realm of human innovation, insights from cellular self-organization can inspire transformative changes in organizational structures and processes. Businesses can adopt distributed models that empower teams to operate independently while still aligning with overarching goals. This mirrors cellular function within an organism, where local interactions drive global order. Companies like Valve Corporation exemplify this model, allowing employees to choose projects and form teams organically, resulting in a dynamic and innovative environment. Embracing autonomous coordination principles can foster creativity, enhance agility, and boost overall performance.

Exploring the potential of cellular self-organization presents both opportunities and challenges. While its decentralized nature offers flexibility and resilience, it necessitates mechanisms to ensure coherence and prevent disorder. Thought-provoking questions arise: How do we balance autonomy with alignment in human systems? What safeguards are critical to maintaining order without stifling innovation? Addressing these requires a nuanced understanding of self-organizing principles and their implications for human endeavors. By studying and emulating behaviors found in cellular systems, we can unlock new possibilities for growth and innovation, crafting solutions that are efficient and adaptive in our ever-evolving world.

Implications of Cellular Self-Organization for Human Innovation

Delving into the realm of cellular coordination unveils a wealth of knowledge that holds the potential to transform human innovation. Central to this concept is the capacity of cells to manage intricate tasks independently, relying on local interactions and feedback rather than a central command. This mirrors the synchronized movements of bird flocks or fish schools, where each unit reacts to its surroundings to create a cohesive and effective group behavior. Within cellular systems, each cell operates autonomously yet remains interconnected, allowing the entire system to adapt, heal, and flourish. This decentralized model provides inspiration for designing human systems that can adapt and remain robust, especially in fields like organizational management and urban planning, where traditional hierarchical models often struggle with complexity.

Advancements in computational biology and systems theory have illuminated the precise ways in which cells organize themselves. Scientists are discovering how cells use chemical gradients, electrical signals, and mechanical cues to reach collective decisions. This concept translates to human contexts as we adopt distributed networks and real-time data for decision-making. For example, businesses can use these insights to develop flexible organizational structures that react swiftly to market fluctuations. By mimicking cellular communication pathways, companies can establish networks where information flows seamlessly, enabling prompt decision-making at the action's origin, reducing delays, and enhancing responsiveness.

A striking example of cellular coordination is evident in regenerative medicine. Stem cells, for instance, exhibit an impressive ability to form complex tissues and even entire organs, driven by inherent self-regulating mechanisms. This regenerative capability could inspire novel approaches in urban development and infrastructure design. Picture cities designed not only to endure challenges but to evolve and renew themselves, much like living organisms. By incorporating principles of autonomous coordination, urban planners can create adaptable environments that meet evolving needs, promoting sustainability and resilience.

Diverse viewpoints on cellular coordination pave the way for innovation. Some researchers advocate for biomimetic strategies, directly emulating cellular processes to address human challenges. Others suggest hybrid models that combine biological inspiration with technological advancements. Swarm robotics, for instance, draws from cellular coordination, enabling simple robots to collectively perform tasks exceeding individual capabilities. These innovations extend to logistics and disaster response, where decentralized decision-making and adaptability can significantly boost efficiency and effectiveness.

Considering the implications of cellular coordination raises a broader question: How can we leverage these natural strategies to create systems that not only endure but thrive amidst uncertainty? Adopting this perspective encourages a shift from rigid, top-down models to more fluid, adaptable structures. By nurturing environments where individual elements contribute to a greater whole, we unlock the potential for sustained creativity and growth. The future of human systems lies not in merely copying nature's solutions but in understanding their underlying principles and applying them creatively to our unique challenges.

Implementing Self-Organization in Business Structures

In recent years, the business landscape has undergone a significant transformation, embracing self-organized models inspired by nature's decentralized systems. Companies are discovering that emulating these natural structures can lead to remarkable flexibility and creativity. This shift moves organizations away from rigid hierarchies, fostering a more adaptable and responsive way of operating. Just as nature finds harmony through complex networks of interaction, businesses are learning to thrive by encouraging environments where creativity and efficiency naturally flourish. This change is not merely a passing trend but a fundamental rethinking of organizational structures in a rapidly evolving world. The appeal of self-organized systems lies in their capacity to adapt and grow, akin to the graceful coordination of bird flocks that journey vast distances through shared insights rather than a singular command.

This evolution prompts a closer look at how decentralized decision-making can empower employees, enhancing agility and robustness in business. By leveraging feedback loops, companies can achieve self-regulation, maintaining a balanced and adaptive approach to change. Central to this transformation is nurturing a culture of independence and empowerment, where individuals are encouraged to take initiative and openly share their insights. By integrating flexible systems, organizations can allocate resources dynamically, allowing them to swiftly adapt to new challenges. These ideas coalesce to create a business environment where innovation emerges naturally, guided by principles that have supported life on Earth for eons. As we delve into these themes, the path to embracing self-organization in business becomes clearer, offering a strategic edge grounded in nature's wisdom.

Leveraging Decentralized Decision-Making for Agility

Decentralized decision-making is a transformative approach in business, acting as a catalyst for organizational agility. By distributing authority across various levels, companies can quickly adapt to changing conditions, leveraging the collective intelligence and creativity of their workforce. This strategy not only speeds up decision-making but also empowers employees to take initiative, fostering a culture of ownership and accountability. Consider the innovative structure of Valve Corporation, where employees self-organize into project teams based on their interests and expertise. This dynamic setup allows for rapid shifts and continuous innovation, keeping the company at the cutting edge.

Recent studies highlight the advantages of decentralized models, noting their enhanced resilience and adaptability, especially in turbulent markets. These organizations, unburdened by bureaucratic obstacles, can seize opportunities and mitigate risks more effectively. In contrast, traditional hierarchies often struggle with decision-making delays due to bureaucratic inertia. Moreover, decentralized systems align with modern workforce expectations, valuing autonomy and empowerment, which attract and retain top talent.

To implement decentralized decision-making successfully, organizations must foster an environment where communication is open and transparent. Establishing robust channels for knowledge sharing and collaboration is crucial. Collaborative platforms and digital tools can facilitate seamless interactions across diverse teams, ensuring insights and information flow freely. Leaders should transition from directive roles to facilitators, supporting and guiding rather than controlling. This shift requires trust and a willingness to embrace experimentation, accepting that occasional missteps are part of innovation.

As businesses embrace decentralized models, they must address potential challenges. Balancing autonomy with alignment to overarching goals is vital. A clear vision and shared objectives help maintain focus and coherence, ensuring decentralized activities align with the company's strategic direction. Leaders can achieve this by cultivating a strong organizational culture that reinforces core values and mission, providing a common framework for autonomous operation.

Imagine a global corporation adopting decentralized decision-making, allowing regional teams to tailor strategies to local market dynamics. This approach enhances responsiveness and leverages diverse perspectives and expertise. By empowering employees to adapt and innovate within their unique contexts, the organization gains a competitive edge, navigating complex landscapes with precision. Embracing decentralized decision-making not only transforms business structures but also unlocks the full potential of human creativity and ingenuity, paving the way for sustained success.

Harnessing Feedback Loops to Enhance Self-Regulation

Self-regulation in organizations thrives when feedback loops are strategically integrated, drawing inspiration from nature's ability to maintain balance in complex systems. These loops form the core of self-organizing entities, allowing them to adjust and adapt dynamically without centralized control. In business, this often takes shape through real-time data analytics, which offer continuous insights into operations, prompting swift strategy and process adjustments. By embedding such loops into organizational structures, companies can create environments that prioritize continuous growth and learning over static procedures and rigid hierarchies.

Technological advancements, particularly in artificial intelligence and machine learning, have greatly enhanced feedback systems. These technologies simplify data collection and enrich the analysis of complex datasets. Predictive analytics, for example, can anticipate market shifts, enabling preemptive strategy changes. Similarly, AI-driven customer feedback systems can discern consumer behavior patterns, facilitating personalized and responsive services. By leveraging these advanced tools, businesses can build strong feedback mechanisms, ensuring they remain agile and responsive in ever-evolving markets.

Creating a feedback-rich corporate culture involves more than technology; it requires a cultural shift towards transparency and open communication. Organizations that actively seek and act on feedback tend to flourish. Encouraging a mindset that views feedback as a growth tool rather than criticism is key. Regular reflection sessions, open forums, and collaborative platforms can channel feedback effectively, empowering stakeholders to contribute insights that drive innovation. This democratization of feedback not only enhances self-regulation but also aligns with the broader goal of fostering a culture of autonomy and empowerment.

The principles of biological feedback loops highlight the need for balance between positive and negative feedback. In business, positive feedback reinforces successful strategies, while negative feedback points out areas needing improvement, preventing stagnation and fostering resilience. A prime example is the agile framework in project management, where iterative feedback cycles refine products incrementally. This ensures each development stage benefits from direct stakeholder input, resulting in refined, market-ready solutions. By modeling such natural processes, organizations can achieve a balance between innovation and stability.

To effectively implement feedback loops, businesses must be proactive. Regularly reviewing and refining these mechanisms ensures alignment with organizational goals. Leaders should establish clear success metrics and integrate feedback seamlessly into daily operations. Encouraging teams to experiment and learn from outcomes, both positive and negative, can lead to breakthroughs in efficiency and creativity. By engaging actively with feedback loops, organizations not only adapt to change but also anticipate it, turning challenges into opportunities for growth.

Cultivating a Culture of Autonomy and Empowerment

Cultivating a culture of autonomy and empowerment in organizations mirrors the self-organizing patterns found in nature, where individual elements operate independently yet in harmony, resulting in complex adaptive systems. In a business context, this translates to creating an environment where employees are free to make decisions and take initiative without constant oversight. Such an approach not only boosts job satisfaction but also fuels innovation, as team members feel appreciated and motivated to share their unique insights and skills. Recent organizational behavior research indicates that companies promoting high levels of employee autonomy often see increased productivity and reduced turnover, underscoring the tangible benefits of such a culture.

A foundational pillar of fostering autonomy is trust. Just as ant colonies depend on individual ants' instincts for survival, businesses must have faith in their employees' judgment and capabilities. Trust-based cultures promote open communication and risk-taking, essential for nurturing creativity and effective problem-solving. By flattening hierarchical structures, companies can minimize bureaucratic delays, allowing employees to act quickly and effectively. This principle aligns with distributed leadership, where decision-making power is shared across various organizational levels, enabling more agile and responsive operations.

Empowerment complements autonomy by not only granting freedom to act but also providing individuals with the necessary tools and resources for success. This might involve offering continuous learning opportunities, access to advanced technology, and a supportive network of peers and mentors. Companies that invest in employee development often see returns in the form of enhanced skills and a more engaged workforce. By prioritizing learning and growth, businesses can foster a vibrant culture of innovation, akin to ecosystems thriving through diversity and resource exchange.

To further strengthen a culture of autonomy and empowerment, organizations should focus on cultivating feedback-rich environments. In nature, feedback loops are vital for maintaining balance and encouraging adaptation, and a similar approach can be beneficial in business. Regular, constructive feedback enables individuals to recognize their strengths and areas for improvement, guiding them to make informed decisions and take ownership of their roles. This ongoing dialogue between employees and management creates a dynamic workplace where continuous improvement is the norm, propelling both personal and organizational growth.

Consider success stories like Google's '20% Time' policy, which encourages employees to dedicate part of their workweek to projects they are passionate about. This initiative has led to groundbreaking innovations such as Gmail and AdSense, illustrating the potential of an empowered workforce. For organizations looking to implement similar strategies, starting with pilot programs and gradually expanding can help tailor the approach to fit the company's unique culture and objectives. By adopting these strategies, businesses can leverage the power of self-organization, resulting in a more resilient and innovative organization capable of thriving in an ever-changing environment.

Integrating Adaptive Systems for Dynamic Resource Allocation

In today's fast-paced business environment, the ability to quickly adjust to changing conditions is crucial. Flexible systems provide the framework for this adaptability by reallocating resources based on real-time data and evolving demands. Drawing inspiration from nature's ecosystems, where resources are managed without central oversight, businesses can establish systems that respond fluidly to market changes and internal shifts. Consider ant colonies, which exemplify efficient resource management as ants modify their roles and paths to optimize foraging under varying environmental conditions. Similarly, companies can create adaptable frameworks to ensure resources are directed to where they are most needed.

A key element of adaptive business systems is leveraging advanced technology to collect and analyze data. Cutting-edge analytics and machine learning tools can handle vast data volumes, identifying patterns and predicting trends to guide resource decisions. This process is akin to how neural networks in the human brain process sensory data for immediate adjustments. By adopting such technologies, businesses can refine decision-making, ensuring strategic and efficient resource use. For instance, a retail company might employ predictive analytics to forecast inventory needs, adjusting stock levels according to consumer behavior and market dynamics, thus minimizing waste and boosting profitability.

The success of adaptive systems relies not just on technology but also on nurturing a company culture that values flexibility and innovation. Empowering teams to work autonomously and make informed decisions creates an environment where adaptive systems can flourish. This is similar to the self-organizing actions seen in migratory bird flocks, where each bird independently adjusts its movements based on its neighbors, resulting in efficient and harmonious travel. By fostering a culture that prizes adaptability and independence, businesses can cultivate an atmosphere where employees are motivated to tackle challenges and seize opportunities in real time.

Adopting adaptive systems also requires a shift in leadership style. Leaders need to move away from traditional command-and-control models to roles that emphasize guidance and support. This involves setting clear goals and providing the necessary tools for teams to effectively self-organize. This leadership approach resembles that of a conductor guiding an orchestra to achieve a dynamic and cohesive performance without dictating every note. By promoting adaptive systems and encouraging decentralized decision-making, leaders can bolster organizational resilience and responsiveness, keeping the business competitive in a constantly changing market.

To successfully implement adaptive systems, organizations must commit to continuous learning and refinement. Regular evaluation of resource allocation strategies and iterative improvements are essential. A feedback-driven approach, similar to those found in biological systems, enables companies to learn from both successes and failures, enhancing their adaptive strategies over time. By fostering a culture of experimentation and ongoing improvement, businesses can sustain a dynamic resource allocation system that evolves alongside internal and external needs. Through this continuous process, organizations can leverage adaptive systems for lasting growth and innovation.

As we wrap up this chapter, our journey into the realm of autonomous coordination unveils a compelling paradigm where order naturally arises from the interactions of individual elements, free from centralized control. The elegance of nature shines through in the seamless unity of bird flocks and the intricate orchestration of cellular systems, illustrating how simplicity breeds complexity. These natural wonders provide valuable insights for human enterprises, demonstrating that decentralized structures can nurture creativity and adaptability. By adopting this approach, organizations can foster environments that promote independence and innovation, leading to operations that are both robust and nimble. This chapter highlights the transformative potential of emergent systems, challenging us to rethink traditional hierarchies in favor of more fluid and responsive models. As we ponder the opportunities that autonomous coordination presents, we are encouraged to consider how these principles might reshape our personal and professional lives. The wisdom gleaned from nature propels us forward, inviting the application of these insights to build more harmonious and efficient systems in our ever-changing world.

Chapter Seven

Sustainable Resource Management Nature S Closed Loop Systems

Picture a thriving forest where every fallen leaf transforms into rich soil, seamlessly nourishing the trees that shed them. This elegant cycle of renewal showcases nature's innate ability to turn waste into wealth, offering a profound lesson in resource management. In this endless dance of life and decay, nothing is discarded; everything finds a role and a purpose. Such natural choreography challenges us to rethink our own resource strategies, urging us to consider: How can we mirror this effortless efficiency in our industries and communities?

Natural systems, from dense woodlands capturing carbon to microorganisms recycling nutrients in the earth, present a time-tested model of sustainability. These systems reveal that what we often perceive as waste is simply a resource in disguise, waiting for transformation. As we delve into this exploration, we'll uncover how nature's processes can spark innovative solutions in industrial design and beyond. By emulating nature's circular economies, we have the opportunity to transform how we produce and consume, moving away from the linear, wasteful habits of the past.

The insights from these systems aren't mere ecological musings; they offer tangible potential for addressing today's pressing challenges. In a world facing resource scarcity and environmental decline, learning from nature's methods is not just advantageous—it's essential. This chapter invites you to explore the practical applications of these proven strategies, revealing how they can guide us towards a sustainable future. Let's venture into the heart of natural innovation, where each conclusion is a new beginning, and every challenge presents an opportunity to be embraced.

Circular Economies in Ecosystems: Waste as a Resource

Visualize a world where waste signifies not an ending but a fresh start, where every discarded item is revitalized in an endless cycle of renewal. This isn't merely a hopeful vision in nature; it's a fundamental reality. Across various ecosystems, waste is cleverly repurposed into a valuable asset, promoting growth and sustaining ecological balance. Nature's intricate systems offer profound lessons in managing resources responsibly. By observing how ecosystems thrive without producing excess, humans can develop strategies for creating self-sustaining cycles that revolutionize our approach to materials and byproducts. The natural world demonstrates a flawless sequence where every output becomes an input for another process, exemplifying the promise of circular economies that can inspire innovative solutions to our challenges.

At the core of this ecological wonder is the complex interplay of nutrient cycling, directed by unseen yet essential decomposers. These organisms decompose organic matter, returning vital nutrients to the soil to support new life. Beyond decomposition, nature fosters symbiotic relationships, where species exchange resources in mutually beneficial interactions, highlighting the effectiveness of resource sharing. Faced with resource scarcity, ecosystems exhibit remarkable adaptability, optimizing the use of available materials. This blend of efficiency and adaptation offers valuable insights for human systems. By adopting integrative waste-reduction methods, industries can emulate nature's ingenuity, transforming byproducts into opportunities for innovation.

Nutrient Cycling and the Role of Decomposers

Nutrient cycling is fundamental to nature's resource management, with decomposers playing a vital role in converting waste into life-sustaining elements. Organisms such as fungi and bacteria break down dead organic matter, releasing nutrients back into the ecosystem. This complex process supports plant growth and ensures ecosystem stability. New research highlights how mycorrhizal fungi form partnerships with plant roots, enhancing nutrient exchange and boosting growth. These natural systems embody circular processes, offering insights for designing human industries that aim to minimize waste and maximize efficiency.

Decomposers do more than break down nutrients; they are crucial in carbon regulation and climate change mitigation. As organic material decomposes, carbon is released into the atmosphere or stored in soil, impacting global carbon cycles. Innovative research suggests that boosting specific decomposers' activity could enhance soil carbon storage, offering a strategy for carbon mitigation. Understanding these processes helps develop agricultural practices that improve soil health and contribute to environmental goals, illustrating the intersection of ecological knowledge and sustainable development.

Exploring decomposers' adaptability in changing environments highlights their resilience to shifts like temperature changes or nutrient variations. This adaptability offers potential for bio-inspired innovations in human systems, where flexibility is increasingly important. By studying how these organisms thrive under diverse conditions, we can create adaptive systems that dynamically respond to challenges, from climate variability to resource scarcity. Such insights encourage us to rethink system design to be robust and responsive.

One innovative approach involves integrating nutrient cycling principles into urban planning and industrial design. By emulating decomposers' efficiency, cities and industries can create systems that recycle materials and reduce waste. For example, biomimetic waste management systems are being developed to mimic natural decomposition, transforming organic waste into useful byproducts like biofuels and fertilizers. These innovations not only cut landfill dependency but also promote resource conservation, aligning human activity with nature's sustainable principles.

Imagine a world where human systems mirror nature's decomposers' efficiency. Businesses could adopt circular models that mimic nutrient cycling, optimizing each product lifecycle stage for minimal waste and maximum recovery. Local communities could implement composting initiatives that harness decomposer activity, turning organic waste into a resource for local agriculture. These scenarios challenge us to innovate with nature as a guide and redefine our approach to sustainability.

Symbiotic Relationships and Resource Exchange

The intricate web of symbiotic relationships within ecosystems offers a fascinating glimpse into the world of mutual advantage and resource exchange, serving as a blueprint for eco-friendly practices in human systems. In diverse ecosystems, organisms engage in complex partnerships that promote survival and efficiency, transforming potential rivalry into cooperation. Take, for example, the interaction between mycorrhizal fungi and plant roots. This relationship exemplifies a sophisticated exchange where fungi boost nutrient absorption for plants, which in turn provide carbohydrates. These interactions highlight the potential for developing human systems where resource exchange is similarly optimized, reducing waste and boosting productivity.

Research into the myriad mechanisms of symbiosis offers a window into the adaptability and resilience inherent in these natural partnerships. Recent studies have uncovered the complex communication networks that sustain these interactions, such as the chemical signaling between leguminous plants and nitrogen-fixing bacteria. This relationship not only enriches soil but also lessens the need for synthetic fertilizers, presenting a natural solution to agricultural issues. By understanding and emulating these biological strategies, industries can explore innovative methods to create integrated cycles that minimize waste while maximizing resource efficiency.

One of the most compelling aspects of symbiotic relationships is their ability to thrive in resource-limited environments, a lesson particularly pertinent to contemporary challenges like climate change and resource depletion. In arid ecosystems, certain plants and fungi form partnerships that allow them to endure extreme conditions by sharing resources and optimizing water use. This model of mutual dependency can inspire the development of resilient urban infrastructures that emphasize resource sharing and adaptability, transforming how cities manage limited resources.

Incorporating principles of symbiosis into industrial design can fundamentally reshape business operations, fostering collaboration over competition. The circular economy model, inspired by nature's resource exchange systems, encourages the repurposing of byproducts as valuable inputs for other processes. By fostering partnerships across industries, companies can create networks that emulate the symbiotic relationships found in nature, leading to innovative solutions that benefit both the economy and the environment. This approach not only conserves assets but also creates new economic opportunities, driving sustainable growth.

To apply these insights practically, organizations can start by fostering cross-sector collaborations that mimic natural symbiotic systems. Encouraging diverse teams to co-create solutions can lead to breakthroughs that would be unattainable in isolation. Additionally, businesses can audit their processes to identify waste streams that might serve as resources for other operations, transforming liabilities into assets. By cultivating a mindset of interconnectedness and cooperation, inspired by nature's examples, humanity can tackle complex modern challenges with the same ingenuity that thrives in the natural world.

Adaptive Strategies in Resource Scarcity

In ecosystems, the challenge of limited resources is familiar terrain. Organisms in nature have evolved sophisticated methods to make the most of scarce materials, ensuring their survival and growth. One such method involves refining metabolic processes to extract maximum energy from minimal resources. Take desert plants like cacti, for example. They have adapted to arid environments by using CAM photosynthesis, which allows them to photosynthesize with minimal water loss. By opening their stomata at night, they conserve water—a clever adaptation that highlights how life forms can adjust their physiological functions to thrive in challenging conditions. Such adaptations can inspire innovative approaches to resource management in human systems.

Beyond physiological changes, behavioral adaptations also play a significant role in managing resources within ecosystems. Social insects, such as ants, exemplify this with their complex resource-sharing networks. Ant colonies use collective foraging techniques to efficiently gather and distribute food, ensuring the colony's survival even in times of scarcity. By observing these cooperative behaviors, businesses and organizations can learn how to optimize resource allocation and create collaborative environments that mimic these natural systems, boosting efficiency and sustainability.

Resource scarcity also drives the evolution of symbiotic relationships, where organisms work together to access resources more effectively. A typical example is the mutualistic relationship between fungi and plant roots, known as mycorrhizae. In this partnership, fungi extend the root system's reach, helping plants access otherwise inaccessible nutrients and water, while plants supply carbohydrates to the fungi. This symbiosis illustrates the potential of cooperative strategies to overcome resource limitations, encouraging industries to form partnerships that leverage mutual strengths, enhancing resilience and reducing waste.

In the realm of human innovation, nature's adaptive strategies provide a blueprint for creating robust systems resilient to resource shortages. Biomimicry in industrial design has led to products and processes that mimic nature's efficiency. Companies, for instance, are exploring how to replicate the structure of diatom shells—tiny algae with intricately patterned silica shells—to develop lightweight yet strong materials for engineering. These innovations demonstrate the potential to turn resource scarcity into a driver for creativity and progress.

Addressing resource scarcity calls for reimagining waste as a resource, akin to nature's closed-loop systems. Forward-thinking industries are beginning to adopt circular economy principles, minimizing waste and repurposing by-products into valuable assets. By learning from ecosystems, where waste seamlessly reintegrates into the nutrient cycle, businesses can develop sustainable practices that conserve resources and contribute to a regenerative economy. Embracing these natural strategies encourages a shift in perspective, fostering a culture of innovation where limitations are opportunities for growth and transformation.

Integrative Approaches to Waste Minimization in Human Systems

In today's world, minimizing waste is not just an aspiration but a crucial necessity that requires a holistic approach, aligning with nature's self-sustaining cycles. Central to this mission is the idea of eliminating waste by design, a concept mirrored in natural ecosystems where waste from one organism becomes nourishment for another. This interconnectedness forms an efficient cycle of resource use, offering a model for human systems striving for zero waste. Inspired by nature's seamless efficiency, modern industries are increasingly focusing on designs that utilize biodegradable materials and modular components, making products easier to disassemble and reuse.

Advancements in biomimicry and materials science have led to innovative methods for managing resources sustainably in industrial design. A notable example is the creation of self-repairing materials, modeled after the regenerative abilities of certain plants and animals. These materials enhance product durability, reducing the need for frequent replacements and thus cutting down on waste. Furthermore, closed-loop manufacturing processes have gained traction, where byproducts from one production cycle are repurposed as inputs for another. Companies like Interface, a leader in eco-friendly flooring, have set the standard by turning old carpet tiles into new ones, demonstrating how waste can be transformed into a valuable resource.

Transitioning towards waste reduction also involves redefining consumption and ownership concepts. The growing popularity of the sharing economy, exemplified by platforms such as Zipcar and Airbnb, marks a shift towards prioritizing access over ownership. This model not only minimizes waste but also maximizes the use of available resources, drawing from the collaborative interactions found in nature. Such strategies challenge traditional linear economic paradigms, advocating for systems where products are leased and returned, enabling companies to reclaim and recycle materials continuously.

Despite these promising initiatives, questions about scalability and implementation across various sectors remain. Addressing potential challenges, such as the economic feasibility of sustainable practices and the need for regulatory backing, requires thoughtful consideration. Infrastructure, consumer behavior, and technological innovation are critical in the shift from linear to circular models. How can industries reshape their business strategies to align with these eco-friendly principles, and what role will consumers play in driving this change? These questions highlight the complexity of integrating natural wisdom into human systems, urging stakeholders to collaborate in developing comprehensive solutions.

To turn these concepts into actionable steps, industries can start with waste audits to pinpoint major areas for improvement, focusing on redesigning products for longevity and repairability. Encouraging cross-industry collaboration can facilitate the exchange of best practices and technological innovations. Education is also crucial in fostering a sustainability-oriented mindset, empowering individuals and organizations to make informed decisions that align with nature's integrated cycles. By embracing a comprehensive approach that considers ecological, economic, and social dimensions, society can move towards a future where waste is minimized, and resources are treasured as vital elements in a continuous cycle of renewal.

Carbon Sequestration in Forests and Soil

In recent years, there's been a growing recognition of the vital role carbon capture plays in addressing climate change. Often overlooked, forests and soil work tirelessly, capturing and storing carbon dioxide from the atmosphere. These natural systems exemplify nature's resourcefulness, transforming potential challenges into opportunities for balance and renewal. Through the lens of carbon capture, we witness a complex interplay of elements, with photosynthesis at the helm, converting carbon into life-giving energy and illustrating how ecosystems function as cohesive units.

The connection between soil and forest ecosystems reveals a fascinating tapestry of life, from the hidden microbial exchanges underground to the majestic trees above. Each component aids in carbon retention uniquely, underscoring the sophistication and efficiency of nature's design. When forest management aligns with these natural processes, it can significantly enhance carbon storage, offering valuable insights into sustainable management. Advanced modeling techniques now empower us to foresee and refine these interactions, merging natural wisdom with human innovation. As we delve into these topics, the opportunity to mimic and apply these strategies to our resource management challenges becomes increasingly clear, heralding a future where human endeavors coexist as seamlessly as the ecosystems we strive to protect.

The Role of Photosynthesis in Carbon Capture and Storage

Photosynthesis is fundamental to Earth's ecosystem, converting sunlight into chemical energy while capturing and storing atmospheric carbon dioxide. This exceptional process not only supports plant life but is also pivotal in managing the planet's carbon cycle. During photosynthesis, plants absorb carbon dioxide from the air, transforming it into glucose and oxygen. This transformation is essential for building plant biomass, which acts as a carbon sink. Each carbon dioxide molecule incorporated into plant structures contributes to atmospheric carbon reduction, aiding climate regulation. By unraveling the complexities of photosynthesis, we can leverage its mechanisms to enhance carbon sequestration efforts, shaping strategies to combat climate change.

Recent botanical research has shed light on the varied strategies plants use to optimize photosynthesis in different environments. Some species have developed C4 and CAM pathways, adaptations that enable efficient carbon fixation in high temperatures or water-scarce conditions. By studying these adaptations, scientists can find ways to improve agricultural practices and create resilient crop varieties that enhance carbon uptake. Exploring these diverse photosynthetic mechanisms inspires innovative carbon management approaches in both natural and human-designed environments.

In forests, the combined photosynthetic activity of trees and understory plants forms a dynamic carbon sink, capable of sequestering significant carbon over time. Old-growth forests, with their vast biomass and intricate ecological relationships, excel in carbon storage. They not only capture carbon but also store it effectively in their woody structures and soil. Forest management practices, like selective logging and reforestation, can impact these landscapes' photosynthetic capacity and carbon storage potential. By adopting methods that boost photosynthesis and minimize disturbance, we can enhance forests' carbon sequestration ability, contributing to climate resilience.

The advent of advanced technologies like remote sensing and spectral analysis has transformed our capacity to monitor and model photosynthesis on ecosystem scales. These tools offer vital insights into the spatial and temporal variations in photosynthetic activity, allowing for more accurate predictions of carbon fluxes across landscapes. Utilizing these technologies, scientists and policymakers can devise targeted strategies to boost photosynthesis and carbon sequestration in critical regions. Monitoring photosynthetic efficiency over large areas provides an unprecedented opportunity to optimize land management practices and assess their impact on the global carbon balance.

As we envision a future where human innovation aligns with nature's tried-and-true methods, we're encouraged to consider how photosynthesis can inform sustainable development strategies. The potential to mimic photosynthetic processes in artificial systems, such as bio-inspired solar cells or carbon capture technologies, presents exciting research and application opportunities. Drawing inspiration from nature, we can deepen our understanding of how to engineer solutions that are both effective and ecologically harmonious. Exploring these possibilities, we must consider how to translate the insights of photosynthesis into actionable frameworks that tackle today's pressing environmental challenges.

Soil Microbial Interactions and Their Impact on Carbon Retention

Beneath the surface of the earth, soil microbes are instrumental in the carbon cycle, often acting as the unsung champions of sustainable carbon retention. These tiny organisms, including bacteria, fungi, and archaea, conduct intricate biochemical activities that transform organic matter into stable carbon compounds. As plant material decomposes, microbes break it down, releasing carbon dioxide as a byproduct but also converting part of it into humus, a stable, carbon-rich organic matter. This process not only enhances soil fertility but also boosts carbon storage, providing a natural solution to reduce atmospheric carbon levels.

Recent scientific discoveries have highlighted the profound interaction between soil microbes and plant roots, unveiling a sophisticated exchange where plants supply carbohydrates to microbes in return for essential nutrients like nitrogen and phosphorus. This mutually beneficial relationship promotes an environment that supports enhanced carbon sequestration. Advanced research using metagenomics and isotopic tracing is shedding light on these complex interactions, offering insights into how microbial communities can be managed or engineered to optimize carbon retention. This knowledge is crucial for creating agricultural practices that enhance carbon sequestration, potentially transforming farmlands into significant carbon sinks.

Microbial communities show varying efficiencies in carbon retention, influenced by factors such as soil type, moisture, and temperature. In tropical rainforests, rapid decomposition by microbes leads to a dynamic carbon cycle, while in boreal forests, slower decomposition results in greater soil carbon accumulation. These ecological differences emphasize the need for context-specific strategies for enhancing carbon retention. By understanding microbial ecology's nuances, scientists and land managers can develop tailored approaches that leverage specific microbial communities to amplify carbon sequestration in different ecosystems.

Innovative practices like applying biochar and using cover crops are proving effective in manipulating soil microbial activity and increasing carbon storage. Biochar, a type of charcoal from organic material, provides habitat for beneficial microbes, enhancing their carbon-sequestering abilities. Similarly, cover crops prevent soil erosion and supply organic matter that fuels microbial processes, leading to increased carbon retention. These practices illustrate how integrating microbial ecology into land management can yield substantial productivity and sustainability benefits.

As we consider the role of soil microbes in carbon dynamics, intriguing questions arise about the potential for biotechnological interventions. Could genetically modified microbes enhance carbon sequestration, or might they disrupt existing ecosystems? These considerations invite a thoughtful examination of ethical and ecological implications while encouraging innovation. By understanding microbial contributions to carbon retention, we can develop strategies that address climate change and foster a deeper connection to the living world beneath our feet.

The Influence of Forest Management Practices on Carbon Sequestration Efficiency

Effective forest management practices are essential for enhancing carbon capture and storage, which is crucial in combating climate change. By strategically applying these practices, we can significantly boost forests' ability to sequester carbon. Techniques such as selective logging, reforestation, and afforestation focus not just on increasing tree numbers but on improving the overall health and carbon retention of ecosystems. For example, selective logging, when executed carefully, can encourage the growth of young trees and enhance biodiversity, thus increasing carbon absorption. These approaches emphasize the need to view forests as dynamic systems requiring customized management strategies to maximize their environmental benefits.

Recent ecological research has highlighted the significant role of undergrowth and soil composition in carbon storage, stressing the importance of comprehensive forest management. The interaction among tree roots, soil organisms, and the forest floor forms a complex network that influences carbon retention. Forests managed to maintain diverse plant species and healthy soil ecosystems demonstrate enhanced carbon sequestration efficiency. This approach challenges traditional forestry methods that often prioritize timber production over ecological balance. By integrating the latest research into management practices, forestry professionals can devise strategies that support robust ecosystems capable of capturing more carbon.

Innovative perspectives in forest management are reshaping our approach to carbon capture by incorporating indigenous wisdom and community-based practices. Indigenous communities have long managed forests sustainably, balancing resource use with conservation. Their methods, grounded in deep ecological knowledge, offer valuable insights into sustainable management practices. Incorporating these approaches not only respects cultural heritage but also enhances the effectiveness of carbon capture efforts. By collaborating with indigenous communities, forest managers can develop more comprehensive strategies that benefit both the environment and local populations.

Emerging technologies are transforming the development and assessment of forest management practices. Tools such as remote sensing and satellite imagery enable continuous monitoring of forest health and carbon dynamics, providing real-time data that guides adaptive management strategies. Machine learning algorithms analyze this data to predict carbon sequestration potential under various management scenarios, allowing for more informed decision-making. These technological advancements support a more responsive approach to forest management, where practices can be swiftly adjusted to respond to changing environmental conditions. This adaptability is crucial in the face of climate change, where rapid shifts in weather patterns and biodiversity can affect carbon capture processes.

Envisioning the future of forest management requires a commitment to ongoing learning and adaptation. By integrating diverse perspectives, advanced technologies, and a deeper understanding of ecological processes, we can enhance the carbon sequestration potential of forests. Thought-provoking questions arise: How can we balance economic needs with environmental stewardship? What role do forests play in the broader context of global carbon management? By exploring these questions and applying innovative forest management practices, we lay the groundwork for a sustainable future. This forward-thinking approach not only addresses current challenges but also presents new opportunities to harness nature's wisdom in combating climate change and preserving ecological balance.

Advanced Modeling Techniques for Predicting Carbon Sequestration Dynamics

In the ever-evolving digital era, innovative methods are being developed to understand and predict the complex processes of carbon capture and storage in forests and soil. At the forefront of this exploration are advanced modeling techniques that provide profound insights into ecosystem carbon dynamics. These models synthesize extensive datasets, such as satellite images, climate forecasts, and biological data, to create dynamic simulations of carbon flow within natural environments. As a result, they reveal previously hidden patterns and interactions, enabling researchers to understand the diverse factors influencing carbon retention with exceptional precision.

A particularly fascinating feature of these models is their ability to simulate future scenarios under different conditions. For example, they can forecast how various forest management strategies, like selective logging or afforestation, may affect carbon capture rates over time. This forecasting ability empowers policymakers and land managers to make informed choices that balance ecological and economic priorities. By considering factors like soil composition, tree species diversity, and climate change, these models provide a nuanced view of how ecosystems respond to both natural and human-induced influences.

Recent advancements in machine learning have significantly enhanced the potential of carbon modeling. Machine learning algorithms, adept at processing complex datasets, refine these models to be more precise and adaptable. They uncover subtle correlations and causal relationships that traditional methods might miss. By continuously updating with real-time data, machine learning improves predictive accuracy, ensuring models remain relevant amid shifting environmental conditions. This approach also allows for tailored strategies in forest and soil management, customized to specific ecosystems and carbon objectives.

While these sophisticated models generate valuable insights, they also invite critical examination. Some scientists argue that models must be consistently validated against empirical data to avoid overreliance on simulations that might not fully capture ecosystem complexities. This highlights the importance of integrating field studies with computational models, creating a feedback loop where field data refines digital simulations. Such integration not only enhances model credibility but also deepens our understanding of the ecological processes involved in carbon capture.

As these modeling techniques advance, they inspire innovative thinking about resource management and climate strategies. They prompt questions about the trade-offs between different land-use practices and their long-term impacts on carbon storage. What are the consequences of prioritizing certain forests or regions for carbon credits? How might policies change with accurate predictions of carbon dynamics? These questions promote a holistic approach, blending cutting-edge technology with ecological insights, offering actionable strategies for sustainable practices on a global scale.

Turning Waste into Opportunity in Industrial Design

Let's begin with a fundamental inquiry: In what ways can the wisdom of the natural world revolutionize our approach to waste management in industrial design? Nature exemplifies efficient cycles where every element serves a purpose, offering a blueprint for sustainability that can significantly alter industrial methodologies. Within ecosystems, nothing is superfluous; each byproduct is integral to the system's vitality and function. This natural cycle of renewal starkly contrasts with the conventional linear model of industry, where materials are often used once and then discarded. By studying and emulating these self-sustaining systems, industries can redefine waste as a resource, fostering innovative design solutions that marry economic viability with environmental stewardship.

This viewpoint encourages a profound shift in how industrial waste streams are perceived, advocating for the adoption of biomimicry and eco-friendly design. Inspired by nature, biomimicry offers a pathway to transform waste into opportunity, enabling industries to implement solutions that reflect circular economy principles. These principles drive the redesign of products and processes, ensuring that waste is reintegrated into the production cycle rather than serving as an endpoint. Incorporating waste-to-energy technologies can enhance product design, converting byproducts into viable energy sources. Advanced material innovations through upcycling not only reduce waste but also enhance material properties, creating new, valuable assets. As we delve into these concepts, the potential of nature-inspired design to revolutionize industrial practices emerges not just as a vision but as an achievable reality.

Biomimicry in Transforming Industrial Waste Streams

Biomimicry provides a fresh perspective on transforming industrial waste streams by emulating nature's resource management systems. In natural ecosystems, the concept of waste is nonexistent; every byproduct is repurposed as a resource for another organism or process. This idea can be applied to industrial design by reinterpreting waste as a starting point rather than an endpoint. For example, the byproducts from one manufacturing process could become the raw materials for another, fostering a symbiotic industrial ecosystem. Such an approach not only mitigates environmental impact but also enhances sustainability and economic efficiency. Just as in the nutrient cycles of forests or coral reefs, industries can significantly reduce waste by ensuring every output is a valuable input elsewhere.

To integrate biomimicry effectively, interdisciplinary collaboration is essential. Engineers, biologists, and designers must join forces to create systems that emulate nature's efficiency. An example is the development of biodegradable materials inspired by plant cellulose structures, demonstrating how biological insights can drive innovation in material science. By examining how fungi decompose organic matter into nutrients, companies can devise new methods to convert industrial byproducts into valuable materials. This demands not only technical skills but also a paradigm shift—viewing waste as a potential asset rather than a burden.

The emerging field of synthetic biology further highlights biomimicry's potential to transform waste streams. Through the engineering of microorganisms to metabolize industrial byproducts into valuable substances, industries can establish closed-loop systems akin to those in nature. Genetically modified bacteria could be engineered to consume plastic waste and produce biofuels or biodegradable materials. This approach not only tackles plastic pollution but also offers a sustainable alternative to reliance on fossil fuels. Such advancements illustrate the intersection of biology and technology, where natural processes inspire innovative solutions to contemporary challenges.

Significantly, the shift toward biomimetic waste transformation requires reassessing traditional industrial practices. It challenges existing norms, urging industries to replace linear models with circular ones. Companies must invest in research and development to explore how nature's strategies can be tailored to their specific contexts. This might involve rethinking product design to facilitate disassembly and recycling, akin to how natural organisms decompose and reintegrate into the ecosystem. Such a shift not only yields environmental benefits but also opens new pathways for innovation and competitive advantage in the market.

To fully harness biomimicry's potential, stakeholders must cultivate a culture of continuous learning and adaptation. Encouraging curiosity and experimentation can lead to unexpected breakthroughs, as seen in industries that have successfully adopted biomimetic strategies. By posing questions like "How would nature solve this challenge?" or "What natural processes can we emulate?" businesses can discover novel approaches to resource management. This mindset, coupled with a commitment to sustainability, can revolutionize how industries perceive and manage waste, transforming potential obstacles into opportunities for growth and innovation.

Circular Economy Principles and Their Design Implications

Circular economy principles have transformed the way designers manage resources, encouraging a shift from the traditional linear approach of production and consumption to a self-sustaining system. This change is evident in the focus of industrial design on the entire lifecycle of a product, from creation to reintegration into the ecosystem. Designers now go beyond functionality and aesthetics, implementing strategies that prioritize minimizing resource depletion and waste. By observing natural ecosystems, where every byproduct becomes a resource for something else, designers can craft products that fulfill their primary function while also contributing to a cycle of regeneration through reuse.

Embracing circular design principles demands a deep understanding of material flows and the interconnectedness of industrial processes. For example, the growing trend of modular design allows products to be disassembled and upgraded, extending their lifespan and reducing discard. This mirrors the adaptability seen in nature, where organisms evolve to optimize resource use and minimize energy waste. By designing with end-of-life in mind, materials can be reclaimed and repurposed rather than disposed of, conserving resources and fostering innovation in materials science and engineering.

Progressive companies are already advancing in this area. The apparel industry, for instance, is incorporating recycled fibers and biodegradable materials into designs, addressing environmental concerns and appealing to consumers who value eco-friendliness. These practices are inspired by the resilience of natural systems, which thrive on diversity and redundancy, ensuring stability despite challenges. By adopting such natural principles, industrial design can balance economic viability with environmental responsibility.

Advanced material innovation is key to embracing circularity, transforming waste into valuable assets. Techniques like upcycling convert discarded materials into products of higher quality, challenging the notion of waste itself. This approach mirrors nutrient cycles in ecosystems, where organic matter is continuously repurposed, supporting diverse life forms. By viewing waste streams as reservoirs of potential, designers can create groundbreaking products that meet the demands of a sustainable future, advancing beyond traditional manufacturing and consumption paradigms.

To fully realize the potential of circular economy principles, designers must adopt a mindset that embraces complexity and interdependence. This involves questioning traditional assumptions about product utility and exploring innovative avenues for resource recovery. Imagining scenarios where waste is nonexistent can stimulate creative problem-solving and drive the development of regenerative design practices. By fostering a culture of continuous learning and adaptation, practitioners can not only address current challenges but also anticipate and mitigate future ones, ensuring the longevity and health of both their products and the planet.

Integrating Waste-to-Energy Technologies in Product Design

Integrating waste-to-energy technologies into product design unveils a fascinating realm of sustainable innovation, where the remnants of one process become the fuel for another. This concept, inspired by nature's cyclical systems, encourages a fresh perspective on sourcing, utilizing, and repurposing materials. By tapping into the energy potential within waste, designers can develop products that not only reduce environmental impact but also bolster a regenerative economy. Notably, advancements in microbial fuel cells and anaerobic digestion have opened new avenues for converting organic waste into usable energy, offering a model for industries eager to lower their carbon emissions while maintaining productivity.

Recent innovations have proven the feasibility of embedding waste-to-energy solutions within product lifecycles. For example, bio-digesters incorporated into agricultural machinery can transform farm waste into biogas, powering equipment in remote areas with limited traditional energy access. Likewise, urban buildings are beginning to integrate systems that convert sewage and organic refuse into electricity, pioneering structures that sustain themselves by utilizing their waste. Such developments illustrate how waste-to-energy technologies can revolutionize product design, turning waste management from a logistical issue into a core aspect of a product's functionality.

A crucial factor in this integration is the creation of adaptable and modular materials and systems. Designers are increasingly adopting flexible frameworks that accommodate evolving waste-to-energy technologies. This adaptability not only protects products from becoming technologically obsolete but also encourages continuous enhancements based on real-world performance data. Through modular designs, companies can effortlessly upgrade components or replace outdated technologies, ensuring products remain at the forefront of sustainability and efficiency throughout their lifespan.

As industries adopt these technologies, they must also consider the broader impacts on supply chains and business models. Transitioning to waste-to-energy systems requires a reevaluation of conventional production and distribution practices, prompting companies to embrace more localized and decentralized operations. This shift can yield economic benefits by reducing reliance on external energy sources and fostering resilient infrastructure capable of withstanding global disruptions. Additionally, it meets the rising consumer demand for transparency and sustainability, offering businesses a competitive advantage in an increasingly eco-conscious market.

To fully harness the potential of waste-to-energy integration, stakeholders must nurture a culture of innovation that promotes experimentation and cross-disciplinary collaboration. By forging partnerships among engineers, biologists, and designers, companies can draw from a diverse pool of knowledge and skills, sparking breakthroughs that would be impossible in isolated environments. This collaborative approach not only accelerates the development of new technologies but also ensures their effective and ethical implementation. In this context, asking questions like "How can we redesign existing products to incorporate waste-to-energy systems?" or "What partnerships are essential to facilitate the adoption of these technologies?" can ignite the strategic thinking needed to turn ambitious concepts into practical realities.

Advanced Material Innovation Through Upcycling Techniques

In the dynamic realm of material science, upcycling is reshaping how industrial byproducts become valuable materials. This inventive process redefines product life cycles, transforming discarded items into assets with renewed purpose and utility. Upcycling diminishes environmental impact and ignites creativity in material design, offering numerous opportunities for industries to adopt eco-friendly practices. By reimagining waste, designers and engineers unlock new possibilities, crafting materials with superior properties and enhanced functionality. This shift goes beyond recycling to reimagine waste as a core resource in the design process.

Upcycling drives advanced material innovation, particularly in developing composite materials that exceed the limitations of their original elements. Collaborations between scientists and designers have led to robust construction materials by integrating plastic refuse with natural fibers. These composites not only increase strength but also provide thermal and acoustic insulation, transforming undervalued materials into essential components of green architecture. Such innovations challenge traditional manufacturing norms, urging industries to view waste as a foundation for innovation rather than a byproduct.

Biotechnology plays a crucial role in upcycling, enabling the transformation of waste into novel materials through biological processes. Microbial and enzymatic pathways convert organic waste into biodegradable polymers and other valuable compounds. This dual approach reduces waste's ecological footprint while generating materials safer for the environment. Cutting-edge research in this area has led to bio-based materials that can replace conventional plastics, providing a sustainable alternative that aligns with circular economy principles.

In fashion and consumer goods, upcycling offers a unique opportunity where creativity meets eco-consciousness. Designers increasingly use textile waste to create fashionable items appealing to environmentally aware consumers. By adopting techniques like 3D knitting and digital fabrication, the fashion industry can reduce waste and produce custom garments that reflect personal style without environmental costs. This blend of technology and design curtails waste and supports a sustainability culture that challenges fast-fashion norms.

To fully harness upcycling's potential, industries must adopt a mindset focused on adaptability and collaboration. Cross-disciplinary partnerships can spark transformative solutions as diverse perspectives converge to tackle complex challenges. By fostering a culture of experimentation and openness to new ideas, businesses can pioneer innovative materials, redefining waste as a resource. Imagining scenarios where waste is non-existent can motivate industries to adopt upcycling practices that ensure a sustainable future. Strategically implementing upcycling techniques allows companies to reduce environmental impact and gain a competitive market edge by offering unique, eco-friendly products.

By observing nature's seamless recycling processes, we gain valuable insights into responsible resource management. Natural ecosystems show extraordinary efficiency, turning byproducts into essential materials and maintaining balance. Studying these self-sustaining systems reveals how what we often discard is vital to life's cycle, hinting at the potential for similar models in human industries. The way forests and soils naturally capture and store carbon exemplifies nature's capacity to manage essential elements, providing us with strategies to lessen our environmental footprint. These lessons extend beyond theory, urging us to reimagine industrial practices where waste serves as a foundation for innovation. As we absorb these teachings, the broader themes of this book highlight nature's unmatched ingenuity, encouraging us to adopt a perspective that prioritizes resilience and ecological harmony. This exploration of nature's methods challenges us to integrate these enduring principles into our endeavors, ensuring our progress aligns with the environment. What new opportunities might arise if we genuinely embed nature's wisdom into our approach to unresolved challenges?

Chapter Eight

Structure And Form Efficiency In Design

Picture yourself in a meadow at dawn, the grass wet with dew as the first rays of sunlight unveil a spider web glistening in the gentle breeze. This seemingly delicate creation is a marvel of natural engineering, crafted with precision to balance strength and minimal material use. Nature abounds with such wonders, where elegance meets functionality, offering timeless lessons in design perfected over ages. This chapter invites you to explore nature's studio of innovation, where every form, from the tiniest detail to the grandest scale, tells a story of cleverness and efficiency.

As we navigate this chapter, view the spider's web not just as a trap, but as a symbol of intelligent design. Its radial symmetry and spiraling threads illustrate resilience and economy—principles vital in our pursuit of sustainable solutions. Similarly, the structure of bones, with their complex internal networks, demonstrates how nature achieves lightness while supporting weight, a challenge engineers and architects strive to replicate. These natural forms hold secrets that modern science is just beginning to unravel, promising a future where our environments align with nature.

Design efficiency goes beyond the physical, shaping how we tackle challenges in technology and business. By grasping the core principles behind natural architecture, we can inspire breakthroughs in various fields, from urban skyscrapers to digital innovations. This chapter draws insights from biology, architecture, and engineering to show how nature's enduring strategies can lead us to more inventive and sustainable paths, encouraging a fresh perspective on design.

The Structural Efficiency of Spider Webs

Envision a world where architectural wonders find inspiration in the intricate designs crafted by spiders. These natural engineers create webs that showcase a remarkable blend of structural refinement and resourcefulness. Each silk strand, meticulously positioned, reveals a tale of geometric precision and optimal material use. This captivating natural framework intrigues scientists and designers, igniting a pursuit to decode the secrets woven into these delicate threads. Spider webs, with their ability to endure environmental challenges while remaining astonishingly lightweight, offer profound lessons in human innovation. By observing how spiders achieve a balance of strength and flexibility, we can draw insights for designing resilient and sustainable structures.

As we delve into the art of web construction, a fascinating exploration unfolds through the realms of geometry, material science, and adaptive design. We begin by examining how web structures achieve both elegance and functional brilliance. Following this, the extraordinary properties of silk come into focus—a material as strong as steel, crafted with minimal energy. This natural efficiency challenges us to rethink our production methods. Moreover, spiders' adaptability to environmental demands serves as a compelling model for dynamic and responsive design. Translating these natural principles into human architecture and engineering unlocks new possibilities, inspiring innovative approaches that beautifully merge form with function. In this synergy between nature and innovation, spider webs underscore the untapped potential within the natural world.

Analyzing the Geometric Precision of Web Structures

Spider webs exemplify geometric precision, highlighting nature's talent for merging form and function with remarkable effectiveness. These complex structures illustrate how organisms achieve maximum strength and utility while using minimal resources. By studying the radial and spiral patterns of spider webs, scientists have uncovered principles of tension distribution that translate into efficient load-bearing designs. The interaction between these patterns ensures the web's stability and enhances its ability to catch prey, serving as a dual-purpose design that has inspired architects and engineers. This natural ingenuity encourages a reevaluation of traditional design methods, fostering innovative approaches that balance aesthetic appeal with structural durability.

Recent research delves deeper into spiders' remarkable ability to adapt their web designs to their surroundings, revealing a sophisticated approach to spatial problem-solving. The precise angles and spacing between silk threads are strategically adjusted to handle environmental stressors like wind or rain without losing the web's strength. This adaptability offers valuable lessons for human-engineered systems, where rigid designs often struggle under changing conditions. By embracing the concept of adaptive geometry, we can develop structures that intelligently respond to their environments, increasing their lifespan and functionality. Potential applications range from disaster-resistant buildings to adaptable urban infrastructure, paving the way for sustainable development.

The material properties of spider silk further highlight the web's efficiency. Known for its high tensile strength and elasticity, silk combines qualities rarely found together in synthetic materials. This dual characteristic allows webs to absorb significant energy without breaking, a trait being studied for its potential in advanced composites and textiles. The energy-efficient production of silk, which occurs at ambient temperatures using readily available resources, challenges industries to rethink resource-intensive manufacturing processes. Emerging research into the genetic and biochemical pathways of silk production holds promise for biofabrication techniques that minimize environmental impact while maximizing material performance.

Drawing inspiration from these natural designs, architects and engineers are developing 'web-inspired' frameworks that mimic the efficient layouts and adaptive features of spider webs. These innovations are evident in lightweight, high-strength materials and structures that sustain significant loads with minimal resources. Such designs prioritize decentralized support systems, distributing forces to enhance structural resilience. Projects like the Eden Project in the UK and the Water Cube in Beijing demonstrate how bio-inspired geometry can inform iconic architecture, integrating ecological considerations with cutting-edge design.

Studying spider webs prompts a shift in perspective, from viewing nature as separate to recognizing it as a model for sustainable innovation. By adopting nature's design principles, we can tackle contemporary challenges with solutions that are efficient and environmentally harmonious. This chapter not only highlights the elegance of web structures but also encourages readers to apply these insights across diverse fields, from urban planning to product design. As we explore new possibilities, spider webs remind us that the most sophisticated solutions often emerge from simplicity and adaptability.

Material Properties and Energy Efficiency in Silk Production

Spider silk, an extraordinary natural fiber, exemplifies efficiency and energy conservation in material production, offering insights into sustainable design. Unlike synthetic fibers, which require energy-intensive processes and chemicals, spiders spin silk at room temperature using water-based solutions. This method significantly reduces energy consumption and results in a material that is both strong and flexible. Researchers are keenly interested in spider silk due to its potential applications in various industries, including textiles and biomedical engineering.

Advancements in genetic engineering have enabled the production of spider silk proteins in organisms like bacteria and yeast, paving the way for scalable production while preserving the silk's remarkable qualities. This biomimetic approach could transform industries by creating biodegradable fabrics and medical sutures that integrate seamlessly with human tissue. The shift toward bio-fabrication aligns with global sustainability goals, reducing reliance on petrochemicals and promoting materials that are both strong and elastic.

The silk's molecular structure is key to its exceptional properties. The arrangement of proteins within silk threads achieves a balance between toughness and elasticity. Crystalline regions interspersed with amorphous segments allow the material to absorb and dissipate energy under stress. This quality is inspiring engineers and architects to explore novel construction materials and techniques that can withstand environmental pressures.

Adaptive silk production offers further potential for innovation. Spiders can modify silk properties to suit different environmental conditions, highlighting the importance of adaptability in design. Understanding the mechanisms behind this adaptability could lead to materials that dynamically respond to their surroundings, enhancing performance and longevity. Imagine building materials that adjust thermal properties based on external temperatures, improving energy efficiency in buildings.

Exploring spider silk challenges us to rethink conventional materials and processes, integrating natural efficiencies into human creations. This exploration inspires designers and scientists to push the boundaries of what's possible, fostering a new generation of materials that are efficient, resilient, and harmonious with the ecosystem. As we learn from these arachnid architects, we can shape modern design and engineering in innovative ways.

Adaptive Web Design for Environmental Resilience

Spider webs, with their complex architecture, demonstrate a remarkable ability to adapt to environmental challenges. Central to this adaptability is the spider's skill in customizing its web to suit changing conditions. This flexibility ensures that webs remain functional despite variables like wind or prey availability. For example, spiders often adjust the anchoring points and tension of their silk to endure strong winds, reflecting an innate grasp of structural integrity and aerodynamics. This capability to modify and strengthen their constructions provides valuable insights into designing structures that are both durable and adaptable in uncertain environments.

In recent years, scientists have begun unraveling the genetic and biochemical processes enabling spiders to produce silk with extraordinary precision and versatility. This silk, known for its impressive strength and elasticity, is composed of proteins that spiders can manipulate to address specific environmental demands. By altering the silk's composition and diameter, spiders create webs that are not only robust and flexible but also efficient in terms of energy use for construction and maintenance. This control over material properties highlights the potential for bio-inspired materials in human engineering, especially in developing smart materials that can respond to environmental changes.

Architects and engineers are drawing inspiration from spider webs to create adaptive structures that respond to environmental variations. For instance, modern architecture employs adaptive façade systems equipped with sensors and actuators to adjust to light, temperature, and wind, mimicking the responsive nature of spider webs. These innovations aim to boost energy efficiency and enhance occupant comfort. By adopting the principles of adaptive web design, designers can develop buildings and structures that are not only visually appealing but also resilient and sustainable, minimizing the need for energy-intensive climate control systems.

The design of spider webs also prompts reflection on how minimal resources can achieve maximum structural efficiency. In our pursuit of resilient design, we must consider how to accomplish more with less, a challenge that spider webs elegantly address. By strategically arranging minimal resources for optimal load distribution and energy efficiency, spiders provide a model for sustainable design practices. This minimalist yet effective approach encourages a reevaluation of traditional engineering processes, advocating for strategies that conserve resources without compromising performance.

The study of spider webs offers a meaningful framework for understanding resilience and adaptability in design. By observing how spiders naturally optimize their web structures, we can draw actionable insights for creating environments that are both robust and adaptable. Fostering a mindset that values flexibility and resourcefulness, this exploration challenges us to innovate beyond conventional methods. By integrating these principles into practice, we enhance the durability and efficiency of our designs while contributing to a more sustainable and resilient future.

Translating Web Architecture into Architectural Innovation

Exploring the sophisticated design of spider webs offers a groundbreaking perspective on modern construction techniques. Spiders have developed webs that are not only feather-light and adaptable but also incredibly robust, demonstrating nature's skill in optimizing material use. These webs, with their complex geometric forms, achieve maximum strength with minimal resources, a principle ripe for architectural innovation. By examining the radial and spiral structures of a web, architects can derive methods to build using fewer materials while ensuring stability, which can lower costs and lessen environmental impact.

Spider silk exemplifies biological engineering at its finest, being five times stronger than steel of the same thickness and remarkably light. This extraordinary combination of features has driven researchers to create synthetic materials that replicate the strength and elasticity of spider silk. Progress in material science has led to bio-inspired composites poised for use in construction, presenting a sustainable alternative to traditional resources. These advances promise to improve the durability and flexibility of structures, enabling them to better withstand environmental challenges while reducing the carbon impact commonly linked with conventional building methods.

Adaptive web designs showcase the ability to respond to environmental shifts, a characteristic modern architecture can adopt to develop intelligent buildings. Such structures could feature responsive exteriors that adjust to light, wind, and temperature, enhancing energy efficiency. By incorporating sensor technology and advanced materials, architects can design buildings that dynamically change in response to external conditions, much like a spider modifies its web to meet different demands. This approach not only boosts the comfort and functionality of buildings but also supports sustainability efforts by cutting energy use and conserving resources.

Integrating web-like architecture into urban settings calls for a shift in design philosophy, embracing organic shapes and modularity. Biomimetic architecture encourages a move away from rigid, linear designs toward the fluidity and adaptability found in nature. This shift can lead to the creation of structures that are visually appealing and capable of evolving to meet changing needs. By adopting modular construction inspired by the interconnectedness of spider webs, architects can design buildings that are easily adaptable and scalable, supporting urban expansion without harming the environment.

To truly innovate, one must consider the broader implications of adopting nature-inspired architecture. What would cities resemble if they embodied the efficiency and adaptability of a spider's web? How might our urban planning strategies shift if we prioritized resilience and resourcefulness? Encouraging architects to think beyond traditional boundaries and explore these questions can lead to groundbreaking solutions that redefine our built environment. By fostering a deeper understanding of nature's design principles, we can inspire a new generation of architects and engineers to create structures that are not only efficient and resilient but also harmonious with the natural world. Through this lens, spider webs transform from mere biological curiosities into blueprints for a sustainable future.

Bone Density and Load-Bearing Structures

Consider the subtle interplay of forces within a bone—a quiet symphony balancing robustness with grace. These seemingly solid structures are marvels of natural engineering, refined through ages to maximize strength with minimal resources. At their core lies a brilliant strategy: harnessing optimal strength with the least material. This efficiency is seen in the intricate balance of density and shape, where each curve and cavity is purposeful, redistributing load and minimizing stress. Such natural ingenuity prompts us to rethink our approach to contemporary engineering and design, urging us to emulate nature's meticulous precision. Upon closer examination, we find not a static frame but a dynamic, living system continuously adapting and evolving.

Exploring bone density and load-bearing structures opens the door to understanding how nature's designs can transform our built environment. By comparing the way nature distributes loads, we begin to see similarities between the quiet workings of bones and the monumental designs of bridges and skyscrapers. These insights extend beyond theory, driving biomimetic innovations that inspire architects and engineers to craft structures reflecting resilience and efficiency akin to their natural models. Advanced computational tools further advance this exploration, allowing for simulation and refinement of these natural mechanics, effectively merging evolutionary wonders with human creativity. As these connections become clear, we find a path forward: by embracing the lessons embedded in the living blueprints of bones, we can fundamentally rethink the art of design.

Evolutionary Advancements in Bone Density Optimization

In evolutionary biology, the marvel of bone density optimization exemplifies nature's engineering prowess. This sophisticated process has allowed numerous species to evolve skeletons that are both lightweight and incredibly strong, serving as a model for modern structural design. Bones achieve an efficient balance between material use and strength, a result of evolutionary fine-tuning over millions of years. By studying bone microarchitecture, we observe how nature optimally arranges trabeculae, the small rod-like formations within spongy bone, to enhance strength while reducing weight. Bone remodeling, a continuous process that adjusts density in response to stress, ensures optimal bone structure for various functions. The dynamic interaction between osteoblasts and osteoclasts, the cells responsible for bone formation and breakdown, highlights a system of balance that architects and engineers strive to emulate.

Recent research has deepened our understanding of how bone density optimization varies across species, revealing how evolutionary forces shape skeletal adaptations. For example, the dense bones of terrestrial mammals are designed for weight-bearing and absorbing impacts, contrasting with the lighter, hollow bones of birds adapted for flight. This diversity in bone structures offers insights into tailoring designs for specific functional needs. Exploring these evolutionary adaptations provides principles applicable across fields like aerospace engineering and prosthetics. The adaptability of bone tissue, with its capacity to reorganize and strengthen under mechanical stress, presents a model for creating self-reinforcing materials that could revolutionize construction and manufacturing.

In the growing field of biomimicry, architects and engineers increasingly draw inspiration from bone density optimization to create innovative designs. This interdisciplinary approach has led to the development of materials and frameworks that mimic the efficiency and adaptability of bone. For instance, lattice structures in 3D-printed materials replicate the trabecular arrangement found in bones, offering a lightweight yet strong alternative to traditional materials. By adopting the concept of distributed load-bearing, designers can construct structures that are both efficient and sustainable, minimizing material use. This aligns with the trend toward sustainable architecture, emphasizing reduced environmental impact while maintaining function and aesthetic appeal.

Advancements in computational modeling have enhanced the application of bone mechanics in modern design. Advanced algorithms now simulate complex stress interactions within bone, enabling researchers to predict how changes in density and structure impact overall strength. This capability allows exploration of new design possibilities, such as adaptive structures that self-modify in response to external forces, akin to bone remodeling. By integrating these computational insights with material science, engineers can craft novel solutions bridging biological inspiration and practical application. Such innovations hold the potential to transform industries, fostering the creation of more efficient, resilient, and adaptive infrastructures.

As we look to the future of design, lessons from evolutionary advancements in bone density optimization offer a wealth of inspiration. By emulating nature's strategies, we can tackle modern challenges with creativity and foresight. Imagine buildings that adjust structural density in response to seismic activity, or vehicles that alter form to enhance aerodynamics based on conditions. While these scenarios may seem futuristic, they are within reach as we continue to uncover the secrets of nature's engineering. Delving into bone biology not only enriches our understanding of the natural world but also sparks imagination, challenging us to redefine the boundaries of what's possible in design and innovation.

Comparative Analysis of Load Distribution in Natural Structures

Natural structures, with their complex designs, offer invaluable insights into optimizing load distribution. Consider the marvel of bone density in animals, where bones provide more than mere support; they are engineering masterpieces shaped by evolution to balance strength and lightness. The trabecular, or spongy bone, located at the ends of long bones, exemplifies this balance. Its lattice-like framework efficiently manages stress and strain, adapting to various demands. Unlike human-made materials that often focus on uniformity, these natural structures prioritize adaptability. By studying the diverse bone configurations across species, researchers can derive principles of load distribution applicable to modern architecture and engineering.

Recent studies in bone mechanics reveal how nature achieves this delicate balance. With advanced imaging techniques like micro-CT scanning, scientists can examine bone microarchitecture in remarkable detail. These analyses have shown that the orientation of trabecular struts aligns with primary mechanical load directions, a strategy that minimizes material use while enhancing strength. Such discoveries suggest a potential shift for architects and engineers, who can adopt these natural principles to design buildings and structures that are resource-efficient yet durable. Embracing bio-inspired designs might lead to a sustainable construction era, reducing both material costs and environmental impact.

The field of biomimicry, which draws inspiration from nature's design strategies, is already influencing architecture. Notable projects include buildings that emulate the lightweight yet robust internal structures of bones. Designers increasingly use 3D printing to replicate these intricate patterns, creating structures that are both strong and light. These innovations are not just theoretical; practical applications are emerging, with buildings and bridges echoing the efficiency of bone structures. Such developments highlight the potential for biomimetic approaches to redefine structural engineering possibilities.

A crucial factor in applying these concepts involves developing sophisticated computational models that simulate bone mechanics. These models incorporate data on bone growth patterns and stress responses to enhance accuracy. By simulating bones' adaptive capabilities, these models provide architects and engineers with a powerful tool to predict how structures will respond to various loads over time. This capability can lead to designing buildings that not only withstand natural forces but also adapt to them, akin to dynamic and resilient natural structures.

To advance these ideas, one might envision a transformation of our built environment if architects and engineers embraced nature's load distribution principles. Imagine urban landscapes designed with the same efficiency and adaptability as a bird's skeleton. This thought experiment challenges the status quo, encouraging professionals to reconsider traditional approaches and explore innovative pathways for sustainable design. By deepening our understanding of nature's time-tested strategies and translating them into actionable frameworks, we can create a future where human ingenuity and natural wisdom coexist harmoniously.

Biomimetic Applications for Modern Architectural Design

In recent years, the realm of biomimicry has significantly influenced architectural design by drawing inspiration from nature's intricate structures. Bone, with its superb balance of strength and lightness, serves as a model for creating more efficient and sustainable buildings. Engineers and architects examine how bone manages weight through its internal lattice, known as trabeculae, which modifies density based on stress. This natural adaptation has led to the creation of innovative materials and frameworks that promise to transform construction practices, making them more adaptable and re-source-efficient.

One intriguing application of bone-inspired design is the development of materials that replicate its hierarchical structure. Researchers are working on composite materials that mimic bone's ability to achieve exceptional strength-to-weight ratios. For example, advances in 3D printing have allowed for the creation of complex structures with varying densities, similar to how bone becomes denser in areas experiencing greater stress. This approach not only enhances the mechanical properties of construction materials but also reduces the use of raw materials, aligning with sustainability goals.

Modern architectural projects also benefit from the self-healing principles found in bone. This natural ability to repair micro-damages has inspired the development of self-repairing materials. These materials incorporate microcapsules filled with healing agents that release upon damage, initiating the repair process. Such innovations are being integrated into building facades and infrastructure, extending the lifespan of structures and lowering maintenance costs, which aligns with the growing emphasis on resilience and durability in architecture.

Another captivating aspect of biomimetic design is the exploration of load distribution techniques observed in natural structures. The efficient way bones handle stress through their geometry and composition has inspired architects to rethink traditional load-bearing systems. For instance, the Gaudí-inspired Sagrada Família in Barcelona uses hyperbolic and parabolic designs that reflect the natural load distribution seen in bones, combining aesthetic appeal with structural efficiency. This fusion of beauty and functionality demonstrates how nature's designs can lead to groundbreaking architectural solutions.

The pursuit of biomimetic architecture encourages a multidisciplinary approach, integrating insights from biology, materials science, and engineering. This collaboration enhances our understanding of how natural systems can inform human design. As we continue to explore nature-inspired architecture, it is essential to apply these principles beyond individual projects, influencing urban planning and sustainable development on a larger scale. By challenging traditional design paradigms and embracing nature's wisdom, architects and engineers are paving the way for a future where human environments coexist harmoniously with the ecosystems they inhabit.

Advanced Computational Models for Simulating Bone Mechanics

Advanced computational models have transformed our understanding of bone mechanics, offering remarkable insights into the delicate balance between strength and weight. By employing finite element analysis (FEA), researchers can simulate the intricate microarchitecture of bone, allowing for a detailed study of how bones endure various loads. This simulation capability opens a window into the evolutionary marvels of bone optimization, showcasing nature's ability to achieve maximum efficiency with minimal mass. These models are pivotal in analyzing the anisotropic properties of bone—its varying strengths and weaknesses depending on force direction. By embracing these advanced models, scientists and engineers can decode the inherent wisdom found in natural structures, paving the way for innovative applications in human-made systems.

The scope of these computational models extends beyond mere observation; they serve as a blueprint for innovation in architectural and engineering design. Through biomimetic approaches, architects draw inspiration from bone's adaptive strategies to create structures that are robust yet lightweight. This has led to the development of novel structural forms, challenging traditional paradigms by using minimal material while maintaining structural integrity. For example, the design of the Eden Project's biomes in the UK exemplifies how understanding bone mechanics can inspire resilient and resource-efficient architecture. By applying principles derived from bone structure, designers craft spaces that reflect nature's elegance and efficiency.

Furthermore, these computational tools encourage collaboration among biologists, engineers, and architects in a shared pursuit of sustainable design solutions. They enable the exploration of multi-material structures, similar to the composite nature of bone, where different materials fulfill distinct functions.

Advanced models simulate the interaction between these materials, optimizing their distribution and arrangement for enhanced performance. This interdisciplinary synergy ignites a new wave of creativity, pushing the boundaries of what is possible in design and engineering. As a result, designers are equipped with the tools to create environments that are not only aesthetically pleasing but also environmentally conscious.

While the promise of these models is immense, they also invite critical examination and innovation. Researchers continually refine algorithms to capture the dynamic processes of bone remodeling, where the structure adapts in response to mechanical stimuli over time. This ongoing refinement challenges researchers to think beyond static models, incorporating elements of time and adaptability into their simulations. These efforts underscore the importance of embracing dynamic systems in design, offering a more holistic understanding of structural efficiency and resilience. By integrating these insights, designers can anticipate and respond to changing conditions, much like living organisms.

Thought-provoking scenarios emerge when considering the implications of these models on future design practices. Imagine a world where buildings adapt to environmental changes, much like bones adjust to mechanical stress. How might this shift the landscape of urban planning and construction? The possibilities are vast, and embracing the lessons embedded in bone mechanics could redefine our approach to design. The challenge lies in translating these complex simulations into tangible solutions, prompting a reimagining of both natural and built environments. As we continue to explore these computational frontiers, the dialogue between nature and innovation grows ever more profound, offering a rich tapestry of possibilities for the future of design.

Bio-Inspired Architecture and Engineering

Imagine a world where the buildings around us are not mere static entities but dynamic organisms that adapt, mend, and coexist seamlessly with their surroundings. This concept, once limited to science fiction, is steadily moving towards reality, thanks to the innovative field of bio-inspired architecture. Nature, with its vast array of clever designs, offers architects and engineers a wealth of knowledge for developing sustainable and efficient solutions. In the natural realm, form and function are intricately linked; every shape and surface has evolved over time to serve a specific purpose. By studying these natural structures, we can uncover vital lessons in resilience and effectiveness, helping us to rethink how we construct our environments.

Central to this endeavor is the aspiration to replicate the grace and ingenuity found in nature. Whether it's the leaves of a forest capturing solar energy with precision or the complex structure of a bird's bone that achieves both strength and lightness, nature provides a remarkable example of design efficiency. Building materials inspired by natural compounds hold the promise of a reduced ecological impact, while adaptive constructions that echo the responsive traits of plants and animals have the potential to transform urban settings. As we explore energy efficiency through biomimetic design and consider self-repair mechanisms drawn from biological processes, the divide between biology and engineering becomes less distinct. This paves the way for a future where our buildings not only harmonize with nature but also become an extension of it.

Nature's Principles in Sustainable Building Materials

In the field of sustainable building materials, nature offers a wealth of strategies that can transform how we design and construct structures. Picture a world where buildings not only serve their purpose but also exist in harmony with their surroundings, much like a tree flourishing within its ecosystem. Central to this vision is the concept of biomimicry, where inspiration from natural materials and processes leads to innovative design and construction techniques. For example, the light yet immensely strong structure of a bird's bone can inspire the creation of composite materials that use fewer resources while maintaining strength. This approach not only lessens environmental impact but also boosts the durability and efficiency of building materials.

Adopting biomimicry principles in sustainable building materials also involves an understanding of the materials' life cycle, similar to how leaves fall and decompose, enriching the soil. The idea of cradle-to-cradle design, drawing from nature's cyclical processes, highlights materials that can be reused or regenerated instead of discarded. Recent progress in biopolymers, sourced from renewable resources, exemplifies this concept. These materials, mimicking the function and decomposition properties of natural polymers, offer a promising substitute for conventional plastics, reducing waste and energy use in construction.

One intriguing aspect of nature's design is its capacity to adapt and flourish under various conditions. This adaptability is reflected in the development of smart materials that change properties in response to environmental stimuli, reminiscent of how some plants adjust to optimize sunlight absorption. Recent studies on phase-change materials, capable of storing and releasing thermal energy, illustrate this idea. By integrating these advanced materials into construction, buildings can self-regulate temperatures, significantly cutting down on external energy needs and enhancing energy efficiency.

Nature's lesson in efficiency extends beyond material selection to the construction process itself. The precise patterns found in seashells, for instance, have inspired modular building components that fit seamlessly together, reducing the need for extra resources and labor. This precision mirrors the careful assembly of a spider's web, where every strand is placed with purpose. Modern engineering methods, such as 3D printing, have learned from these natural processes, enabling the creation of complex structures with minimal waste and optimal efficiency.

Exploring nature's principles in sustainable building should also consider the potential for self-healing buildings, similar to how a lizard regrows its tail. The use of self-healing materials, which can autonomously repair damage over time, presents an exciting frontier in sustainable construction. Inspired by biological processes, these materials promise to extend the longevity of structures while reducing maintenance costs and resource use. As this field advances, it invites architects and engineers to rethink traditional methods, advocating for a future where buildings are not static entities but dynamic, living systems.

Adaptive Structural Designs Inspired by Flora and Fauna

The intricate designs in nature offer profound insights into adaptive structures, drawing inspiration from the elegant forms and functional capabilities of plants and animals. Nature's ability to create structures that dynamically respond to environmental changes serves as a remarkable model for human engineering. These natural designs are not static; they are living architectures that adjust to varying conditions. For example, the leaves of the mimosa plant fold in response to touch or wind, illustrating responsive adaptability. Such mechanisms can inspire buildings that modify their shape or function in response to changes in climate or occupancy, enhancing both efficiency and user comfort.

Recent advances in biomimicry have paved the way for innovations in architecture and engineering, where adaptive designs are increasingly employed to create more sustainable and resilient structures. A notable example is the Eastgate Centre in Zimbabwe, which draws inspiration from termite mounds. These natural formations maintain a stable internal temperature despite external fluctuations, thanks to their complex system of vents and tunnels. Similarly, the Eastgate Centre uses passive cooling techniques, reducing the need for artificial air conditioning by up to 90%. This approach not only minimizes energy consumption but also exemplifies how adaptive structures in nature can be translated into efficient, eco-friendly human constructions.

Incorporating adaptive design principles from nature involves a multidisciplinary approach that integrates biology, engineering, and material science. Researchers are exploring how the structural dynamics of tree branches, which bend without breaking in response to wind forces, can inform the development of flexible and resilient building materials. By studying the geometry and material composition of these natural structures, engineers can create adaptive façades and frameworks that optimize load distribution and enhance structural integrity. This cross-pollination of disciplines fosters innovation and empowers designers to craft buildings that harmonize with their environment.

The potential of adaptive design extends beyond static architecture to encompass dynamic engineering solutions. Bio-inspired robotics, for instance, often mimic the adaptive capabilities of animals, such as the octopus, which can alter its body shape to navigate through tight spaces. This concept can be applied to create adaptive infrastructure, like bridges that change form in response to load conditions or seismic activity, maximizing safety and durability. Such innovations underscore the versatility and applicability of adaptive designs, offering a blueprint for future engineering endeavors that prioritize both functionality and harmony with nature.

Envisioning the future of adaptive designs raises intriguing questions about their potential applications and implications. How might buildings that dynamically respond to air quality or noise pollution transform urban living? What role could adaptive infrastructure play in mitigating the impacts of climate change? These considerations invite engineers and architects to push the boundaries of conventional design, embracing nature's wisdom to craft environments that are not only sustainable but also symbiotic with their surroundings. By channeling the adaptive ingenuity of nature, a new era of design can emerge, seamlessly integrating with the natural world and fostering innovation and sustainability in tandem.

Energy Efficiency Through Biomimetic Design

The delicate interplay of energy efficiency in biomimetic architecture connects the wonders of nature with the needs of contemporary buildings. Picture structures that emulate the way leaves breathe, turning sunlight into energy, or designs that mirror the insulation of polar bear fur. These concepts are grounded in the tangible potential of biomimicry, not mere fantasies. Studying plant photosynthesis provides a model for crafting solar panels that capture light with unprecedented precision. By imitating how leaves optimize light intake, scientists are creating solar cells that function efficiently even in low-light environments, ushering in a transformative era for sustainable energy.

Recent strides in crafting energy-efficient buildings draw inspiration from the natural world, where species have refined resource conservation over countless generations. The passive cooling system found in termite mounds, for instance, has influenced architects to design structures that maintain temperature with minimal energy. The Eastgate Centre in Harare, Zimbabwe, illustrates this concept by adopting the self-cooling properties of termite mounds, ensuring a comfortable climate with reduced reliance on conventional air conditioning, significantly cutting energy use.

Biomimetic principles also shape the materials used in construction. The lotus effect—where the leaf's texture repels water and grime—has inspired the creation of self-cleaning surfaces for buildings, minimizing the need for water and harsh chemicals. These innovations not only streamline maintenance but also boost the durability and sustainability of buildings, echoing nature's drive for optimized function.

As societies confront energy consumption challenges, studying ecosystems reveals immense potential. The spatial arrangement of certain plants, designed for optimal space and light efficiency, inspires urban planners to rethink city layouts. These natural patterns can guide the creation of urban areas that better utilize wind and sunlight, reducing dependence on artificial lighting and heating. Thus, biomimetic design fosters a harmonious relationship between urban settings and their natural contexts, underlining the importance of symbiosis.

Imagining the future of energy-efficient architecture invites us to consider how self-regulating systems found in nature could reshape our built environment. Buildings that dynamically adjust to environmental shifts, akin to a chameleon's changing colors, could transform energy management strategies. Embracing such bio-inspired advances allows designers and engineers to create spaces that fulfill human needs while respecting ecological wisdom. The quest for energy efficiency transcends technology, representing a philosophical shift that encourages us to view nature as a mentor, offering lessons vital for a sustainable future.

Integrating Self-Healing Mechanisms in Modern Engineering

In modern engineering, the development of self-repairing systems takes inspiration from nature's remarkable regenerative abilities, such as a gecko regrowing its tail or human skin healing. These natural phenomena have catalyzed advancements in materials science, leading to innovations that autonomously mend damage. This concept is revolutionary in fields like construction, aerospace, and the automotive industry, where reducing maintenance costs and downtime is crucial. For example, researchers have created concrete that releases healing agents to seal cracks and restore structural integrity, extending infrastructure lifespan and reducing environmental impact by minimizing repairs.

The momentum behind integrating self-healing technologies into engineering is fueled by progress in material science and nanotechnology. These advancements have resulted in polymers that mimic the self-repair capabilities of living organisms. When damaged, these materials release embedded healing agents that bond the affected area, similar to biological clotting. This innovation not only enhances material longevity but also bolsters safety by preventing cat-astrophic failures. In the automotive sector, self-healing coatings repair minor scratches, preserving both the appearance and structural integrity of vehicles. The applications for this technology range widely, from consumer products to critical infrastructure and beyond.

The exploration of self-healing mechanisms opens exciting possibilities for adaptive structures. Consider a building that can repair itself after an earth-quake, maintaining safety and integrity without immediate human interven-tion. Recent breakthroughs in smart materials, like shape-memory alloys and self-healing composites, make this vision feasible. These materials can detect damage and initiate repair processes, adapting to environmental changes and reducing human oversight. This capability aligns with sustainable design prin-ciples by minimizing resource use and maximizing structural efficiency. As research advances, the dream of fully autonomous, self-sustaining structures becomes more attainable.

Incorporating self-repair systems into engineering requires a shift in de-sign philosophy. Engineers must move beyond traditional maintenance models, adopting a holistic view that considers the entire lifecycle of materials and struc-tures. This shift encourages interdisciplinary collaboration, blending insights from biology, chemistry, and physics to create innovative solutions. Engineers and designers are challenged to rethink how we construct and maintain our world, using nature's wisdom to build resilient, self-sufficient systems. Provoca-tive questions arise: How can we create urban environments that not only endure but actively recover from natural disasters? What role can self-healing materials play in mitigating climate change? These inquiries push the limits of current engineering practices, nurturing a culture of innovation.

For practitioners and innovators eager to apply these concepts, a strategic approach is essential. Start by identifying areas within existing systems prone to wear and failure, assessing how self-healing mechanisms can address these weak-nesses. Collaborate with material scientists to explore cutting-edge technologies and tailor them to specific applications. Launch pilot projects to test and refine these innovations, collecting data to guide future applications. By embracing these strategies, engineers and designers can harness self-healing materials to revolutionize their industries and the built environment, paving the way for a more resilient and sustainable future.

Exploring the intricate designs found in nature teaches us valuable lessons about creating solutions that harmonize form and function. For instance, the architecture of spider webs demonstrates a perfect blend of resilience and flex-ibility, allowing them to endure environmental challenges while using minimal resources. Similarly, the structure of bones showcases nature's expertise in bal-ancing weight and density to support various forces. These biological models have driven innovation in fields like bio-inspired architecture and engineering, fostering developments that prioritize sustainability and resourcefulness. By analyzing these natural constructs, we can derive insights into crafting designs that are not only robust but also adaptable. This chapter highlights the transformative potential of biomimicry, encouraging a reimagined approach to design by learning from nature's unmatched creativity. As we continue to explore further natural inspirations, reflect on how these principles of efficiency can influence your projects and initiatives, challenging the conventional to forge a future where nature and human innovation advance together.

Chapter Nine

Sensing And Responding Real Time Decision Making

As dawn breaks over the sprawling savanna, a lioness moves with purpose, her eyes locked on a distant herd of grazing antelope. Every whisper of wind and sway of grass is meticulously analyzed, shaping her actions with unerring precision. This scene embodies not just the stark beauty of the wild but also the extraordinary sensory and cognitive skills honed through countless generations. The natural world is a tapestry of intricate systems, where both predator and prey navigate their environments with unparalleled agility and accuracy. These finely-tuned mechanisms have sparked innovations beyond the wild, offering transformative lessons in adaptive decision-making that hold relevance in our own fast-paced lives.

In this chapter, we delve into the captivating realm of nature's sensory and response networks. We will uncover how predators and their quarry employ sophisticated sensory tools to maneuver through a complex landscape of risks and rewards, revealing insights into the art of agile decision-making. Even plants exhibit remarkable adaptability, responding to their surroundings with a level of sophistication that rivals human technology. These natural phenomena provide valuable guidance on the art of real-time decision-making, a crucial skill in an ever-changing world.

By drawing parallels between these biological wonders and the forefront of artificial intelligence, we can outline a framework for crafting responsive systems that echo the intuitive decision-making found in nature. As you explore this chapter, envision the potential of harnessing nature's wisdom to drive innovation. Whether you're developing AI technologies or refining your personal decision-making abilities, the lessons embedded in the natural world offer a reservoir of inspiration. The insights from these ecosystems are not mere relics of the past but a vibrant guide to forging a more responsive and resilient future.

The Advanced Sensory Systems of Predators and Prey

Imagine a chameleon, seamlessly shifting its hue to match its surroundings, or picture an owl gliding soundlessly through the night to capture its prey. These aren't merely captivating natural wonders; they demonstrate nature's extraordinary sensory capabilities and swift adaptability. In nature's realm, both hunters and their targets rely on an intricate network of sensory cues honed over eons, where the sharpest senses often draw the line between life and death. This dynamic interplay is not just about survival—it's about flourishing in a world of constant change. The natural world, in its unfolding tale of sensory mastery, offers invaluable lessons in rapid decision-making and adaptability.

Delving into the sensory abilities of predators reveals their astonishing precision in detecting even the faintest movements or subtle shifts in light. On the other hand, prey have developed advanced alert systems and stealthy tactics, turning evasion into a sophisticated skill. The coordination of multiple senses allows both predator and prey to execute complex survival strategies with remarkable speed and accuracy. This sensory fusion provides insights into enhancing our capabilities, particularly in artificial intelligence. The neurological innovations that drive these rapid response mechanisms can inspire the creation of technologies that react and adapt with similar agility. As we explore these themes, we connect the sensory strategies of the natural world with their potential to drive human innovation forward.

Evolutionary Adaptations in Predator Sensory Acuity

Predators in the wild boast an impressive array of sensory enhancements that elevate their ability to sense, pursue, and capture prey with pinpoint accuracy. These evolutionary advancements often manifest as heightened sensitivity in particular senses, allowing these hunters to maneuver through intricate environments with grace. Take, for example, the keen eyesight of raptors like eagles, whose retinas are densely packed with photoreceptors, giving them the ability to spot small mammals from afar. Likewise, the acute sense of smell in wolves enables them to detect scents over vast distances, allowing them to track prey even when out of sight. These adaptations showcase nature's ingenuity in honing sensory capabilities to fit specific ecological roles, offering valuable insights into how sensory integration can improve efficiency and success in practical situations.

Beyond individual sensory enhancements, many predators demonstrate multisensory integration—a complex process that combines information from various senses to create a comprehensive understanding of their environment. This can be observed in the hunting tactics of big cats, which utilize a blend of vision, hearing, and smell to successfully ambush prey. Such multisensory processing not only enhances the precision of their perceptions but also accelerates decision-making, enabling quick reactions to changing stimuli. These principles hold vast potential for technological innovation, particularly in developing advanced AI systems that must analyze diverse data streams to make precise, instantaneous decisions.

The evolutionary contest between predators and prey has spurred the development of remarkable sensory abilities, resulting in a continuous cycle of adaptation and counter-adaptation. As predators refine their sensory skills, prey species develop corresponding defenses, such as camouflage or mimicry, to avoid detection. Bats, for instance, have evolved echolocation to hunt in darkness, while some moths have adapted to detect these ultrasonic calls and evade capture. This ongoing interaction highlights the importance of adaptability and innovation in sensory systems, offering a blueprint for designing resilient and adaptable technologies capable of thriving in ever-changing environments.

Recent studies in the neurobiology of sensory systems illuminate the mechanisms that enable rapid responses. Predators' brains are adept at swiftly processing critical information, thanks to specialized neural circuits and synaptic efficiencies. Advances in neuroscience reveal how these circuits facilitate the rapid transmission of sensory data, enabling split-second decisions crucial for survival. Understanding these processes opens new avenues for enhancing human-designed systems, particularly in areas requiring real-time data processing and decision-making, such as autonomous vehicles and robotics.

Learning from nature's sensory systems prompts us to reconsider how we perceive and interact with our surroundings. By drawing on these evolutionary strategies, designers and engineers can create systems that mimic nature's capacity for dynamic response to stimuli, paving the way for innovations that are efficient and sustainable. Encouraging reflection on how these adaptations can be applied invites us to ask: What aspects of our current technological systems could benefit from a more nuanced, nature-inspired approach to sensory processing? By exploring this question, we unlock potential for transformative advancements in technology and beyond.

Prey Detection Mechanisms and Stealth Countermeasures

In the natural world, predators and prey engage in a relentless cycle of adaptation, each honing their skills for survival. Predators enhance their sensory abilities to detect even the faintest signals. Owls, for instance, have asymmetrical ears that enable them to locate prey in pitch darkness, demonstrating nature's remarkable ingenuity in sensory refinement. Meanwhile, prey species develop stealth tactics to avoid detection. Moths, for example, have wings that absorb sound waves, making them elusive to echolocating bats. This ongoing evolutionary conflict reveals an enduring arms race, where innovation becomes vital for survival.

The ability to process multiple sensory inputs is crucial for survival, allowing organisms to interpret and react swiftly to their surroundings. The mantis shrimp illustrates this concept with its extraordinary visual acuity, capable of detecting polarized light and a broader color spectrum than humans. Such advanced sensory integration allows it to identify prey and threats with precision. This synthesis of sensory information leads to a comprehensive environmental understanding, enabling rapid responses. This concept can inspire the development of AI systems that replicate nature's efficiency in processing complex data streams, enhancing decision-making capabilities.

In the plant world, dynamic responses complement sensory systems, providing real-time adaptation to environmental changes. Despite their immobility, plants display incredible sensitivity to stimuli like light, gravity, and touch. The sensitive plant, Mimosa pudica, rapidly folds its leaves when touched, a defensive tactic against herbivores. This swift response to external stimuli highlights a form of sensory perception often underestimated in flora. Understanding these mechanisms can inspire advances in robotics, where quick adaptation to environmental shifts is critical for performance and safety.

Recent neurobiological research has unraveled the complexities of rapid response systems in animals, highlighting the neural pathways that enable quick reactions. The C-start escape response in fish, for instance, involves a neural network that triggers a rapid, reflexive escape maneuver. This response, executed within milliseconds, is orchestrated by neurons processing sensory information and initiating muscle contractions. Insights into these natural systems can guide the development of advanced robotics and autonomous technologies, improving their ability to respond swiftly to unexpected events.

Translating these natural strategies into practical frameworks could revolutionize AI systems by mimicking biological sensory and response mechanisms. By integrating diverse sensory inputs and processing them in real time, AI can achieve exceptional situational awareness. This capability is transformative for fields like autonomous vehicles, where detecting and responding to changes is crucial. Readers are encouraged to explore how integrating multisensory data and rapid response capabilities can drive innovation in their fields, drawing inspiration from nature's intricate designs.

The Role of Multisensory Integration in Survival Tactics

In the complex interactions of predator and prey, the ability to integrate multiple sensory inputs is vital for survival. By combining data from diverse senses, animals can make quick and informed decisions. For instance, a bat uses more than just sound waves in its echolocation; it combines auditory, tactile, and sometimes visual cues to navigate and hunt efficiently in the dark. This multisensory coordination allows predators to target prey with precision while prey develop intricate systems to detect and escape threats. Recent research has unveiled the neural processes behind this integration, showing how animals like owls and dolphins can process multisensory information in milliseconds, significantly enhancing their reaction times.

This intriguing process is not exclusive to animals. Stationary plants also demonstrate their own version of multisensory integration. Some plants can detect subtle changes in light, gravity, and even chemical cues from neighboring flora or potential herbivores. This capability to perceive and react to various environmental stimuli allows them to optimize resource use, growth, and defense. For example, the sensitive mimosa plant folds its leaves upon touch, integrating sensory input to minimize damage from predators. These plant behaviors reveal another aspect of multisensory integration, offering insights into how stationary organisms engage with their environment.

Translating these natural strategies into human innovation has led to advancements in responsive technologies. Engineers and designers find inspiration in biological systems to develop adaptive mechanisms in robotics and artificial intelligence. A growing area of research focuses on enhancing AI through multisensory integration, enabling machines to process visual, auditory, and tactile inputs simultaneously. This approach not only improves real-time decision-making but also grants AI systems a nuanced understanding of complex environments, akin to the perceptual capabilities found in the natural world.

Exploring these natural models raises intriguing questions about technology's future and its applications. How might understanding multisensory integration shape the design of next-generation autonomous vehicles, allowing for more intuitive navigation and interaction with their surroundings? Could integrating multiple sensory inputs lead to more effective human-computer interfaces, improving accessibility and user experiences? By considering these questions, researchers and innovators can pave the way toward more sophisticated and responsive technologies.

The practical applications of multisensory integration are already impacting numerous industries. From developing more effective security systems using multiple data streams to creating smart, adaptive environments that respond to human presence, the possibilities are extensive. Innovators can adopt a biomimetic approach, identifying specific sensory integration strategies in nature and translating them into actionable frameworks. This approach unlocks nature's wealth of knowledge, applying time-tested strategies to contemporary challenges and paving the way for breakthroughs that enhance efficiency, resilience, and adaptability in human systems.

Neurobiological Innovations in Rapid Response Systems

Neurobiological advances in swift reaction mechanisms showcase nature's extraordinary creativity. These complex systems have evolved over millions of years, equipping organisms with the ability to respond rapidly to various stimuli. Both predators and prey have developed advanced neural structures that allow for quick and precise processing of sensory data. The neural pathways in these creatures are designed to minimize delays, enabling immediate reactions to dangers or opportunities. This high efficiency is achieved through specialized neurons and synaptic arrangements that emphasize speed over detailed analysis, offering valuable insights for designing human-engineered rapid response mechanisms.

Consider the star-nosed mole, which possesses sensory appendages rich with over 100,000 nerve fibers, making them among the most sensitive tactile organs found in nature. The mole's brain is structured to prioritize these sensory inputs, allowing it to detect and catch prey almost instantaneously. Such neurobiological setups demonstrate the power of sensory prioritization in creating systems that can quickly interpret and act on environmental signals. By studying these neurological designs, researchers can explore ways to develop artificial systems that replicate these remarkable capabilities, potentially transforming fields like robotics and autonomous vehicles.

Recent neurobiological research emphasizes the significance of neuromodulators—chemicals that regulate neuron activity—in enhancing rapid reactions. These substances fine-tune neural responses to optimize quickness and efficiency, adjusting the system to different scenarios. For example, the fight-or-flight reaction in mammals exemplifies how neuromodulation readies the body for immediate action, a concept adaptable to creating artificial intelligence systems. By incorporating neuromodulatory principles, engineers can create AI that dynamically alters its processing strategies based on situational needs, leading to more adaptive and responsive technologies.

Understanding multisensory integration helps us appreciate how organisms combine various sensory inputs to make quick decisions. The success of this integration depends on both the speed of signal transmission and the brain's ability to prioritize vital information. For instance, the barn owl's hunting ability in complete darkness is due to its remarkable capacity to merge auditory and visual information, swiftly converting them into coordinated actions. This natural phenomenon inspires the design of systems requiring real-time data synthesis, such as those used in defense or rescue operations, where rapid and precise decision-making is crucial.

To apply these neurobiological insights practically, innovators can focus on developing systems that emulate nature's strategies for prioritization and integration. This involves crafting algorithms that replicate neural pathways, emphasizing the speed and significance of data over exhaustive analysis. By nurturing a culture of interdisciplinary collaboration, where insights from biology inform engineering and AI development, we can discover new paradigms for rapid response technology. Encouraging readers to consider how they can incorporate these evolutionary lessons into their own projects can lead to breakthroughs that not only boost efficiency but also transform our interaction with the world.

Dynamic Response Mechanisms in Plants

Imagine waking up to a world where the silent language of plants unfolds before you, revealing a vibrant tapestry of signals and interactions. These seemingly still organisms, anchored in place, are anything but inert. They engage in a lively exchange of perceptions and reactions, employing intricate mechanisms to navigate ever-shifting surroundings. From the rapid signaling pathways that activate their defenses to the complex hormonal systems that steer growth and adaptation, plants showcase a sophisticated toolkit for making immediate decisions. This concealed realm of plant communication uncovers profound insights for those eager to comprehend and apply the principles of responsive systems, offering a window into nature's blueprint for adaptability and resilience.

As we delve deeper, the crucial role of electrical signals in plant responses emerges, revealing a network similar to a nervous system that enables swift reactions to external stimuli. This is not merely metaphorical; plants genuinely display intricate signaling pathways that allow them to flourish in varied conditions. Furthermore, these processes are dynamic. Through epigenetic modifications, plants possess the extraordinary capacity to adapt over generations, fine-tuning their responses to environmental challenges. Each of these mechanisms offers unique lessons, guiding us toward the development of responsive systems in technology and other fields. As we navigate these topics, the parallels between plant strategies and potential innovations in human-designed systems become increasingly apparent, highlighting the vast opportunities for learning from nature's ingenuity.

Rapid Signaling Pathways in Plant Defense

Plants, often underestimated as passive life forms, demonstrate surprising speed and precision in their defense mechanisms. These intricate communication systems enable them to detect and respond to threats with remarkable efficiency. One notable example is the jasmonic acid pathway, a critical component in the plant's defense against herbivores. When damage occurs, plants emit volatile compounds that not only repel attackers but also signal nearby plants to activate their defenses. This complex interaction underscores the sophisticated strategies plants use to thrive in ever-changing environments.

In examining plant communication, calcium ions emerge as crucial secondary messengers that transmit signals between cells. When under attack, plants exhibit a rapid increase in calcium levels, which sets off a cascade of biochemical reactions, culminating in the synthesis of defensive proteins. This swift response functions like a finely-tuned biological alarm, honed over millennia, providing plants with a vital competitive advantage. The similarities between these natural systems and engineered alarm networks suggest potential for innovative, bio-inspired technologies.

Beyond chemical signals, plants also use electrical impulses, akin to those in animal nervous systems, to quickly relay information. Recent studies have shown these signals can traverse the plant rapidly, triggering defensive responses throughout. This discovery challenges conventional views of plant biology, prompting new insights into how plants blend diverse signal types to mount comprehensive defenses. These findings could inspire advancements in fields like robotics and artificial intelligence, leading to more responsive and adaptive technologies.

Considering the technological implications of plant defense systems, we can derive inspiration for creating efficient, adaptive networks. Observing how plants integrate chemical and electrical signals might inform the development of hybrid communication frameworks that enhance information flow in complex systems. These cross-disciplinary applications go beyond imitation, offering transformative solutions in industries such as telecommunications and emergency response.

Reflecting on the broader potential of plant signaling pathways, one might ponder how our systems could emulate the swift, efficient communication seen in nature. This thought encourages exploration of biomimetic design, where insights from nature's enduring strategies guide the creation of systems that are not only efficient but also sustainable and flexible. By drawing on the profound wisdom found in plant communication networks, we can reimagine real-time decision-making approaches in our rapidly evolving world.

Hormonal Regulation of Growth and Adaptation

Plants, often seen as passive entities, actually possess a sophisticated hormonal network that intricately manages their growth and adaptation to ever-shifting environmental conditions. Central to this network are phytohormones, a varied group of signaling molecules that govern numerous physiological functions. Auxins, for instance, are crucial for guiding cell elongation and differentiation, helping plants to orient towards light—a process known as phototropism. This hormone-driven flexibility allows plants to maximize light absorption, vital for survival in competitive habitats. Gibberellins and cytokinins further bolster this adaptability by promoting cell division and expansion, essential for rapid growth and recovery from physical damage. These hormonal interactions highlight the complex internal communication system that enables plants to flourish despite environmental hurdles.

Recent breakthroughs in plant science have clarified the molecular mechanisms behind hormone signal transduction, offering fresh insights into plant resilience. Notably, the identification of receptor proteins that mediate hormone detection has revealed how plants finely adjust their reactions to external stimuli. By decoding these pathways, scientists are crafting innovative agricultural methods to bolster crop resilience against stressors such as drought and salinity. These advancements are crucial for securing food supplies and hold potential for sustainable farming in the face of climate change. The expanding field of synthetic biology further broadens this potential, enabling the engineering of plants with customized hormonal responses, potentially transforming crop development strategies.

The flexible regulation of hormones is vital for plant adaptation to changing environmental conditions. Abscisic acid, for instance, plays a pivotal role in managing water usage by controlling stomatal closure during drought. This hormone acts as a safeguard, balancing the plant's carbon dioxide uptake with the risk of water loss. Such adaptive strategies underscore the remarkable ability of plants to maintain equilibrium, even in challenging situations. Ethylene, another key hormone, orchestrates responses to biotic stresses like pathogen attacks by modulating defense mechanisms. These examples illustrate the multifaceted role of hormones in helping plants navigate the intricate interplay of environmental signals.

Exploring hormonal regulation in plants offers profound implications for biomimicry, inspiring innovative approaches in technology and design. Businesses can draw parallels between plant hormone networks and organizational decision-making processes, fostering adaptability and resilience. By emulating the way plants balance growth and resource allocation, companies can develop dynamic strategies for resource management and crisis response. Additionally, the concept of hormonal feedback loops can inform the design of self-regulating systems in engineering and artificial intelligence, where adaptability and precision are paramount. These applications illustrate the potential of nature-inspired frameworks to revolutionize various sectors, fostering sustainable and resilient practices.

Engaging with the complexities of plant hormones invites a deeper reflection on the interconnectedness of life and the potential for cross-disciplinary innovation. Consider, for instance, how understanding plant signaling pathways could inform medical research, particularly in the development of new pharmaceuticals. The parallels between plant and human hormonal systems open avenues for groundbreaking therapies and treatments. By questioning conventional approaches and seeking inspiration from the natural world, we can forge new paths in science and technology, ultimately leading to a more harmonious relationship with our environment. As we continue to unravel the mysteries of plant biology, the potential for transformative innovation remains boundless.

The Role of Electrical Signals in Plant Responses

Plants, often perceived as static, are dynamic organisms equipped with an intricate network of electrical signals, essential for their interaction and adaptation to their environment. These signals function similarly to a nervous system in animals, facilitating swift internal communication. This rapid information transfer allows plants to react to stimuli such as light, gravity, and physical damage. Recent research highlights how plants use these electrical impulses to execute complex defense strategies against herbivores, such as closing leaves or producing toxins when attacked. The study of plant electrical signaling is expanding, challenging traditional perspectives and showcasing the active nature of plant responses.

A particularly intriguing aspect of plant electrical signaling is its role in defense. When damaged, such as by a caterpillar feeding on leaves, plants quickly transmit electrical signals throughout their tissues, initiating a series of biochemical responses that discourage the attacker. This can include synthesizing defensive chemicals or activating genes to enhance the plant's resistance. These findings not only reveal the complexity of plant biology but also inspire new agricultural strategies, such as developing crops that resist pests more effectively without heavy reliance on chemical pesticides.

Beyond defense, electrical signals are crucial in regulating growth and adaptation to environmental changes. These signals enable plants to respond to variations in light and temperature, ensuring optimal growth. This ability to sense and react to environmental cues, while not cognitive, resembles decision-making processes. Such adaptability opens exciting possibilities for biomimetic applications, particularly in creating smart materials and responsive technologies that emulate plant behavior for optimized performance in varying conditions.

Advancements in technology now allow scientists to explore plant electrical signaling mechanisms more deeply. Techniques like electrophysiology and bioimaging provide unprecedented insights into how plants process information and coordinate their responses. This growing understanding offers valuable inspiration for designing artificial systems that mimic plant sensing and response capabilities, leading to innovations that are both efficient and environmentally harmonious, paving the way for sustainable progress.

Reflecting on the elegance of plant signaling, one can ponder how these insights might be translated into practical applications. Imagine urban infrastructure that adjusts to changing weather patterns as fluidly as a plant responds to sunlight shifts. Such visionary concepts challenge us to rethink technological paradigms, promoting solutions that are inherently adaptive and resilient. By embracing the lessons from plant signaling, we not only deepen our understanding of nature but also unlock new pathways for addressing the complexities of modern challenges.

Epigenetic Modifications for Environmental Adaptation

Plants, often seen as static, are actually vibrant organisms equipped with the capacity for complex environmental adjustment through epigenetic changes. These changes, distinct from genetic mutations, modify gene expression without altering the DNA sequence, enabling plants to rapidly adapt to shifting conditions and ensuring their survival. For example, some plants can adjust stress-responsive genes in times of drought or high temperatures, fine-tuning their physiological processes to conserve water or endure heat. This extraordinary flexibility has captured the interest of modern researchers, who are exploring how plants utilize epigenetic strategies to combat environmental stressors and maintain balance.

In plant biology, the study of DNA methylation and histone alteration has unveiled how plants can 'remember' previous stress encounters, allowing for a more effective reaction to future challenges. This epigenetic memory grants plants a predictive edge, akin to biological foresight. Recent findings show that this process can be reversed or reinforced based on subsequent environmental signals, offering a versatile and reversible adaptation system. These insights hold significant implications for agriculture, suggesting that manipulating epigenetic markers could boost crop resilience to climate change, potentially revolutionizing food security strategies.

The practical applications of these discoveries extend beyond farming. By understanding how plants employ epigenetic shifts, innovators can explore creative approaches to design systems and products with inherent adaptability. For instance, developing materials or algorithms that emulate this biological flexibility could lead to transformative advancements in robotics, artificial intelligence, and eco-friendly design. Imagine a construction material that adjusts its thermal properties based on environmental conditions, inspired by the principles that allow plants to modify their gene expression in response to temperature fluctuations.

On a larger scale, studying epigenetic adaptation in plants encourages a reevaluation of resilience and sustainability approaches. Embracing reversible and dynamic adaptation prompts the development of strategies that are both responsive and anticipatory. This shift moves away from rigid systems toward continuously evolving and learning frameworks. The potential for cross-disciplinary innovation is vast, opening doors for collaboration among biologists, engineers, and policymakers to address pressing global challenges.

As we explore the ramifications of plant epigenetics, it is crucial to consider the ethical and ecological aspects of applying this knowledge. While the promise of increased resilience and adaptability is appealing, careful thought must be given to the possible effects on biodiversity and ecosystem balance. Provocative questions emerge: How might altering epigenetic processes in plants influence their interactions with other species? Can we ensure that our interventions do not inadvertently disturb ecological harmony? By addressing these considerations, we can harness nature's wisdom in a way that respects and preserves the intricate web of life on our planet.

Creating Responsive AI Systems Inspired by Nature

Picture a morning where the devices surrounding you are no longer mere instruments but active allies, seamlessly adapting to your needs and surroundings. This isn't a fantasy of tomorrow; it's a reality drawing inspiration from nature's sophisticated sensory systems. The natural world excels in instantaneous decision-making, with creatures perpetually interpreting sensory data to navigate intricate ecosystems. Predators, using keen sight and sound, notice even the faintest rustle of prey, while plants, though rooted, respond dynamically to light, gravity, and touch. This natural dance of sensing and reacting provides a model for creating AI systems capable of flourishing in constantly shifting environments.

By embracing the complexity and elegance of biological systems, researchers are crafting AI that learns from and interacts with its environment. Mimicking nature's adaptive algorithms allows AI to transcend basic programmed responses. Neural networks, inspired by organic brains, are being honed to boost responsiveness, enabling AI to process enormous data spans with exceptional efficiency. As these systems start to weave environmental signals into their decision-making, they cultivate a kind of artificial intuition, making contextually aware choices. This exploration into nature-inspired AI involves designing intricate feedback loops, empowering AI to navigate the complexities of dynamic systems with precision. Such advancements promise to redefine our interaction with technology, transforming it into a constant companion in our pursuit of efficiency and adaptation.

Harnessing Sensory Feedback for Adaptive Algorithms

Incorporating sensory feedback into adaptive algorithms takes cues from nature's intricate sensory systems, where organisms constantly scan and respond to their environments. In artificial intelligence, this means developing algorithms that are not only reactive but also predictive, adept at adjusting promptly to new data. Central to this development is the fusion of feedback mechanisms, enabling machines to fine-tune actions based on sensory input, akin to how bats use echolocation for navigation. By embedding these feedback loops, AI systems emulate the way animals continually recalibrate their strategies to thrive and operate efficiently.

Recent strides in sensor technologies and machine learning have led to more advanced adaptive algorithms. The advent of neuromorphic chips, which mimic the brain's neural structures, enables more efficient sensory data processing. These innovations support AI models that learn and evolve like biological networks, enhancing fields such as autonomous vehicles and robotics. For example, autonomous drones now dynamically adjust their flight paths in response to wind changes or obstacles, similar to how birds adapt their flight patterns based on environmental conditions.

Feedback loops play a crucial role in crafting adaptive algorithms capable of succeeding in unpredictable settings. By integrating multi-layered feedback frameworks, AI achieves a responsiveness mirroring the intricacy of natural systems. An intriguing application is in smart agriculture, where AI systems employ sensory feedback to track soil and weather conditions, allowing farmers to optimize irrigation and fertilization. This not only boosts crop yields but also encourages sustainable farming by reducing resource waste.

Exploring different perspectives on adaptive algorithms uncovers a rich array of ideas, underscoring the potential for cross-disciplinary breakthroughs. Some researchers advocate for decentralized systems, drawing parallels to the self-organizing traits observed in ant colonies. Decentralizing control can enhance system robustness and resilience, maintaining functionality even if individual components fail. This viewpoint challenges traditional centralized AI models, suggesting a shift towards distributed systems that better mimic the flexibility and adaptability of natural ecosystems.

The practical applications of utilizing sensory feedback extend beyond technology into healthcare and environmental management. Picture a scenario where AI-enhanced medical diagnostics continually adapt to patient data, offering personalized treatment plans with remarkable accuracy. Or envision environmental monitoring systems that adjust to changing climatic conditions, providing real-time insights for conservation strategies. These possibilities demonstrate the transformative potential of adaptive algorithms, inviting reflection on the broader impact of technology inspired by nature's sophisticated sensory systems.

Mimicking Neural Network Patterns for Enhanced Responsiveness

In exploring artificial intelligence, replicating the complex neural architectures found in nature paves the way for significant advancements in how systems respond. Central to this pursuit is the attempt to emulate the intricate networks enabling rapid information processing in biological entities. Neural systems in animals have evolved to process sensory data with exceptional speed and accuracy, facilitating quick reactions to environmental changes. These biological frameworks provide a model for creating AI algorithms that mirror such responsive intricacies. By examining the parallel processing and adaptability of natural neural networks, researchers are developing AI models that can adjust dynamically to new information, resulting in systems that are not only reactive but also predictive.

A promising focus area is the study of spiking neural networks (SNNs), which mimic the way neurons communicate via electrical signals or "spikes." Unlike conventional artificial networks that use continuous data, SNNs handle information similar to the brain's signaling methods. This approach offers more energy-efficient computation and the potential for instantaneous decision-making, marking a significant leap in developing AI systems that operate under constraints similar to those faced by biological organisms. Recent research has shown that SNNs excel in tasks demanding rapid adaptation to shifting inputs, making them ideal for applications in robotics and autonomous systems where quick responses are crucial.

Integrating nature-inspired neural patterns into AI goes beyond mere imitation; it involves understanding the fundamental principles that make these networks so effective. One such principle is redundancy, where multiple pathways allow for information processing, enhancing robustness and fault tolerance. By incorporating redundancy into AI systems, developers can ensure functionality even when parts of the network malfunction. This strategy not only boosts system reliability but also mirrors the resilience seen in biological systems, where alternative neural pathways ensure survival despite disruptions.

To drive true innovation, exploring diverse perspectives on implementing these natural patterns across various technological fields is essential. In telecommunications, for example, neural network-inspired algorithms can optimize data routing, reducing delays and enhancing connectivity. In healthcare, AI systems designed with these principles can aid in early disease detection by rapidly analyzing extensive datasets for patterns indicating medical issues. Encouraging interdisciplinary collaboration can further refine these AI applications, ensuring they are grounded in both theoretical knowledge and practical use.

Considering the potential of nature-inspired AI, one might wonder how these systems could revolutionize industries or even shape societal norms. As AI continues to advance, the challenge of balancing machine autonomy with human oversight becomes increasingly relevant. By observing how natural systems achieve equilibrium between automated actions and environmental feedback, we can develop frameworks for AI governance that prioritize ethical considerations and human well-being. By applying the insights gained from nature, we are not only progressing in technology but also reimagining the future of human-machine interaction, setting the stage for a world where AI systems enhance rather than replace human capabilities.

Integrating Environmental Cues into AI Decision Frameworks

In the lively choreography of existence, organisms have mastered the art of sensing and adjusting to their surroundings, creating a complex interaction between sensory perception and decision-making. This vibrant exchange provides valuable insights for the evolving domain of artificial intelligence. By weaving environmental signals into AI decision-making frameworks, developers can create systems that mimic the nuanced responsiveness seen in nature. Such systems can detect subtle changes in data streams, similar to how creatures like bats and dolphins use echolocation to navigate and hunt. These natural inspirations underscore the significance of precise sensory mechanisms in helping AI to better interpret and react to real-time data.

Innovative research in bio-inspired algorithms showcases the potential of integrating environmental signals into AI. Observing how plants like the Venus flytrap react to touch, AI researchers are crafting algorithms that emulate this sensitivity to external stimuli. These algorithms emphasize context and flexibility, enabling AI systems to modify their actions based on a continuous influx of environmental information. This strategy is especially useful in areas like self-driving vehicles, where real-time data from surroundings must be processed swiftly and accurately to ensure safety and efficiency. As AI grows more proficient at interpreting these cues, it can develop a level of situational awareness akin to that found in natural ecosystems.

The notion of integrating environmental signals extends beyond simple data gathering; it involves synthesizing and contextualizing information to guide decision-making. Just as migratory birds use Earth's magnetic fields for long-distance navigation, AI systems can incorporate diverse environmental indicators to boost their predictive abilities. This comprehensive approach encourages AI to recognize patterns and anomalies, enhancing its capacity to address challenges or opportunities proactively. By embedding environmental context into AI algorithms, developers can improve the system's ability to function in complex and dynamic settings, reducing dependency on static programming and increasing adaptability.

Emerging machine learning methodologies focus on developing multi-modal systems that draw from various environmental inputs, akin to how different species rely on multiple senses to survive and thrive. For instance, combining visual, auditory, and tactile data streams can lead to AI systems with a more thorough understanding of their environment. Such integration creates a synergy that amplifies the system's decision-making capability, allowing it to respond with greater precision and agility. This multi-modal approach not only enhances the system's ability to adjust to unforeseen circumstances but also fosters innovation in AI applications across diverse sectors.

To apply these insights effectively, practitioners should design AI systems with layered feedback mechanisms that enable continuous learning and adjustment. By establishing feedback loops that mimic the iterative processes of natural evolution, developers can create AI that evolves over time, refining its response strategies based on accumulated experiences. This iterative tuning process is crucial for cultivating AI systems that can operate independently in unpredictable environments. By embracing nature's wisdom in integrating environmental signals, AI can transcend conventional limitations, offering solutions that are not only efficient but also elegantly aligned with the principles of life's enduring ingenuity.

Developing Multi-layered Feedback Loops for Complex System Dynamics

In the sophisticated balance of natural ecosystems, intricate feedback loops play a crucial part in sustaining harmony. These loops involve complex interactions among various components of a system, allowing organisms to detect, react, and adapt to environmental shifts with remarkable accuracy. In the domain of artificial intelligence, replicating these complex feedback systems offers a unique chance to enhance system dynamics and adaptability. By delving into the intricacies of these natural processes, AI can be designed to become more proficient at managing real-time information and adjusting outputs dynamically, much like biological entities.

One of the most fascinating features of natural feedback loops is their capacity to process and assimilate information from multiple sources, achieving a balanced integration of inputs. In AI, this concept can be transformed into the creation of algorithms that gather data from diverse channels, synthesizing it to form a coherent understanding of their surroundings. For instance, research into swarm intelligence, which draws inspiration from the collective behavior of social insects, has led to the development of algorithms based on decentralized control and feedback. These systems exhibit remarkable adaptability and efficiency, highlighting the potential of multi-layered feedback loops to guide AI design.

Developing these sophisticated feedback systems often involves utilizing neural network architectures that emulate biological processes. By embedding multi-layered feedback loops into neural networks, AI can achieve increased flexibility and resilience. This method has shown promise in areas like robotics, where machines must navigate unpredictable environments. Through iterative learning and adjustment, robots equipped with such feedback mechanisms can continually refine their actions, resulting in enhanced performance and decision-making abilities.

Integrating environmental cues into AI decision-making further emphasizes the significance of feedback loops. By incorporating sensors that monitor environmental changes, AI can adjust behavior in real time, similar to how plants modify growth patterns in response to light. Advanced research has concentrated on AI systems that anticipate and respond to user needs, incorporating feedback from user interactions to enhance personalization and relevance. This dynamic adaptability can lead to more intuitive and user-focused technologies, transforming human-machine interaction.

To fully harness the potential of multi-layered feedback loops, it is vital to adopt a holistic approach that supports continuous learning and evolution of

AI systems. This entails a commitment to iterative development, where systems are consistently tested and refined based on fresh data and insights. By fostering an environment of perpetual improvement, AI can evolve to meet society's ever-changing demands, reflecting the adaptive capabilities found in nature. As we progress in this endeavor, the lessons learned from nature's time-tested strategies will continue to illuminate pathways for innovation, inspiring new paradigms in AI design and functionality.

Inspired by nature's incredible capacity to sense and react instantaneously, this chapter has explored the sophisticated sensory networks present in both predators and prey, along with the dynamic ways plants respond to their surroundings. These natural wonders offer valuable insights for crafting innovative technologies, especially in artificial intelligence. By leveraging these lessons, we can design AI systems that emulate nature's accuracy and flexibility, enhancing decision-making efficiency. This chapter emphasizes the deep interconnection among all living things and the vast knowledge embedded in nature's design, reinforcing the book's broader theme: nature serves as a blueprint for groundbreaking innovation. With these insights, readers are now equipped to apply nature-inspired strategies for real-time decision-making. As the journey progresses, we will delve deeper into applying these principles to tackle new challenges, inviting readers to consider how else nature's wisdom might expand our understanding and abilities.

Chapter Ten

Complexity And Simplicity Leveraging The Power Of Simple Rules

As you stroll through a lush forest on a brisk morning, your eyes might catch the spirals of a fern or the intricate web woven by a diligent spider. Though these natural marvels appear intricate, they are guided by straightforward and graceful principles. This blend of simplicity and complexity is a profound concept that nature has honed over millennia. It prompts us to ask: How do these basic principles lead to such elaborate outcomes? By delving into this engaging interplay, we uncover how these fundamental ideas can guide us toward innovative solutions in a world that often feels overwhelmingly intricate.

Nature excels at achieving balance, weaving together ecosystems with basic guidelines that ensure harmony and resilience. In the interactions of hunter and hunted, the cycle of seasons, and the growth patterns of plants, simple principles create the basis for elaborate systems. These natural frameworks hold the key to solving challenges that seem unsolvable. By observing these patterns, we gain insights into how simplicity can be leveraged to tackle the complexities of modern innovation. This understanding not only transforms our approach to problem-solving but also empowers us to create strategies that are both effective and sustainable.

As we explore the dynamics between simplicity and complexity, we will discover how these principles can be translated into practical frameworks. From the mathematical beauty of fractals to the streamlined approaches that fuel successful innovation, we find that the answers often lie in the essentials. This chapter aims to inspire and equip you with the tools to simplify the seemingly intricate challenges of today, echoing the wisdom of the natural world in our quest for progress. Through this perspective, innovation becomes not just an endeavor but a natural progression, guided by the timeless insights of the world around us.

The Mathematical Elegance of Fractals in Nature

Picture waking up to discover the frosty patterns on your window hold a secret—a mathematical rhythm that resonates throughout the cosmos. Welcome to the captivating realm of fractals, where intricacy emerges from simplicity, and nature reveals its timeless wisdom through endlessly repeating patterns. From the network of veins in a leaf to the vast branches of a tree, fractals uncover hidden order amidst chaos, offering insight into the elegant simplicity at the core of nature's most elaborate designs. These patterns are nature's blueprints, shaping the growth of forests, the formation of clouds, and even the structure of galaxies. In this chapter, we embark on a journey through these fascinating patterns, exploring how they provide the key to understanding the balance between complexity and simplicity—a balance that can inspire groundbreaking innovation in our own pursuits.

As we delve into the mathematical beauty of fractals, we will explore the fundamental concepts of fractal geometry, where seemingly random shapes form harmonious order. These self-similar patterns demonstrate how ecosystems maintain their resilience and efficiency through repeating structures. By examining fractals as models for biological growth, we gain insights into how basic principles can guide the development of intricate forms. Finally, we will explore the advanced fractal dimensions present in ecological systems, unlocking a deeper appreciation for the delicate yet robust frameworks that sustain life on Earth. Each aspect offers a layer of understanding, guiding us toward practical applications of these natural patterns in solving complex problems and enhancing our innovation strategies.

Understanding Fractal Geometry in Natural Patterns

Fractal geometry, a concept that blends mathematical beauty with natural patterns, reveals itself in the world around us. At its heart, this branch of geometry deals with structures that maintain self-similarity at various scales. This characteristic appears in diverse phenomena such as the branching of trees, the winding shapes of coastlines, and the intricate networks within leaves. These repeating patterns are not just visually striking; they play a vital role in optimizing space and resources. By studying these geometric forms, we gain insights into the efficiency of natural designs, which achieve complex functions through straightforward principles.

The application of this geometry extends beyond the abstract and finds real-world relevance, particularly in biology. Consider the spiraled shells of mollusks or the unique formations of snowflakes. These are examples of how simple repetitive processes can lead to complex and distinct shapes. Such natural wonders highlight how simplicity can lead to complexity, potentially transforming innovation across various fields. By emulating these patterns, designers and engineers can develop systems that are not only efficient and scalable but also adaptable to evolving conditions, similar to their natural inspirations.

Recent developments in computational modeling have allowed researchers to explore the complexities of fractal patterns more deeply. By simulating these natural processes, scientists can uncover the core principles behind biological growth and development. These discoveries hold the potential to transform fields like architecture and medicine, where fractal-inspired designs could result in more sustainable buildings or groundbreaking medical treatments. As we decode the language of nature's geometry, the possibilities for applying fractal theory multiply, offering new solutions to some of humanity's major challenges.

The true strength of fractals lies in the simplicity of their underlying rules. This paradox encourages a reevaluation of how we approach complex problems, urging us to identify fundamental patterns applicable across various domains. By adopting a fractal mindset, innovators can break down complicated systems into manageable parts, discovering new problem-solving strategies that are both elegant and effective. This approach not only enhances our ability to address current issues but also prepares us to tackle future challenges.

For practical application, fractal geometry offers valuable insights. By identifying and leveraging the self-similar patterns present in both natural and artificial systems, we can design solutions that are inherently robust and flexible. Whether it's creating flexible algorithms that mimic ecological resilience or developing products that emulate the resource efficiency of natural structures, the opportunity for innovation by studying fractals is vast. As we continue to explore the mathematical elegance of nature, the challenge lies in translating these insights into practical strategies that can transform our world for the better.

The Role of Self-Similarity in Ecosystems

Nature's extraordinary talent for crafting intricate systems through straightforward, recurring patterns is embodied in self-similarity, a core feature of fractal geometry. This recursive design is not just an artistic oddity; it is a fundamental principle shaping the complex networks within ecosystems. Self-similarity appears in countless forms, from the way trees branch to the layout of leaf veins, promoting efficiency by maximizing surface area for vital processes like photosynthesis and nutrient uptake. These natural designs serve as a blueprint for innovation, inspiring approaches that emphasize resourcefulness and sustainability. By emulating nature's love for repeating patterns, we can create systems that minimize waste and optimize output, reflecting the success seen in the natural world.

Recent research has highlighted how self-similar structures enhance ecological resilience. These recurring motifs provide redundancy and stability, enabling ecosystems to endure disruptions and adapt to changes. As the pressures from climate change and human activities intensify, understanding and applying self-similarity can guide strategies to strengthen ecosystem services and biodiversity conservation. These insights offer a model for developing resilient human systems, where design redundancy translates into robust functionality. Incorporating self-similar patterns into urban planning or network design, for instance, can foster environments that echo nature's resilience, bolstering both ecological and societal strength.

The influence of self-similarity extends beyond physical structures to affect behavioral patterns within ecosystems. Consider the foraging habits of ants or the migratory routes of birds, which follow fractal-like decision-making processes to optimize energy use and resource management. These behaviors illustrate how basic rules can lead to complex outcomes, a concept that aligns with modern organizational theories. By mimicking these natural strategies, businesses and communities can create adaptive frameworks that respond fluidly to external pressures. This shift toward self-similar, rule-based systems encourages innovation that is both flexible and sustainable, promoting environments where growth is not just possible but assured.

In the realm of technology, self-similarity has become a cornerstone, influencing everything from network algorithms to data compression methods. The digital era increasingly demands solutions that can scale efficiently, a challenge that self-similar designs are well-suited to meet. By harnessing the recursive efficiency of fractal patterns, technology can achieve greater scalability and adaptability. This fusion of nature and technology signals a new wave of innovation, where self-similarity guides the creation of systems that are both intricate and manageable. Exploring these concepts promises to reveal unprecedented efficiencies, mirroring the evolutionary success of natural experiments.

Reflecting on self-similarity invites us to reconsider how simplicity can lead to sophisticated outcomes. Engaging with nature's recursive patterns challenges us to rethink traditional problem-solving approaches, advocating for frameworks that embrace simplicity as a path to complexity. This perspective not only deepens our understanding of natural systems but also provides practical insights for addressing modern challenges. By adopting the principles of self-similarity, we are equipped to design solutions that are inherently efficient, adaptable, and resilient, fostering a harmonious relationship with the natural world. As we continue to unravel the complexities of these patterns, the potential for transformative innovation remains vast, encouraging us to further explore the untapped genius of nature's design.

Fractals as Models for Biological Growth and Efficiency

Fractals captivate with their intricate designs, revealing nature's elegant principles. These patterns are more than aesthetic; they are blueprints for growth and optimization in biology. The fractal branching of trees, rivers, and lung bronchioles maximizes surface area and efficiency, using minimal space. This geometry is not just visually stunning but functionally crucial, enabling organisms to thrive by efficiently managing resources.

Recent research highlights fractals' role in biological growth. For instance, the fractal nature of vascular networks ensures efficient blood flow, delivering nutrients and oxygen to even the most distant cells with minimal energy use. This efficiency extends to plant roots, where fractal branching enhances nutrient and water absorption. Such findings inspire innovative design in technology and architecture, where adopting fractal principles can boost efficiency and sustainability.

Biomimicry explores how fractals influence technological advancements. Engineers incorporate fractal patterns in solar panels, increasing efficiency by mimicking leaves' light-capturing abilities. These designs improve light absorption and energy conversion, drawing directly from nature's solutions. By embracing these patterns, industries can create products that are both efficient and environmentally harmonious, highlighting fractals' potential in bridging natural processes with human innovation.

Mathematical exploration of fractals unveils new insights into ecological balance and resilience. Self-similar patterns in ecosystems, like species distribution in forests or coral reef organization, show how complexity emerges from simple guidelines. This arrangement fosters stability and adaptability, allowing ecosystems to maintain balance despite changes. Applying these principles can guide strategies for managing complex systems, from conservation to urban planning, ensuring human actions align with nature's wisdom.

Understanding fractals encourages a shift from linear thinking to a holistic problem-solving approach. Consider applying fractal principles to organizational structures, where decentralized, fractal-like networks enhance communication and adaptability. By observing nature's use of simplicity to manage complexity, businesses and individuals can devise innovative strategies that are both efficient and resilient. This dynamic interplay between simplicity and complexity enriches our understanding of biological systems and equips us to address modern challenges in a rapidly changing world.

Advanced Fractal Dimensions in Ecological Systems

Within the intricate web of ecosystems, fractal dimensions emerge as the unseen architects of both complexity and efficiency. Far beyond simple mathematical wonders, fractals serve as the fundamental blueprints for numerous biological and ecological networks. Their influence can be observed in the spirals of shells, the branching of trees, and the vast expanse of galaxies. By deciphering fractal geometries, scientists can gain insights into the effective distribution of resources and the robustness of ecosystems. This understanding is crucial for developing sustainable solutions that emulate the elegance and simplicity found in natural designs.

Recent breakthroughs in computational modeling have significantly advanced our grasp of fractal dimensions, providing a new perspective to explore ecological intricacies. These models empower researchers to simulate coral reef growth, investigate fungal networks, and predict animal population dynamics. Fractal analysis in ecology not only enhances our comprehension of ecosystem balance but also guides restoration initiatives. By mimicking the fractal patterns of thriving ecosystems, conservationists can devise strategies that bolster biodiversity and ecological stability.

The allure of fractals lies in their simplicity, yet their impact on ecological systems is profound. The self-repeating nature of fractals ensures ecosystems can endure external challenges. This principle is evident in the fractal design of river networks that optimize water flow and nutrient distribution across landscapes. Such natural efficiencies inspire innovations in water management, agriculture, and urban planning. By adopting fractal geometry principles, industries can create systems that are both efficient and adaptable, reflecting nature's harmonious balance.

Beyond their visual appeal, fractals offer practical insights for solving complex problems with straightforward principles. In innovation strategy, applying fractal concepts can streamline processes and improve decision-making. Businesses might model their organizational structures on fractal principles, fostering networks that are robust and flexible. This approach encourages creativity and resilience, enabling quick adaptation to market changes. By aligning strategic frameworks with natural fractal patterns, leaders can cultivate environments conducive to growth and innovation.

Exploring fractals in ecological systems encourages a reevaluation of how we address complexity in our endeavors. Could the solution to our most pressing challenges lie in nature's simple designs? By drawing inspiration from fractal patterns governing ecosystems, we can craft solutions that are both efficient and sustainable. Embracing fractal geometry's elegance enables us to transcend conventional thinking, envisioning a future where human systems coexist harmoniously with the natural world. Through this lens, transformative innovation is not just possible but inevitable.

Simple Rules That Govern Complex Systems

Imagine that beneath the surface of life's intricate phenomena lies a hidden simplicity, waiting to be uncovered. In the expansive and diverse tapestry of the natural world, a few straightforward principles often orchestrate the complexity we see. From the synchronized dance of starlings in the sky to the self-regulating ecosystems of coral reefs, basic guidelines lead to sophisticated behaviors. These guidelines are not mere constraints; they form the very structure upon which complexity thrives, offering us a perspective to view and address the multifaceted challenges of our modern world. The interplay of simplicity and complexity is not only a natural marvel; it is a blueprint for innovation, suggesting that the key to unraveling life's complexities may lie in identifying and applying these core principles.

As we delve into this exploration, our journey begins with an appreciation of emergent patterns in natural systems, revealing how individual components interact to produce unexpected and often mesmerizing outcomes. To harness such dynamics, we must pinpoint the key drivers that distill intricate systems into their essential elements. By understanding these drivers, we can employ reductionist strategies to dissect and tackle multifaceted challenges with precision. The integration of feedback loops emerges as a crucial strategy, fostering dynamic stability and resilience in both natural and human-made systems. These insights illuminate the path to innovation and empower us to transform complexity into simplicity, crafting solutions as elegant and efficient as those perfected by nature over millennia.

Harnessing Emergent Behavior in Natural Systems

Nature's intricate systems often manifest as a complex web of interconnected elements, yet they function under surprisingly straightforward principles. Emergent behavior, where simple interactions among individual components lead to collective dynamics, exemplifies these systems. In nature, starlings perform mesmerizing murmurations, crafting elaborate patterns in the sky through fundamental rules of alignment and spacing. This simplicity in individual actions leading to astonishing complexity teaches a valuable lesson for human innovation: simplicity often forms the foundation of the most sophisticated systems.

To harness emergent behavior, observing the subtle interplay within natural ecosystems is essential. Take the ant colony, for instance; no single ant possesses a master plan, yet collectively they accomplish intricate tasks like building networks, foraging, and defending their nest. Each ant follows a set of uncomplicated rules, responding to pheromone trails and environmental signals. This decentralized decision-making model can be applied to organizational structures, promoting autonomy and fostering innovation while maintaining cohesion. By adopting similar principles, businesses can create adaptive teams capable of responding fluidly to changes without the need for rigid hierarchies.

Integrating the concept of emergent behavior into human systems demands a deep understanding of feedback loops and self-regulation. Feedback mechanisms, as observed in ecosystem regulation, ensure stability and adaptability, allowing systems to adjust dynamically. This can be mirrored in product design or service delivery, where consumer feedback is continuously incorporated to refine offerings. A company that treats customer feedback as a living, evolving dialogue rather than a static dataset can stay ahead of shifting demands, enhancing customer satisfaction and driving continuous improvement and innovation.

The challenge lies in identifying the fundamental rules that will drive the desired emergent outcomes. Just as biologists study the interactions within a habitat to understand the behavior of its inhabitants, innovators must dissect the underlying processes of their systems. By applying reductionist strategies, one can focus on critical interactions that influence the whole. For instance, tech startups often distill their operational ethos into core values and missions, using these as guiding principles to navigate complex market landscapes. This clarity of purpose simplifies decision-making processes and aligns team efforts toward shared objectives.

Imagine scenarios where emergent behavior could transform current practices. How might decentralized networks enhance urban planning, or how could the principles of swarm intelligence optimize supply chain management? By questioning existing paradigms and exploring nature's solutions, one opens the door to transformative possibilities. Implementing these ideas requires the courage to challenge conventional thinking and the foresight to anticipate the ripple effects of simple changes. In doing so, innovators can cultivate systems that are not only robust and responsive but also infused with the elegance found in the natural world.

Identifying Key Drivers of Systemic Simplicity

In the complex web of natural environments, a paradox emerges where simplicity forms the backbone of intricate systems. This is evident in how ecosystems self-regulate using a handful of core drivers. Identifying these elements helps us appreciate the elegance that governs these systems, offering valuable insights for human innovation. Recent studies in biology and ecology reveal that interactions among a few components—like predators, prey, and environmental conditions—can shape an ecosystem's overall behavior. By grasping these dynamics, we can emulate nature's strategies to simplify complex organizational or technological structures, enhancing their efficiency and adaptability.

Consider an ant colony, a prime example of systemic efficiency. Despite lacking centralized control, ants perform complex tasks by following simple rules and sharing local information, leading to sophisticated collective behavior. This emergent order suggests a reevaluation of organizational design and management. By focusing on fundamental drivers like shared objectives, clear communication, and decentralized decision-making, organizations can create environments where complexity is effortlessly managed. This shift not only boosts operational efficiency but also fosters innovation by empowering individuals to operate autonomously within a unified framework.

The expanding field of biomimicry applies these principles to technological advancements, where nature's simplicity inspires groundbreaking design and engineering. By distilling natural processes, engineers and designers can craft streamlined solutions that emphasize functionality and sustainability. For instance, lotus-inspired self-cleaning surfaces use a simple water-repellent mechanism to stay clean. By identifying and leveraging these basic drivers, innovators can create products that fulfill human needs while reducing resource use and environmental impact.

To apply these insights effectively, methodologies that identify key drivers within complex systems are essential. Systems thinking and network analysis are invaluable tools, providing a deeper understanding of how individual components interact and influence overall dynamics. Mapping these interactions reveals leverage points to simplify and improve system performance. This approach aids problem-solving and encourages proactive innovation, where simplicity becomes a strategic asset.

As we tackle modern challenges, lessons from nature's simplicity offer a compelling framework for innovation. By identifying and embracing key drivers of systemic efficiency, we can transform complex issues into growth opportunities. This journey requires attunement to natural systems' subtleties, openness to interdisciplinary thinking, and a commitment to continuous learning. This unlocks the potential to reshape industries, technologies, and personal practices, paving the way for a future where simplicity and complexity coexist seamlessly.

Applying Reductionist Strategies to Complex Challenges

In the complex interplay of the natural world, reductionist strategies illuminate pathways through intricate systems, providing valuable insights into problem-solving. These strategies fundamentally involve breaking down complex systems into simpler, more manageable parts, much like a prism separating light into its individual colors. While rooted in scientific inquiry, this approach resonates beyond the laboratory, finding applications in various fields. In business innovation, for instance, reductionism aids in unraveling multifaceted challenges, enabling leaders to focus on the core elements that drive outcomes. By identifying and isolating these fundamental components, organizations can devise targeted and efficient strategies, transforming daunting problems into a series of actionable tasks.

In nature, the success of reductionist strategies is evident in species that have mastered simplicity to thrive in intricate ecosystems. Take the leafcutter ant, for example. It navigates the complexities of its bustling colony using straightforward rules: cut leaves, transport them, and cultivate fungal gardens. This basic behavior forms the basis of a sophisticated agricultural system, illustrating how simple, consistent actions can lead to remarkable results. Innovation practitioners can learn from such strategies, stripping away unnecessary details to uncover the essence of a challenge, thus enabling clear and decisive action. This approach not only enhances problem-solving effectiveness but also promotes adaptability in changing environments.

Recent research highlights the power of reductionist methods in cutting-edge fields like artificial intelligence and data analytics. In these domains, the focus has shifted to breaking down vast datasets into smaller, manageable units, allowing for more precise and actionable insights. This mirrors the reductionist strategies observed in nature, where organisms optimize behavior by concentrating on specific, impactful actions rather than attempting to address every variable at once. Innovators can glean valuable lessons: by focusing on the most influential factors within a system, they can direct their efforts more effectively, achieving greater impact with fewer resources.

In exploring these strategies, it's crucial not to overlook the role of creativity and intuition in determining which elements of complexity to simplify. While data and analysis provide a foundation, often it's an intuitive leap that uncovers the true levers of change within a system. The combination of analysis and intuition encourages leaders to trust both empirical evidence and their instincts when simplifying complex problems. This blend of logic and creativity mirrors the adaptive strategies of successful species that seamlessly integrate instinctual behavior with learned experience to navigate their environments.

The application of reductionist strategies extends beyond professional settings into personal growth, where simplifying complex life decisions can lead to deeper satisfaction and achievement. By focusing on core values and priorities, individuals can navigate life's intricacies with clarity and purpose. This approach encourages a reflective practice of identifying the essence of personal aspirations, akin to distilling a rich, complex brew into its most potent flavors. In both personal and professional realms, embracing reductionist strategies provides a powerful toolkit for transforming complexity into clarity, fostering a more intentional and impactful engagement with the world.

Integrating Feedback Loops for Dynamic Stability

Feedback loops are integral to both natural and engineered systems, serving as a mechanism to maintain balance amidst change. In the natural world, they play a crucial role in sustaining equilibrium, allowing organisms and ecosystems to adjust to varying conditions. An example is the regulation of body temperature in mammals, where sensors detect fluctuations and trigger responses to maintain stability. This concept parallels modern innovation strategies, where feedback mechanisms help refine and strengthen complex systems. By continuously integrating feedback, businesses can adapt to market shifts, foresee obstacles, and innovate efficiently, turning potential disruptions into strategic opportunities.

The beauty of feedback loops lies in their ability to simplify complexity. In organizations, they enable continuous learning and adaptation, much like how ant colonies use basic signals to optimize resource collection. These natural systems operate on uncomplicated rules yet achieve incredible efficiency and complexity. In business, effective feedback systems can identify inefficiencies, creating an environment where small improvements accumulate over time. This iterative process not only boosts operational efficiency but also fosters a culture of innovation, encouraging teams to experiment, learn, and evolve through real-time insights.

Modern technology enhances the potential of feedback loops, offering advanced tools to leverage data and insights on an unprecedented scale. Developments in artificial intelligence and machine learning equip organizations to analyze patterns and forecast outcomes, similar to how neural networks process information in the brain. By utilizing these technologies, businesses can develop adaptive systems that self-regulate and continuously optimize performance. These systems, like ecosystems, thrive on the balance between stability and change, enabling proactive adjustments that improve resilience. This technological integration transforms feedback loops from reactive tools into strategic assets, driving sustainable innovation.

A compelling example of feedback loops in action is the development of smart cities, where data-driven systems manage resources and infrastructure dynamically. These urban areas use sensor networks to monitor real-time traffic flow, energy consumption, and environmental conditions. Feedback from these systems allows city planners to make informed decisions, optimizing urban operations and reducing waste. This approach mirrors the efficiency of natural ecosystems, where feedback mechanisms ensure balance and sustainability. By adopting similar strategies, industries can create environments that are both efficient and adaptable to changing stakeholder needs.

To fully leverage feedback loops, it's essential to adopt a mindset of continuous improvement and adaptability. Organizations can achieve this by fostering feedback-rich environments that promote open communication and iterative learning. This involves setting up clear channels for feedback collection, analysis, and action, ensuring insights lead to tangible improvements. Encouraging diverse perspectives can further enhance the robustness of feedback systems, as varied viewpoints often uncover overlooked opportunities and issues. By embracing these principles, businesses and individuals can unlock the transformative power of feedback loops, driving innovation that is both sustainable and forward-thinking.

Simplifying Complex Problems in Innovation Strategy

Imagine waking up to discover that the most perplexing issues in your life have been transformed into a set of clear, elegant guidelines. This might sound like a fantasy, but it reflects the essence of nature's most intricate systems. In the natural world, elaborate complexity often springs from straightforward foundations, directed by simple principles that yield surprisingly sophisticated results. Consider the flight of birds, the spiral of a seashell, or the branching of trees—all follow fundamental guidelines that bring order to chaos. This chapter invites you into a captivating realm where the elegance of simplicity meets the challenges of complexity, offering a novel perspective on innovation strategy. By exploring how nature crafts its masterpieces with a few key strokes, we uncover insights that can be applied to modern challenges.

As we journey through strategic innovation, the following sections will demonstrate how these natural patterns can be leveraged for transformative outcomes. From adapting the efficiencies of biological systems into potent business solutions to creating flexible frameworks inspired by evolutionary successes, each topic builds on the previous one. By interweaving cross-disciplinary insights, we discover new routes through the maze of intricate problem-solving.

This exploration promises to reveal the layers of simplicity hidden within complexity and provide tools to redefine innovation strategies in ways that are both profound and practical.

Harnessing Nature's Simple Patterns for Strategic Innovation

Nature's intricate web illustrates a world where complexity often stems from the interaction of straightforward principles. In strategic innovation, these foundational patterns can serve as powerful frameworks for crafting effective strategies. Consider the murmuration of starlings, where each bird adheres to basic proximity guidelines to maintain cohesion and evade predators. This phenomenon exemplifies how simple directives can orchestrate a symphony of sophisticated behaviors. Businesses can adopt similar principles by establishing core guidelines that promote adaptability and creativity, enabling them to navigate the unpredictable currents of market dynamics.

Advancements in biomimicry reveal striking parallels between biological ecosystems and successful business models. The minimalist communication methods used by ants, reliant on pheromonal trails, can inspire streamlined communication protocols in organizations. By harnessing these natural efficiencies, businesses can enhance internal coordination and reduce information overload, a common obstacle in large enterprises. This approach not only simplifies operational complexities but also fosters an environment where innovation can thrive spontaneously, mirroring the self-organizing patterns seen in nature.

Strategic innovation also benefits from embracing the evolutionary success of certain species, adept at adapting to their environments through iterative processes. This concept aligns with agile development in business, emphasizing incremental improvements and rapid prototyping. By observing how species like the finch adapt their beak structures to exploit available resources, companies can learn to iterate their products and services efficiently. This adaptive framework champions resilience and responsiveness, essential qualities for maintaining a competitive edge in today's fast-paced markets.

Cross-disciplinary insights further enrich the strategic innovation palette, offering fresh perspectives that transcend traditional boundaries. The fusion of biological insights with technological advancements has led to breakthroughs such as bio-inspired algorithms in artificial intelligence, mimicking the problem-solving prowess of natural systems. By integrating diverse viewpoints and methodologies, organizations can cultivate fertile ground for innovation, where unconventional ideas are not only welcomed but actively pursued.

To translate nature's straightforward patterns into actionable strategies, organizations must nurture a mindset of curiosity and openness. Encouraging teams to observe and question natural phenomena can lead to groundbreaking insights that redefine conventional approaches. For instance, exploring how nature achieves balance and harmony can inspire new models of sustainability and efficiency. By empowering individuals to draw connections between the biological world and their strategic objectives, businesses can unlock a wealth of ideas that propel them toward unprecedented innovation.

Translating Biological Efficiency into Business Solutions

In the sphere of business strategy, taking cues from the efficiency of nature offers an intriguing opportunity. Across the natural world, organisms have refined their methods over millions of years, accomplishing extraordinary tasks with minimal resources. For instance, birds conserve energy during long migrations by flying in V-formations, which reduces wind resistance and boosts energy efficiency. Businesses can emulate this approach by simplifying operations and cutting out waste, ensuring resources are used to their maximum potential. This mindset promotes lean methodologies that identify inefficiencies and encourage ongoing improvement, mirroring the natural systems that inspire them.

Biological efficiency is also evident in the collaborative relationships within ecosystems. Species cooperate for mutual benefits, showing that teamwork can enhance productivity and resilience. Businesses can replicate this by developing partnerships that harness complementary strengths, leading to shared value creation. The rise of strategic alliances and open innovation platforms reflects this approach, where organizations unite resources and expertise to spur growth and innovation. These collaborations, similar to natural partnerships, can revolutionize industries by combining knowledge and minimizing individual shortcomings, facilitating breakthroughs that might otherwise remain out of reach.

Another striking example of biological efficiency is found in the communication systems of cells. Cells use chemical signals to coordinate actions, ensuring every function aligns with the organism's broader goals. Businesses can apply this principle by establishing clear communication channels that align employee actions with strategic objectives. Companies like Zappos, known for their exceptional customer service, exemplify this with a flat organizational structure that empowers employees and boosts responsiveness. This model ensures that each team member understands their role in achieving success, creating a cohesive and agile business environment.

To incorporate nature's efficiency into business solutions, a shift towards adaptive frameworks is necessary. Just as organisms evolve to thrive in changing environments, businesses must craft flexible strategies that allow them to quickly adapt to market dynamics. This involves fostering a culture of innovation where experimentation and learning from failures are key. Companies like Google, with their policy allowing employees to dedicate time to personal projects, embody this adaptive mindset. By creating an environment where innovation is not only welcome but expected, businesses position themselves to unlock the full potential of their workforce and navigate the complexities of modern markets.

To fully leverage nature's principles, businesses should integrate insights from various fields, adopting a holistic perspective. This interdisciplinary approach can reveal novel solutions to persistent challenges, much like how nature employs multiple strategies to tackle environmental issues. By encouraging the exchange of ideas, companies can spark creativity and drive innovation. For example, biomimicry in product design, as demonstrated by Velcro's inspiration from burdock seeds, highlights the power of interdisciplinary thinking. This approach not only fosters innovation but ensures businesses remain leaders in efficiency, sustainability, and growth.

Developing Adaptive Frameworks Inspired by Evolutionary Success

Adaptive frameworks, drawing from the dynamic process of evolution, provide valuable insights for navigating the shifting terrain of modern innovation. These frameworks mimic evolution, a process characterized by trial, error, and refinement. Just as species adapt to their surroundings, businesses and technologies can flourish by iterating and responding to changing conditions. The development of adaptive strategies hinges on understanding the principles of variation, selection, and retention—concepts refined over millennia. By applying these principles, organizations can create environments where innovative ideas are nurtured, assessed, and systematically improved.

The essence of adaptation often lies in simplicity. Consider bacteria, which evolve rapidly due to their short generational cycles, allowing swift adaptation to environmental pressures. Businesses can take a leaf from this book by adopting agile methodologies that enable rapid prototyping and feedback loops, ensuring innovations are cutting-edge and market-responsive. In this context, simplicity involves distilling processes to their most effective components, facilitating quick adaptation without unnecessary complexity.

Embracing evolutionary success requires accepting uncertainty and change. In nature, organisms that thrive are those that navigate unpredictability. This is reflected in corporate settings, where the ability to pivot and evolve is crucial. Companies like Netflix exemplify this by continually transforming their business model, from DVD rentals to streaming and content creation, staying ahead of consumer demands. This strategic agility is a hallmark of evolutionary thinking, where the emphasis is on thriving amidst constant change. Encouraging a culture that values flexibility and creative problem-solving can lead to breakthroughs that redefine industries.

Cross-disciplinary insights further enrich adaptive frameworks by encouraging a synthesis of ideas from various fields. Nature excels at this, with ecosystems functioning as interconnected networks where diverse species thrive through collaboration. Similarly, innovation can be sparked by integrating knowledge from different domains, such as combining biology and engineering to develop bio-inspired technologies. This interdisciplinary approach fosters creativity and resilience, enabling solutions that are both novel and robust. By breaking down silos and encouraging collaboration, organizations can harness a multitude of perspectives, leading to more comprehensive and adaptable strategies.

Reflecting on the evolutionary process raises intriguing questions about designing better adaptive frameworks. What can we learn from species that have thrived for millennia? How can we create systems that balance stability with the flexibility to evolve? These questions challenge us to critically evaluate our innovation strategies and inspire actionable steps. By applying evolutionary principles, businesses can cultivate environments that not only withstand change but use it as a catalyst for growth. Encouraging experimentation, embracing diversity, and fostering resilience are vital components of a strategy that mirrors the adaptive success found in nature's own playbook.

Integrating Cross-Disciplinary Insights for Complex Problem Solving

In the dynamic sphere of innovation, blending insights across disciplines unveils solutions to intricate challenges. By drawing from diverse fields, we can develop approaches that are both sturdy and adaptable. Nature exemplifies this through ecosystems that integrate various biological components, creating a synergy that enhances functionality and resilience. This blend of influences forms a foundation for innovation strategies, encouraging us to seek inspiration beyond our immediate areas of expertise. Nature's complex designs invite us to embrace diverse perspectives, crafting solutions that are both effective and sustainable.

Consider the intersection of biology and technology in biomimicry, where engineers have modeled the Kingfisher's beak to design quieter, more aerodynamic bullet trains. This highlights the power of interdisciplinary thought, where insights from one domain spark revolutionary applications in another. Such breakthroughs often emerge from viewing problems through diverse lenses, revealing patterns otherwise hidden. The key lies in fostering environments where ideas move freely across disciplines, promoting collaboration and creative problem-solving.

However, leveraging these insights goes beyond mere observation; it requires a strategic framework for integration. This involves nurturing an openness to new ideas and a challenge to conventional wisdom. Practically, this might involve assembling teams with varied expertise or employing methodologies that encourage lateral thinking, like design or systems thinking. By using these strategies, organizations can tap into the vast knowledge across disciplines, crafting innovative and impactful solutions.

Imagine a company facing a supply chain problem using insights from swarm intelligence in ant colonies. By understanding how ants efficiently organize and distribute resources, the company could create an adaptive logistics network that responds dynamically to changes in demand and supply, optimizing efficiency. This cross-pollination of ideas not only tackles immediate challenges but also fosters ongoing innovation, as teams learn to recognize and apply patterns from diverse sources.

Ultimately, integrating cross-disciplinary insights transforms our approach to complex problems, nurturing a culture of innovation that is both flexible and strong. By harmonizing nature's strategies with human creativity, we unlock the potential to surmount even the most daunting challenges. This journey demands curiosity and a willingness to explore the unfamiliar, but the rewards—solutions that are as elegant as they are effective—are worth the effort. As we continue to draw inspiration from the world around us, the possibilities for innovation are limitless, constrained only by our imagination and our readiness to transcend the conventional.

The journey into the balance of complexity and simplicity uncovers a significant insight: the natural world often relies on straightforward principles to orchestrate elaborate systems. This concept is elegantly demonstrated by fractals, where intricate designs emerge from basic rules. Such understanding offers practical guidance for innovation, suggesting that applying clear, effective guidelines can simplify strategies and tackle intricate challenges. Embracing simplicity within complexity not only enhances efficiency but also sparks creativity and adaptability in addressing contemporary issues. Drawing inspiration from nature's strategies, we see the potential to transform our methods by breaking down complexity into practical simplicity. This perspective encourages a reevaluation of how we approach both professional and personal endeavors, prompting a shift towards innovative solutions that are both deep and accessible. As we move forward to the next chapter, we are encouraged to consider how this refined viewpoint can reshape our interaction with the world, inspiring us to find simplicity's elegance and use it as a driving force for transformative change.

Chapter Eleven

Speed And Agility Rapid Response To Changing Environments

Picture yourself on the vast, sunlit expanse of the African savannah, where speed is crucial for survival. A cheetah lies in wait, muscles tense and ready, eyes fixed on a distant target. With a sudden explosion of power, it surges forward, reaching sixty miles per hour in seconds—a testament to the extraordinary prowess of the natural world. This is where evolution has crafted its most remarkable strategies, illustrating the power of adaptability in a constantly changing environment. As we dive into this exploration, we uncover how the quick reflexes and nimble movements of nature's speedsters offer valuable insights for navigating our fast-paced lives.

Through the lens of nature, we observe astonishing feats of renewal and adaptation—like the starfish and salamander, masters of regeneration. In their tranquil underwater realms or secluded forest habitats, these creatures regenerate lost limbs with ease, displaying an almost magical resilience. Yet, their abilities are rooted in ancient biological processes. Their stories inspire us to consider how we might emulate this adaptability, not by growing new limbs, but by renewing ideas and strategies when faced with challenges.

In today's world, the lessons from these agile hunters and regenerators translate into frameworks of flexibility and speed that individuals and organizations can adopt. In rapidly changing markets, where nothing stays the same, the ability to adapt, innovate, and respond quickly is essential. Just as nature's most adaptable species have thrived, so too can we, by embracing these principles. This chapter delves into the art of quick adaptation through nature's examples, encouraging us to apply these timeless strategies to navigate the complexities of our ever-evolving world. Here lies the fusion of ancient wisdom and modern application—a guide for thriving amidst the chaos of change.

The Fast Reflexes of the Cheetah and Agile Predators

Imagine a realm where the cheetah's swift elegance defines the pinnacle of speed and dexterity, showcasing nature's unparalleled ability to adapt and excel in shifting landscapes. This extraordinary animal, with its streamlined form and lightning-quick reactions, stands as one of the planet's most adept hunters. In mere seconds, a cheetah can accelerate from a standstill to sixty miles per hour, revealing an astonishing harmony of neuromuscular coordination and precision. Each sinew and nerve is perfectly tuned for the hunt, a masterpiece of movement refined over countless generations. Yet, the cheetah's strength is not merely in its velocity; it is an intricate dance of energy conservation and resourcefulness, where every leap and breath are precisely planned to ensure a successful pursuit. This natural marvel compels us to consider how such finely honed systems can inspire nimbleness in human activities, encouraging us to rethink how we navigate rapid shifts in our own environments.

However, the cheetah is but one example among nature's agile hunters, each with unique evolutionary traits enhancing their sensory acuity and strategic thinking. Consider the hawk's sharp vision or the octopus's remarkable ability to blend into its surroundings; these creatures exhibit an exceptional knack for swiftly altering their strategies in unpredictable situations. They illuminate the importance of heightened awareness and the capacity to adjust approaches in ever-changing scenarios. By delving into their intricate worlds, we unearth valuable insights these predators offer into frameworks of adaptability applicable in fast-paced markets. Their instinctive reactions and deliberate tactics provide a guide for maneuvering through complex settings, highlighting the potential for cross-disciplinary innovation. Observing and comprehending these natural phenomena equip us with the tools to design strategies that are as agile and effective as the predators that inspire them, paving the way for a deeper exploration of adaptability in both the natural world and human enterprise.

Neuromuscular Coordination and Precision in High-Speed Pursuits

The cheetah's remarkable ability to coordinate its neuromuscular system is a testament to nature's engineering prowess, offering valuable insights for understanding high-speed precision. At the heart of this prowess is the intricate interaction between its musculoskeletal architecture and nervous system. This dynamic relationship enables cheetahs to reach speeds of 60 miles per hour in mere seconds. Their elongated spine functions like a spring, efficiently storing and releasing energy, while their fast-twitch muscle fibers facilitate rapid contractions for bursts of power. This extraordinary blend of anatomical traits and neuromuscular control provides inspiration for designing systems requiring both speed and accuracy, such as in robotics or prosthetics.

Beyond mere speed, the cheetah's pursuit of prey exemplifies the delicate balance of sensory input and motor response. Research highlights how cheetahs use their acute vision to track and predict prey movements, adjusting their chase in real-time. This sensory-motor feedback loop resembles a well-orchestrated symphony, where each component harmoniously performs its role. These insights extend beyond biology, offering lessons for any field that demands rapid information processing and quick adaptation, such as autonomous vehicles or real-time data analytics.

Cheetahs also excel in energy efficiency during high-speed chases, managing their resources astutely. Despite the intense demands, they optimize energy use by adjusting stride length and frequency, ensuring each movement propels them forward most effectively. This principle of efficient motion holds significant implications for industries focused on energy conservation, from designing more efficient engines to developing algorithms that minimize computational resource usage. Observing this balance between power and economy in nature encourages a reevaluation of energy allocation and conservation in human systems.

Evolution has finely honed the cheetah's abilities, providing insights into how incremental adaptations can enhance performance over time. Their streamlined bodies reduce drag, while specialized nasal passages boost oxygen intake during sprints, highlighting the importance of iterative improvements. This evolutionary perspective is invaluable for innovation, emphasizing that breakthroughs often result from gradual enhancements rather than sudden leaps. It encourages a focus on continuous improvement and adaptation, a strategy relevant to everything from software development to product design.

The cheetah's strategic decision-making during hunts showcases a sophistication that goes beyond instinct. These predators evaluate factors like prey speed, direction, terrain, and their energy reserves, making quick decisions to continue or abandon a pursuit. This capability to assess and respond to complex scenarios serves as a model for decision-making frameworks in fast-paced environments. Organizations can learn from this natural strategy to optimize operations in volatile markets, where rapid assessment and agile responses are crucial. By adopting a mindset that values flexibility and quick thinking, individuals and businesses can navigate uncertainty with increased confidence and competence.

Energy Efficiency and Resource Management in Predatory Dynamics

In the world of nature's most effective hunters, the cheetah is remarkable not just for its unmatched speed but also for its extraordinary energy efficiency during high-speed chases. This swift feline perfectly balances power with conservation, using its limited energy reserves to great effect. Each sprint showcases a seamless blend of muscle power and energy conservation, offering a lesson in resource management that extends beyond the savannah. Recent research highlights that the cheetah's musculoskeletal design is fine-tuned for rapid acceleration and deceleration, minimizing energy waste and boosting endurance. This concept can be applied to human endeavors, where the strategic allocation of resources ensures sustained performance in dynamic settings.

Resource management in predatory behavior is further illustrated by the strategic hunting techniques of wolves. In packs, wolves employ a cooperative approach that optimizes energy use by sharing the physical demands of a hunt among several members. This teamwork not only conserves individual energy but also heightens the chances of a successful hunt. Businesses can take inspiration from this by cultivating collaborative environments where tasks are assigned based on individual strengths, enhancing overall efficiency and effectiveness. By drawing lessons from these predatory dynamics, organizations can achieve greater adaptability and responsiveness in fast-paced markets.

The idea of energy efficiency in the natural world extends beyond physical prowess to decision-making. Predators like the peregrine falcon, known for its swift dives and precise strikes, exhibit an ability to make split-second decisions that conserve energy while boosting success rates. This rapid decision-making is supported by advanced sensory adaptations, enabling the falcon to assess and react to environmental changes almost instantly. In business, this underscores the importance of real-time data analysis and agile decision-making processes, allowing companies to quickly adjust in response to market changes. Integrating artificial intelligence and machine learning can further enhance these capabilities, offering predictive insights akin to the falcon's anticipatory skills.

The connection between energy efficiency and sensory perception is also evident in the hunting methods of sharks. These ocean predators use highly developed sensory organs to detect minute electric fields emitted by potential prey. This sensory precision allows sharks to focus their efforts effectively, reducing the need for exhaustive searches. This principle of targeted efficiency can inform technological innovation, where precise engineering and data analytics lead to the creation of products and services that meet specific consumer needs without unnecessary resource use. By learning from nature's teachings, industries can achieve increased sustainability and customer satisfaction.

Reflecting on these natural models, one might consider how energy efficiency can be applied to personal productivity. Just as predators optimize their actions to conserve energy, individuals can boost their effectiveness by prioritizing tasks and focusing on high-impact activities. This approach aligns with the Pareto Principle, where a small portion of efforts yields the majority of results. Encouraging thoughtful consideration of personal energy allocation invites readers to ponder questions like: How can I streamline my daily activities to achieve my goals with minimal effort? By approaching personal and professional challenges with the mindset of nature's efficient predators, one can discover new pathways to success and innovation.

Evolutionary Adaptations for Enhanced Sensory Perception

In the natural realm, species have developed remarkable abilities to perceive and respond to their surroundings. The cheetah, known for unmatched speed, exemplifies evolutionary advancements in sensory perception. Its sharp vision enables it to spot prey from afar, even during fast chases. This keen sight results from a high number of retinal ganglion cells, which provide an expansive field of view and precise detail recognition. These adaptations are not just beneficial; they are vital for survival in the predator-prey dynamic. The cheetah's refined senses highlight the importance of sharp perception in changing environments, offering a model for technologies that require quick data processing and decision-making.

Apart from vision, cheetahs have exceptional hearing, allowing them to detect subtle sounds in their surroundings. Their ears can pivot to focus on specific noises, aiding in locating prey or identifying threats. This integration of multiple senses ensures a complete understanding of their environment, enabling swift, informed reactions. In technology, such as autonomous vehicles or security systems, combining visual, auditory, and other sensory inputs can enhance accuracy and response speed.

These evolutionary wonders inspire cutting-edge sensory technology research. Scientists and engineers are developing bio-inspired sensors that mimic the sensitivity and specificity of natural systems. For instance, advancements in electronic skins, which imitate the tactile sensitivity of animal skins, are leading to innovations in robotics and prosthetics. These sensors can detect small changes in pressure, temperature, and vibration, similar to the nuanced sensory inputs processed by agile predators. By emulating these biological systems, creators can design technologies that are efficient and adaptable to changing conditions.

Applying these insights involves more than imitation; it requires a deep understanding of the principles involved. A thought-provoking question is how businesses can use these evolutionary strategies to improve their sensory perception in competitive markets. By adopting a multi-sensory approach to data collection and analysis, organizations can gain a deeper understanding of market trends and consumer behavior. This comprehensive perspective enables quick decision-making, akin to the cheetah's rapid choices in the wild, allowing businesses to seize new opportunities swiftly.

As we delve into sensory perception's complexities in nature, the potential for innovation is clear. The challenge lies in translating these natural phenomena into practical strategies that enhance human capabilities. Whether through advanced sensors or integrating multi-sensory data in decision-making, lessons from nature offer a powerful framework for navigating today's fast-paced environments. Embracing these evolutionary insights empowers individuals and organizations to be more agile and responsive, leading to more effective and sustainable solutions.

Strategic Decision-Making in Rapidly Changing Scenarios

In the dynamic theater of the natural world, swift predators like the cheetah offer an insightful lesson in making strategic decisions under pressure. These animals master the art of quick response, skillfully navigating complex and ever-changing environments. Their success is rooted in a combination of sharp sensory perception and coordinated muscle action, allowing them to adapt rapidly to shifting circumstances. Cheetahs, for instance, use a blend of sharp vision and instinct to anticipate and respond to the movements of their prey, highlighting the significance of predictive modeling in decision-making.

The effectiveness of predatory tactics goes beyond mere speed; it involves a sophisticated understanding of how to allocate resources and conserve energy. Agile predators naturally balance the immediate demands of hunting with the need to sustain their energy over time. This balance is achieved through well-timed bursts of speed and slowdowns, demonstrating a precise and efficient approach. By embracing these principles, organizations in fast-moving industries can craft strategies to manage resources adeptly, pivoting swiftly without exhausting their reserves and maintaining performance in volatile markets.

Recent research has shed light on the neural processes that enhance predator agility, emphasizing the role of fast-twitch muscle fibers and synaptic flexibility in boosting reaction times. These findings have significant implications for artificial intelligence and robotics, where emulating such biological efficiencies could transform autonomous systems to better adapt in real-time. By integrating adaptive algorithms, businesses can replicate this natural prowess, creating systems that not only respond to changes but also predict them, gaining a competitive advantage.

In strategic decision-making, the ability to quickly interpret and act on sensory information is crucial. Agile predators excel at processing large amounts of environmental data, recognizing patterns, and making split-second decisions that maximize their success. This capability for swift analysis and action can be translated into organizational decision-making frameworks. By fostering an environment that encourages quick yet informed decision-making, businesses can navigate uncertainties with the same agility and precision observed in nature.

Fostering a culture of agility requires more than understanding natural phenomena; it involves nurturing a mindset open to change and innovation. Organizations can draw inspiration from the strategic flexibility of predators by adopting practices that encourage dynamic thinking and continuous learning. By asking critical questions like "How can we better anticipate and adapt to market changes?" or "What mechanisms can we implement to enhance our decision-making speed?" leaders can guide their teams toward developing robust, adaptive strategies. This approach not only improves immediate responsiveness but also lays the groundwork for long-term resilience and growth.

Rapid Cellular Regeneration in Starfish and Salamanders

Imagine awakening to a world where the enigma of natural regeneration has been decoded, revealing a realm where lost limbs and injured tissues are opportunities for renewal. Creatures like starfish and salamanders, with their extraordinary ability to recreate complex body parts, illustrate the essence of resilience and adaptation in the natural world. Through an intricate dance of cells, these beings effortlessly mend wounds and grow new appendages, showcasing an incredible level of biological flexibility. This extraordinary regenerative ability is not merely a natural wonder but a source of inspiration, steering scientists and innovators toward revolutionary breakthroughs in medicine and technology.

Within the quiet, swift processes of starfish and salamanders, a complex interplay of genetic and molecular pathways orchestrates the regeneration journey. By investigating these pathways, researchers unlock the secrets of cellular renewal, aiming to transform these biological wonders into groundbreaking medical treatments. As we delve into the rapid healing abilities of these species, a comparative analysis unveils the varying speeds at which different organisms achieve restoration, providing valuable insights into nature's efficient design. The implications of this research extend far beyond curiosity, holding the promise of transforming human medical practices, from regenerative medicine to tissue engineering. By understanding and applying these natural principles, we move closer to a future where the human body harnesses the regenerative might of nature, turning the once-impossible into reality.

Mechanisms of Cellular Regeneration in Starfish and Salamanders

The ability of starfish and salamanders to regenerate damaged or lost body parts offers an intriguing insight into the potential for renewal and adaptability in nature. These species have developed unique abilities to regrow limbs and other complex structures, distinguishing them within the animal kingdom. Starfish can regenerate entire arms, while some salamanders can restore limbs, tails, and even parts of their hearts and eyes. This extraordinary capability is driven by complex biological processes that operate with precision. Recent scientific studies have illuminated the cellular mechanisms these creatures use to start and maintain regeneration, offering promising insights for human medical advancements.

Central to this regenerative ability is the activation of specialized cells called progenitor cells. In starfish, these cells gather at the injury site and transform into the required tissue types to rebuild lost limbs. Salamanders utilize a distinct group of cells known as blastemal cells, which are triggered by injury and can differentiate into various cell types. The coordination of signaling pathways, including Wnt, FGF, and BMP, plays a crucial role in directing these cells' actions and steering the regeneration process. By manipulating these pathways, researchers are beginning to uncover ways to enhance regenerative abilities in other species, including humans.

Comparative research has identified notable differences in regeneration speed across species, with salamanders often regenerating faster than starfish. This difference is linked to variations in metabolism, cell proliferation, and genetic factors. For example, starfish rely on a slower, more deliberate cellular assembly, whereas salamanders show rapid cell division and tissue differentiation, enabling quicker regeneration. Understanding these differences not only deepens our knowledge of biological regeneration but also provides valuable insights for improving regenerative therapies in medical contexts.

The potential applications of these biological insights are vast, offering exciting possibilities for advancements in human medicine. The study of regenerative biology, inspired by starfish and salamanders, opens new paths for treating injuries and degenerative diseases. By leveraging the molecular pathways and cellular techniques honed by these organisms, scientists aim to create innovative therapies that could revolutionize tissue engineering and regenerative medicine. These approaches may lead to breakthroughs in healing spinal cord injuries, regenerating heart tissue after a heart attack, or even growing complex organs for transplant.

To translate these biological wonders into practical solutions, interdisciplinary collaboration is essential. Engaging in discussions that bridge genetics, molecular biology, and bioengineering can drive the development of regenerative technologies that mimic the natural processes observed in starfish and salamanders. This raises thought-provoking questions about how these regenerative processes can be ethically and effectively integrated into medical practice. By embracing these challenges and exploring diverse perspectives, researchers and innovators are poised to unlock nature's secrets to repair and rejuvenate, potentially transforming the future of medicine.

Genetic and Molecular Pathways Driving Regenerative Processes

In the field of regenerative biology, the genetic and molecular pathways of starfish and salamanders reveal a captivating array of possibilities. Starfish are renowned for their exceptional ability to regenerate entire limbs, while salamanders can regrow complex structures such as limbs and even parts of their hearts. These creatures exemplify nature's ingenuity through a complex interplay of genes and molecular signals that drive regeneration. For instance, salamanders initiate regeneration by reactivating embryonic genes within adult cells, a process that has fascinated scientists eager to decode the molecular mechanisms at play.

A key element in these regenerative processes is the Wnt signaling pathway. This pathway, essential for regulating cell growth and fate, is crucial in both starfish and salamander regeneration. By controlling cell proliferation and differentiation, the Wnt pathway enables these organisms to effectively replace lost or damaged tissues. Advances in genetic editing, such as CRISPR-Cas9, have allowed researchers to manipulate this pathway, shedding light on its functions and potential applications in human medicine. These studies suggest that similar regenerative mechanisms could be harnessed to treat human injuries and degenerative diseases, bridging the gap between natural phenomena and medical innovation.

Beyond signaling pathways, the genetic architecture of these organisms includes a network of genes responsible for cellular dedifferentiation and proliferation. In starfish, for example, certain genes activate to revert differentiated cells back to a pluripotent state, similar to stem cells, which then multiply and differentiate to form new tissues. This genetic reset is vital for initiating regeneration and presents a promising avenue for human applications, where cell reprogramming could lead to groundbreaking therapies. By examining these genetic processes, scientists are starting to unravel the molecular symphony that underlies regeneration, paving the way for revolutionary advancements in regenerative medicine.

While these molecular pathways are intricate, their potential applications are remarkably practical. Envision a future where humans can repair damaged tissues or even regenerate lost limbs by emulating the genetic and molecular strategies of these organisms. By understanding and replicating these natural processes, we could transform medical treatments and recovery methods. The challenge lies in translating these complex biological systems into practical clinical applications, requiring a nuanced grasp of both the science and the ethical considerations involved.

Current research continues to expand our understanding of regenerative biology, prompting us to rethink the boundaries of human healing. As we delve deeper into the genetic and molecular intricacies of starfish and salamanders, the possibility of applying these insights to human health becomes more feasible. These investigations invite us to consider the future: How might our healthcare systems change if we could tap into these regenerative abilities? What ethical questions must we address as we incorporate these natural blueprints into modern medicine? These inquiries not only drive scientific exploration but also inspire a deeper connection between human creativity and the wisdom found in nature.

Comparative Analysis of Regeneration Speeds Across Species

Starfish and salamanders have captivated scientists with their extraordinary ability to regrow lost body parts. This ability highlights the diverse ways life adapts to its environment. Although both species can regenerate, their methods and efficiency differ, influenced by unique evolutionary pressures. For instance, starfish can regrow entire arms, a process that takes several months, while salamanders can restore complex structures like limbs in just a few weeks. Understanding these differences not only illuminates the biological mechanisms involved but also offers potential applications in human medicine.

At the core of these regenerative abilities are distinct genetic and molecular pathways. Starfish utilize a decentralized nervous system to coordinate regeneration, triggering a cascade of cellular activities that lead to tissue regrowth. In contrast, salamanders have a centralized neural network that promotes rapid cellular proliferation and differentiation. These processes involve numerous signaling molecules and genetic factors ensuring precise and efficient regeneration. Recent studies have identified specific genes, such as ERK and Wnt, that play crucial roles, opening up exciting possibilities for biomedical advancements.

Comparative research has provided fascinating insights into why regeneration speed varies among species. Factors like metabolic rates, environmental conditions, and predatory threats dictate the urgency and extent of regeneration. Salamanders, often facing predators in aquatic habitats, have evolved to regenerate quickly to enhance survival. Starfish, living in relatively stable marine environments, might prioritize energy conservation over speed. These differences highlight the importance of ecological context in shaping regenerative strategies, offering a nuanced understanding of how organisms balance resource allocation with survival needs.

The implications of these findings extend beyond understanding nature's complexities. By examining the regenerative abilities of starfish and salamanders, scientists are developing innovative approaches to regenerative medicine. Techniques like tissue engineering and stem cell therapy draw inspiration from these natural processes, aiming to repair or replace damaged human tissues. The challenge lies in translating these complex biological systems into practical applications, a task that requires interdisciplinary collaboration and continued exploration of nature's secrets.

As we delve into the potential of regenerative biology, we are encouraged to consider how nature's designs can address humanity's most pressing challenges. What can we learn from starfish and salamanders that might inform the development of more resilient healthcare solutions? How might we harness these natural strategies to drive innovation in other fields, such as robotics or sustainable technology? By contemplating these questions, we gain a deeper appreciation for the marvels of the natural world and open new pathways for innovation that align with the intricate tapestry of life.

Implications of Regenerative Biology for Human Medical Advancements

The field of regenerative biology has seen incredible progress, inspired by the natural ability of starfish and salamanders to regenerate lost or damaged tissues. These creatures' remarkable capabilities captivate medical researchers who aim to replicate such processes in human medicine. As scientists explore the intricacies of regeneration, they're uncovering the complex genetic and molecular pathways that make it possible. By decoding these natural instructions, researchers are developing groundbreaking approaches to tissue engineering and regenerative therapies, envisioning a future where human bodies heal more efficiently from injuries and degenerative diseases.

In the realm of pioneering research, the study of regenerative pathways has unveiled crucial signaling molecules and genetic factors that govern cellular growth and specialization. Molecules like Wnt, BMP, and FGF, essential in the regenerative abilities of starfish and salamanders, are being investigated for their potential to trigger similar responses in human tissues. These discoveries have propelled the development of bioengineered scaffolds and stem cell therapies designed to mend damaged organs and tissues. By leveraging the principles of natural regeneration, scientists are edging closer to breakthroughs in treating conditions like spinal cord injuries and heart disease.

The impact of these findings goes beyond individual treatments, introducing a shift in medical approaches to healing. Regenerative biology advocates for less invasive procedures that tap into the body's inherent repair capabilities. This transition not only reduces recovery times and enhances outcomes but also lowers the risks associated with traditional surgeries. Such advancements are particularly significant in orthopedics, where regenerative techniques are improving joint repair and enhancing the quality of life for patients with joint degeneration.

As regenerative medicine advances, ethical considerations and practical applications remain central to discussions. The possibility of altering cellular processes raises important questions about long-term effects and potential unintended consequences. Researchers are diligently examining these issues to ensure that regenerative therapies prioritize safety and effectiveness. The ongoing dialogue between scientific innovation and ethical responsibility is vital in directing future research and integrating these therapies into standard medical practice.

Regenerative biology holds promise beyond immediate medical applications, offering a broader perspective on human health and longevity. By deepening our understanding of the body's regenerative potential, society stands to redefine aging and disease management. This knowledge invites us to envision a future where age-related decline is mitigated, and chronic diseases are managed with precision therapies inspired by nature's proven strategies. As we explore this new frontier, the lessons from starfish and salamanders serve as a beacon of hope and a testament to the transformative power of the natural world in revolutionizing human health.

Applying Agility Frameworks in Fast-Moving Markets

Imagine a world where businesses navigate the turbulence of market shifts with the agility of a cheetah dashing across the plains. In our rapidly evolving global environment, the ability to adapt quickly and efficiently to new challenges is not just beneficial—it's essential for survival. Nature has perfected this art of adaptability, with creatures like starfish growing new limbs and salamanders swiftly adjusting to environmental changes. These natural marvels provide valuable lessons for companies striving to flourish amidst perpetual transformation. By learning from the strategies found in nature, businesses can foster a mindset that embraces change, building resilience and sparking innovation even in unpredictable times.

As we explore the landscape of agile practices, the potential for business transformation becomes strikingly clear. Adopting frameworks inspired by nature isn't just theoretical; it's a practical approach to achieving real change. Companies that integrate adaptive strategies can confidently tackle market fluctuations, much like a nimble predator adjusting its tactics to capture prey. Cross-functional teams become the core of this agile methodology, enhancing both speed and creativity in addressing market needs. Meanwhile, predictive analytics shines a light on the future, helping businesses anticipate and respond to the ever-changing market dynamics. Through this lens, the fusion of nature's wisdom and contemporary business strategy unfolds, offering a roadmap to thrive in today's fast-paced markets and beyond.

Harnessing Nature-Inspired Agile Practices for Business Transformation

The natural world has always served as an unmatched source of inspiration for businesses aiming to navigate today's fast-paced markets with flexibility. In nature, agility is not merely a survival tactic; it is a refined art. Picture a flock of birds seamlessly adjusting their flight to evade a predator—their synchronized movements reveal the strength of collective adaptability. Companies can adopt similar strategies to improve their responsiveness and flexibility. By mirroring the decentralized decision-making and real-time communication found in ecosystems, businesses can transform their processes to become more fluid, embedding adaptability into every function.

To leverage nature-inspired agile practices for business transformation, adopting a mindset that prioritizes flexibility and swift adaptation is crucial. This involves rethinking organizational structures to enable quick shifts and iterative methods, akin to the flexible ecosystems in nature. Recent studies in organizational behavior indicate that businesses embracing decentralized models—similar to self-organizing ecosystems—see increased innovation and resilience. These structures allow teams to make autonomous decisions, much like ant colonies efficiently manage resources without centralized oversight. Embracing such frameworks can enable businesses to swiftly identify and seize opportunities, turning potential disruptions into avenues for growth.

Embedding agility into business transformation also requires nurturing a culture that promotes experimentation and learning. Nature thrives on diversity and experimentation, with countless species evolving various strategies to adapt to environmental shifts. Businesses can draw from this evolutionary mindset by fostering environments where new ideas can be tested and refined, rather than stifled by rigid rules. Companies like Google and 3M exemplify this approach by allocating resources for employees to explore projects beyond their immediate duties, thus creating fertile ground for breakthrough innovations. Encouraging a culture of thoughtful risk-taking and continuous learning can significantly boost an organization's ability to adapt and excel in unpredictable markets.

Additionally, agility in business can be enhanced through foresight and scenario planning, similar to how animals anticipate seasonal changes and adjust their behaviors accordingly. Cutting-edge research in predictive analytics and artificial intelligence provides businesses with unprecedented tools to forecast market trends and consumer behavior. By integrating these technologies, companies can gain a proactive edge, allowing them to anticipate shifts and respond with nimbleness. This approach not only strengthens a company's competitive position but also aligns with nature's inherent ability to sense and adapt to changes in the environment, ensuring long-term sustainability and success.

Consider the potential for cross-disciplinary collaboration, reflecting the interconnectedness seen in ecosystems where different organisms rely on each other for survival. By fostering partnerships across industries and sectors, businesses can tap into diverse expertise and innovative perspectives, much like the symbiotic relationships in nature that drive mutual growth. This collaborative flexibility can lead to the development of groundbreaking solutions that transcend traditional industry boundaries. As organizations embrace these nature-inspired practices, they unlock new pathways for transformation, resilience, and sustained success in an ever-evolving marketplace.

Implementing Adaptive Strategies for Real-Time Market Shifts

In today's fast-paced markets, adaptive strategies are crucial for distinguishing thriving businesses from those that falter. Inspired by nature's dynamic systems, companies can enhance their agility by mimicking the adaptability of organisms like the octopus, known for its unparalleled flexibility in changing environments. This biological agility can be reflected in business through modular strategies that allow swift reconfiguration while maintaining overall coherence. Such strategies not only enable organizations to respond effectively to unexpected changes but also foster an environment where innovation thrives, unimpeded by rigid structures.

In business, strategic foresight is indispensable. Companies leveraging predictive analytics are better equipped to anticipate market shifts and act decisively. Just as migratory birds adjust their routes based on environmental cues, businesses can use data-driven insights to navigate market fluctuations with agility. Advanced analytics tools provide a comprehensive view of potential trajectories, allowing organizations to craft strategies that are both reactive and proactive. This dual approach ensures companies are not just responding to changes but are also shaping pathways toward future opportunities, nurturing a culture of continuous growth.

A key component of adaptive strategies is fostering a culture of innovation and idea-sharing. Nature demonstrates the value of diverse ecosystems where varied elements collaborate for mutual benefit. In the corporate world, this translates to forming cross-functional teams that bring together diverse skills and perspectives, driving innovation through collaboration. By promoting open communication and knowledge sharing across departments, businesses can break down silos, creating an agile environment where new ideas can be tested and implemented swiftly. This collaborative ethos enhances problem-solving and imbues the organization with resilience needed to withstand market uncertainties.

Agility involves not just speed but also precision and informed decision-making. Like a cheetah calibrating its speed for a successful hunt, businesses must balance rapid action with strategic deliberation. This requires cultivating a mindset that values informed risk-taking and iterative learning, viewing setbacks as opportunities for growth. By adopting a cycle of continuous feedback and refinement, companies can maintain momentum while aligning efforts with long-term goals. This iterative approach enhances agility and protects against the pitfalls of hasty decisions.

Exploring adaptive strategies encourages reflection on the broader implications of agility in a rapidly changing world. As markets grow more complex, real-time responsiveness becomes a competitive edge. By considering scenarios where agility has led to transformative outcomes, the discussion opens a dialogue on the potential of adaptive frameworks to redefine business success. Questions like "How can we ensure our strategies remain flexible yet focused?" or "How can we embed adaptive thinking into our organizational DNA?" prompt readers to apply these insights to their contexts. These reflections underscore the theme that nature's strategies offer a blueprint for innovation, inspiring those bold enough to embrace change.

Integrating Cross-Functional Teams to Enhance Agility and Innovation

In today's ever-changing business environment, leveraging cross-functional teams is a powerful way to boost adaptability and drive innovation. These teams, made up of diverse professionals from various departments, bring together a wide array of skills and viewpoints, similar to the complex interconnections within natural ecosystems. Just as a rainforest flourishes through the cooperation of its inhabitants, organizations can thrive by fostering cross-functional collaboration. This strategy not only cultivates a culture of creativity but also allows for swift adjustments to market shifts, as team members offer unique insights to solve complex issues.

Research indicates that companies with well-integrated cross-functional teams navigate unpredictable markets more effectively. Their strength lies in quickly synthesizing information and crafting solutions that are both inventive and practical. By dismantling traditional departmental barriers, these teams enable open communication and a fluid exchange of information, much like the nutrient networks found in nature. Companies like Spotify and Apple attribute much of their success to the collaborative mindset and diverse knowledge that cross-functional teams provide.

To fully capitalize on these teams, organizations should nurture an environment that encourages experimentation and rewards innovative thinking. This involves setting clear goals aligned with the company's broader vision while giving teams the freedom to explore new solutions. Leaders should act as supporters, offering the necessary resources and support for team members to push beyond conventional problem-solving. By embracing a culture where calculated risks are valued, businesses can unlock the creative energy within their workforce.

A key component of successful cross-functional teams is the use of technology to facilitate collaboration and efficiency. Advanced tools such as collaborative software and real-time data analytics allow team members to share insights and feedback instantly, bridging the gap between ideas and implementation. This mirrors how some natural species use complex communication systems to respond quickly to environmental changes. As technology evolves, organizations must remain flexible, adopting innovative tools to sustain a competitive advantage in fast-paced markets.

Consider this scenario: Envision a leading company facing unprecedented market upheaval. How could it utilize cross-functional teams to not just endure but excel in this new environment? Reflect on the potential outcomes if these teams are empowered to challenge existing norms and pursue unconventional solutions. By adopting the principles of collaboration and adaptability, businesses can transform obstacles into opportunities, ensuring continued success in a rapidly changing world.

Leveraging Predictive Analytics to Anticipate and Respond to Market Dynamics

In today's rapidly changing markets, businesses must quickly anticipate and adapt to shifts to stay competitive. Predictive analytics, combining statistical algorithms with machine learning, is a vital asset in this dynamic environment. By examining past data and identifying trends, predictive analytics allows companies to forecast market movements and consumer behavior with impressive precision. This foresight empowers businesses to refine strategies, optimize resource allocation, and capitalize on new opportunities ahead of their rivals.

Take a retail company using predictive analytics to project product demand. By analyzing purchase patterns, seasonal fluctuations, and social media insights, the company can fine-tune its inventory, minimizing waste and enhancing customer satisfaction. For example, predictive models might reveal a spike in demand for certain products during the holiday season. Equipped with this information, the company can adjust its supply chain to ensure products are available when needed, boosting sales and customer loyalty. The nimbleness provided by predictive analytics enhances operational efficiency and fortifies the company's market standing.

Beyond demand forecasting, predictive analytics is crucial in identifying and mitigating potential risks before they escalate. Financial institutions, for example, rely on predictive models to spot fraudulent activity by detecting irregularities in transaction patterns. By incorporating these insights into their risk management processes, banks can proactively address threats, protecting assets and building consumer trust. This proactive approach exemplifies how predictive analytics fosters resilience and adaptability in fast-paced markets.

Integrating predictive analytics into an organization's framework requires fostering cross-functional collaboration. By bringing together data scientists, marketers, and strategists, companies can ensure that analytics-driven insights are both technically sound and strategically relevant. This collaborative effort taps into diverse expertise, encouraging innovation and ensuring predictive models are robust and actionable. Consequently, predictive analytics becomes a catalyst for organizational flexibility, enabling businesses to swiftly adapt to market dynamics.

To effectively leverage predictive analytics, companies must nurture a culture of ongoing learning and adaptation. Encouraging teams to question assumptions and refine predictive models enhances their accuracy and relevance. By promoting an environment where experimentation is encouraged, businesses can sharpen their analytics capabilities, keeping them at the forefront of innovation. As markets continue to evolve, successful organizations will be those that not only adopt predictive analytics but also embed it deeply within their strategic frameworks, driving flexibility and sustained success.

As we close this chapter, the study of quickness and adaptability in the natural world offers valuable insights for thriving in our rapidly changing environments. The cheetah, with its unmatched speed, and the starfish, with its extra-ordinary ability to regenerate, exemplify nature's expertise in swift reaction and flexibility. These creatures remind us that in today's ever-evolving world, being nimble and ready to adjust is not just beneficial but crucial. By applying these natural strategies to business and technology, we can create effective frameworks for success in unpredictable markets. Embracing these lessons underscores the need for flexibility and the willingness to change course, prompting us to re-think how we tackle challenges in our respective fields. This understanding not only boosts our capabilities but also aligns us with the enduring wisdom of the natural world, equipping us to face future uncertainties with assurance. As we progress, consider how these natural principles can inspire more agile and responsive systems, pushing us to innovate beyond traditional boundaries with nature as our guide.

Chapter Twelve

Longevity Designing For Durability

Amidst the ancient embrace of a forest where sunlight filters through a living tapestry of leaves, stands nature's quiet custodian of wisdom: the venerable tree. These enduring giants, with bark etched by time and branches reaching into the sky, silently narrate tales of resilience and survival. Standing in their shade prompts reflection: What hidden truths about lasting vitality might they offer, and how can we draw from these insights in our quest for enduring influence?

Nature, the master builder, creates life forms that not only persist but flourish across millennia. From the tortoise's remarkable ability to regenerate to the intricate repair systems in flora and fauna, these wonders of biology present a wealth of lessons for those seeking lasting success. In a world often dominated by fleeting trends, these natural exemplars challenge us to reconsider how we design enduring products, systems, and enterprises. The beauty of nature's solutions lies in their straightforward yet profound effectiveness, encouraging us to look past the obvious and adopt a perspective that values longevity.

In this chapter, we embark on a journey to uncover how these principles of endurance can be applied across various fields, from self-improvement to business strategy. By exploring how nature achieves stability, we can identify parallels that not only enhance our projects but also align with the broader goal of sustainable living. Let the ageless insights of the natural world inspire us to create innovations that endure, leaving a legacy as steadfast as the ancient woods and the tenacious beings that inhabit them.

The Long Lifespans of Trees and Tortoises

As we embark on this exploration, let's marvel at the extraordinary endurance of trees and tortoises, two of nature's most resilient beings. These life forms, with their ancient presence, narrate stories of adaptation and strength across the ages. Trees, standing tall with unwavering roots, have developed unique methods to survive countless environmental changes. Tortoises, on the other hand, with their measured pace and protective shells, have traversed time with a calm yet determined persistence. These majestic survivors reveal crucial insights into the science of long life, an aspiration humans hold dear and nature exemplifies. Their extensive lifespans are not mere happenstance but the result of intricate evolutionary processes that have allowed them to flourish where many others have faded. By delving into their survival strategies, we uncover a rich tapestry of biological knowledge that enhances our understanding of endurance and sustainability.

In the upcoming chapter, we will dissect the evolutionary techniques that bestow upon trees and tortoises their remarkable longevity, focusing on the cellular and genetic mechanisms at play. We will explore how their environments and ecosystems contribute to their extended lifespans, providing a window into the intricate relationship between organism and habitat. Each element of their existence offers lessons in eco-friendly design and sustainable practices, with applications reaching far beyond the natural world. By translating these insights into frameworks for human innovation, we can strive to develop systems and structures that echo the durability of these remarkable organisms. As we navigate these themes, the link between nature's age-old practices and our modern goals will become evident, enriching our approach to designing a future that values lasting endurance.

Evolutionary Strategies for Longevity in Trees and Tortoises

Trees and tortoises, celebrated for their extraordinary lifespans, reveal fascinating evolutionary tactics for enduring over time. These organisms have fine-tuned their survival methods across millennia, adapting to diverse environmental challenges. Trees, some of which can thrive for thousands of years, have developed strong defenses against disease and decay. Their bark acts as a robust shield against pathogens, while their ability to isolate damaged tissues ensures the rest of the organism remains healthy. Similarly, tortoises have evolved slow metabolisms and efficient energy use, reducing bodily wear and tear over time. These adaptations demonstrate the value of structural toughness and energy efficiency in fostering long life, offering inspiration for innovations in design and technology.

Recent studies delve into the cellular and genetic complexities that support these longevity strategies. Trees maintain impressive genetic stability through effective DNA repair mechanisms, preserving genetic integrity for centuries. Tortoises, too, have unique cellular pathways that enhance their capability to repair and regenerate, contributing to their long lives. Cutting-edge research suggests these mechanisms could lead to breakthroughs in biotechnology, particularly in areas like regenerative medicine and genetic engineering. Understanding the molecular basis of longevity in these species helps researchers identify potential methods to extend human health spans and improve resilience in materials and systems.

Environmental and ecological factors significantly influence the longevity of trees and tortoises. Trees thrive in varied environments, from arid deserts to lush rainforests, each presenting unique challenges that shape their survival strategies. Tortoises, conversely, have adapted to resource-scarce environments, perfecting their ability to endure long periods without food or water. These adaptations highlight the importance of adaptability and resourcefulness in achieving long life. By examining how these organisms interact with their habitats, we can gain insights into sustainable practices that balance resource use with environmental stewardship, influencing everything from urban planning to conservation.

Nature's lessons in endurance have profound implications for human design challenges. By emulating the adaptive strategies of trees and tortoises, innovators can create products and systems that withstand the test of time. For example, incorporating modularity and self-repair features into product design can enhance durability and reduce waste. Organizations might adopt business models that focus on long-term value rather than short-term profits, inspired by nature's emphasis on sustainability and resilience. By fostering a mindset that values durability, individuals and organizations can develop strategies that not only meet immediate needs but also ensure future viability.

As we reflect on the durability of trees and tortoises, we are encouraged to rethink our approach to design and innovation. Imagine buildings that could heal like trees or electronic devices that could conserve energy like tortoises. These imaginative scenarios challenge us to push beyond traditional boundaries and explore nature-inspired possibilities. By applying these insights, we can develop solutions that harmonize with the natural world, promoting a future where human creativity and nature's wisdom coexist. Through this perspective, longevity becomes not just a goal but a guiding principle shaping our pursuit of sustainable progress.

Cellular and Genetic Mechanisms Underpinning Extended Lifespans

The impressive lifespans of trees and tortoises are rooted in extraordinary cellular and genetic adaptations honed over countless generations. Trees exemplify a fascinating ability for continuous growth, lacking a fixed lifespan. This trait is largely attributed to meristems, clusters of embryonic cells that perpetually generate new tissues, enabling trees to grow and repair themselves, achieving great size and longevity. In contrast, tortoises possess a genetic structure prioritizing maintenance and repair over reproduction. Their genetic pathways, such as those responsible for DNA repair and stress resistance, minimize cellular damage, significantly extending their lifespan.

Recent studies on telomeres, the protective chromosome ends, have shed light on cellular endurance. In many species, telomeres shorten with each cell division, leading to cellular aging or death. Yet, long-lived species like tortoises have mechanisms to preserve telomere length, bolstering cellular health. This preservation is often facilitated by telomerase, an enzyme that replenishes telomere sequences, effectively rejuvenating cells. Insights from these processes offer valuable ideas for human-designed systems aiming for durability akin to natural self-preservation strategies.

Ecologically, both trees and tortoises have adapted to their surroundings in ways that favor longevity. Trees utilize extensive root systems to access deep water reserves, enhancing survival during droughts. Their ability to shed and regrow leaves optimizes photosynthesis and reduces water loss. Meanwhile, tortoises thrive in arid environments, thanks to their slow metabolism and water storage capabilities. By examining how these organisms interact with their habitats, innovators can develop systems that are not only robust but also environmentally harmonious, ensuring sustainable longevity.

Programmed cell death, or apoptosis, is crucial for maintaining longevity in nature. This process removes damaged or harmful cells, preventing disease and sustaining organismal health. In trees, apoptosis is visible in the seasonal shedding of leaves, removing damaged tissue and conserving resources for new growth. Tortoises similarly utilize apoptosis to uphold cellular health, ensuring only the fittest cells contribute to longevity. By integrating these natural strategies into human technology and design, we can create systems that proactively manage damage and promote renewal, emulating nature's enduring tactics.

Reflection on the cellular and genetic foundations of longevity offers abundant inspiration for modern innovation. By harnessing the principles of cellular maintenance and genetic resilience found in nature, designers and engineers can create robust, adaptable systems. Imagine buildings that self-repair like growing trees, or technology systems that heal themselves like tortoises managing cellular stress. Encouraging critical thinking on translating these natural mechanisms into practical applications not only sparks innovation but also deepens our appreciation for life's intricacies.

Environmental and Ecological Factors Influencing Lifespan

The natural world vividly illustrates the complex interplay of environmental and ecological factors that shape the lifespan of various organisms, such as trees and tortoises. These species have thrived for centuries, their longevity a testament to the blend of genetic traits and external conditions they experience. The impressive lifespans of bristlecone pines and Galápagos tortoises, for example, are closely tied to their stable habitats, which reduce stress and disturbances. This idea of environmental stability being crucial to extended lifespans is vital when designing systems and products meant to last. Emphasizing a balanced interaction with nature can lead to innovative designs that focus on sustainability and durability.

Ecological research highlights the importance of resource availability and competition in lifespan development. In nutrient-rich settings, trees like the giant sequoia efficiently allocate resources to growth and repair, enhancing their endurance. This strategic resource management parallels opportunities in engineering and architecture, where wise material use can prolong the life of structures. Meanwhile, the ability of tortoises to survive in resource-poor environments suggests that designing for durability often requires optimizing limited resources. This insight encourages the creation of efficient, minimalist designs that maximize functionality and minimize waste, aligning with the growing focus on sustainability across industries.

Interdependence within ecosystems significantly influences species longevity. Trees, for instance, form symbiotic relationships with fungi to enhance nutrient absorption, which bolsters their health and lifespan. These ecological partnerships offer valuable lessons for cultivating business ecosystems, where collaboration and mutual support can strengthen organizational resilience. Similarly, tortoises benefit from a balanced ecosystem, inspiring strategies that emphasize harmony and balance in human systems. By applying these ecological principles, businesses can create environments that support long-term growth and stability.

Research on climate change effects on species longevity highlights adaptability as crucial for survival amid environmental shifts. Trees and tortoises that adjust their physiological responses to changing climates demonstrate the importance of adaptive strategies. This adaptability can be mirrored in business models and technological systems designed to be flexible and responsive to external changes. The ability to pivot strategies according to market dynamics or technological advancements is increasingly seen as essential for organizational longevity.

Reflecting on these natural paradigms prompts a reevaluation of design and planning approaches, raising questions about integrating these insights into our endeavors. How can we incorporate ecological balance and resource efficiency into our design processes? What lessons can we draw from nature's adaptability in diverse environments? By embracing these insights, we can craft innovative solutions that endure over time and positively contribute to the ecosystems they inhabit. Moving forward involves leveraging nature's wisdom to create a more sustainable and enduring future.

Applying Nature's Longevity Lessons to Human Design Challenges

To integrate the enduring qualities of nature into human design, we must first explore the remarkable longevity of organisms like trees and tortoises. These species exemplify how durability is intricately embedded in their existence through sophisticated biological and environmental strategies. Take the Bristlecone pine, for example, which thrives in severe climates by adopting slow growth and resource conservation, ensuring survival over millennia. Tortoises, in contrast, benefit from a slow metabolism and effective cellular repair, allowing lifespans exceeding a century. By emulating these strategies, designers and engineers can create products and systems that emphasize durability, thus minimizing waste and promoting sustainability.

Incorporating nature's lessons into human design necessitates understanding the cellular and genetic mechanisms that afford these extended lifespans. Research into senescence—the cellular aging process—provides valuable insights. Cellular repair processes like autophagy and DNA repair are essential for maintaining an organism's integrity over time. In materials science, these processes inspire the creation of self-repairing materials that function much like a tortoise's cells. Utilizing advances in biotechnology and nanotechnology, we can develop materials and structures that emulate nature's capacity for renewal and endurance, offering transformative possibilities for various industries, including construction and consumer electronics.

The theme of sustainability naturally arises when applying nature's longevity lessons to human design challenges. The circular economy, increasingly recognized today, mirrors nature's cyclical resource use and regeneration. Just as decomposing leaves enrich the soil, products can be designed with their end-of-life in mind, facilitating reuse, recycling, and biodegradability. This approach not only extends the lifespan of resources but also aligns with ecological principles governing natural ecosystems. As businesses adopt these circular practices, they can draw on nature's proven strategies, promoting sustainable growth while reducing environmental impact.

Embracing nature's strategies for longevity requires fostering a design mindset that values resilience and adaptability. This means not only creating enduring products but also designing systems that can adjust to evolving conditions. Just as trees endure storms and tortoises survive temperature fluctuations, human-designed systems must be robust enough to thrive amidst uncertainty. This can be achieved through modular designs for easy updates and repairs or adaptive technologies that dynamically respond to user needs and environmental changes. By embedding resilience into the core of design, we can develop solutions that last and evolve over time.

Imagine integrating these concepts into daily life and industries: buildings that self-repair after natural disasters or electronics that adapt and improve over time. Posing such questions opens the door to a future where human ingenuity is seamlessly intertwined with nature's enduring wisdom. Applying these lessons from nature challenges us to think beyond the conventional, fostering innovation that is both visionary and practical. This synergy between biology and human design promises a more sustainable and enduring future, guided by the very principles of life toward greater achievements.

Cellular Repair Mechanisms That Maintain Longevity

Imagine the intricate ballet unfolding within every cell, where a seamless blend of repair and rejuvenation quietly shapes the span of life. In nature's vast laboratory, cellular repair mechanisms act as vigilant guardians of life's blueprint, continuously preserving and restoring the essence of existence. These processes are nothing short of extraordinary, enabling organisms—from the towering trees of the forest to the ancient dwellers of the sea—to endure the relentless passage of time. At the heart of this biological symphony are processes that identify and remedy DNA damage, laying a foundation for longevity that rivals the most sophisticated human designs. As we delve into these cellular strategies, we unveil secrets not just for survival but for thriving over decades and even centuries.

In this realm of cellular strength, telomeres, autophagy, and mitochondrial upkeep form a trio of resilience. Telomeres, the protective ends of chromosomes, slowly erode like the tips of shoelaces, influencing cellular aging and division. Autophagy, akin to a cellular cleanse, removes damaged components, ensuring cells remain vibrant and functional. Meanwhile, mitochondria, the cell's powerhouses, manage oxidative stress, balancing energy production with the need to counteract harmful byproducts. Together, these processes weave a fabric of biological endurance, providing a wellspring of inspiration for creating systems that last. As we explore these topics, we uncover parallels between cellular longevity and strategies for sustaining enterprises, discovering how nature's tried-and-true solutions can illuminate the path to enduring success.

DNA Damage Detection and Repair Pathways

DNA, the essential blueprint of life, faces constant threats from various stressors, both internal and external. This vulnerability necessitates intricate repair pathways to ensure cellular endurance. The DNA damage response (DDR) stands at the forefront of these mechanisms, comprising a complex system that detects, signals, and repairs DNA damage. Acting as a vigilant guardian, this system preserves genomic integrity and thwarts potentially disastrous mutations. Recent research underscores the crucial role of DDR pathways in enhancing lifespan across species, from the tenacious tardigrade to humans. For example, the enzyme poly(ADP-ribose) polymerase (PARP) plays a vital role in identifying single-strand breaks and facilitating repair, highlighting nature's ingenuity in maintaining cellular fidelity.

Delving deeper into DNA repair, the process is segmented into several meticulously orchestrated stages, each designed to address specific types of damage. Double-strand breaks, among the most hazardous forms of DNA damage, are primarily managed through homologous recombination and non-homologous end joining. These pathways exemplify nature's dual approach to problem-solving, balancing precision and speed as needed. Advanced research has revealed the potential to enhance these pathways to extend cellular life, sparking interest in developing therapeutics aimed at strengthening DNA repair mechanisms in age-related diseases. Such innovations underscore the importance of understanding and harnessing these biological processes to extend human healthspan.

Emerging theories suggest that DNA repair is not merely a sequence of reactions but a highly regulated process influenced by various cellular signals. Epigenetic modifications, for example, significantly impact repair efficiency by altering chromatin structure, which can either facilitate or hinder access to damaged sites. This discovery opens new research avenues, particularly in personalized medicine, where modulating epigenetic markers could lead to tailored interventions for enhancing DNA repair capacity. The interplay between genetic and epigenetic factors in DNA repair showcases the complexity and adaptability of biological systems.

In a broader context, the principles underlying DNA repair pathways can inspire robust frameworks for organizational problem-solving. Consider a business environment where challenges resemble DNA damage—requiring timely detection, assessment, and resolution. By emulating the DDR's systematic and adaptive approach, organizations can develop resilient strategies that address immediate issues and fortify their long-term viability. This paradigm encourages a proactive stance, where continuous monitoring and flexible response mechanisms are integral to organizational success. These insights offer a fresh perspective on cultivating durability in various sectors, from technology to healthcare.

To apply these concepts practically, envision an organization implementing a "DNA repair protocol" for its operations. This could involve establishing a detection system for identifying potential threats or inefficiencies, akin to PARP's role in recognizing DNA breaks. Subsequent steps might include analysis and resolution pathways, drawing parallels to homologous recombination and non-homologous end joining, tailored to the specific challenge at hand. By fostering a culture of adaptability and continuous improvement, inspired by natural strategies, entities can enhance their resilience and sustainability, paving the way for enduring success in an ever-evolving landscape.

The Role of Telomeres in Cellular Aging

Telomeres, the end caps of chromosomes, play a vital role in cell longevity by preventing chromosomal ends from fraying, akin to shoelace tips preventing unraveling. With each cell division, telomeres become shorter, acting as a biological clock indicating when a cell can no longer divide. This shortening is key to cellular aging and, by extension, the organism's aging. Recent research highlights telomerase, an enzyme that can partially reverse telomere shortening in certain cells, offering hope for prolonging cellular health and vitality.

Emerging studies are advancing our understanding of telomere dynamics. Researchers have found that lifestyle choices, such as diet, exercise, and stress management, can influence telomere length, potentially delaying cellular aging. The interplay of genetic and epigenetic factors in telomere biology is also gaining attention, providing fresh insights into how organisms manage cellular lifespan. These findings challenge the idea that genetics alone dictate telomere length, paving the way for personalized strategies to enhance cellular strength.

The impact of telomere research reaches beyond biology, offering lessons for creating sustainable systems in various fields. Drawing parallels between telomere maintenance and business strategies can help organizations cultivate a culture of durability. Just as telomeres safeguard genetic information, robust risk management can protect a company's core assets. This analogy emphasizes the value of proactive measures in ensuring the health and vitality of organizational structures, achieving long-term success and adaptability.

Exploring telomere biology inspires innovative thinking about aging and sustainability. Imagine strategies inspired by telomeres guiding urban planning, leading to cities that evolve without losing their foundational integrity. This concept invites reflection on natural systems' management of longevity, urging us to incorporate these lessons into our efforts to create enduring solutions. By fostering a mindset that values preservation and proactive care, we can develop environments that not only endure but thrive amidst change.

Practical steps for individuals and organizations to harness telomere insights include adopting a holistic approach to health and well-being. Encouraging practices like balanced nutrition, regular exercise, and stress reduction can help maintain telomere length. On a broader scale, organizations can implement policies that promote work-life balance and emotional well-being, aligning with principles of cellular endurance. By embracing these insights, we can pave the way for a future where the durability of both cells and systems becomes a tangible reality.

Autophagy and Its Contribution to Cellular Longevity

Autophagy is a crucial cellular process that plays a significant role in promoting longevity by removing and recycling damaged cellular components. This mechanism acts like an efficient waste management system, ensuring cells remain functional by breaking down and repurposing malfunctioning proteins and organelles. Recent studies have underscored autophagy's importance in countering age-related decline, highlighting its potential as a target for therapies aimed at extending healthy lifespan. By enabling cellular renewal, autophagy not only supports an extended lifespan but also strengthens resilience against various stressors, making it fundamental in the pursuit of prolonging life.

Advancements in biotechnology have unveiled complex mechanisms that regulate autophagy, offering insights into how this process can be harnessed to encourage longevity. Researchers have pinpointed key genetic and molecular pathways that can be adjusted to boost autophagic activity, thereby enhancing cellular health. This growing field explores the potential of pharmacological agents and dietary interventions, such as calorie restriction and intermittent fasting, which have been shown to activate autophagy and bolster cellular robustness. Understanding these pathways opens doors to innovative strategies that could transform approaches to aging and age-related diseases.

Autophagy's role goes beyond simple cellular housekeeping; it is intricately linked with cellular adaptation and survival strategies. In response to environmental changes and nutrient shortages, cells intensify autophagic processes to optimize resource use and energy production. This adaptability underscores autophagy's evolutionary importance as a survival mechanism, refined over millennia. The relationship between autophagy and other cellular processes, like apoptosis and senescence, highlights its complexity and necessity in maintaining cellular balance. By examining these connections, researchers can gain insights into how organisms have evolved to balance growth and maintenance, offering parallels for designing systems that prioritize extended lifespans.

In a broader context, autophagy provides a model for sustainability and resource optimization. Just as cells efficiently recycle their components, businesses and technologies can draw inspiration from autophagy to create systems that minimize waste and maximize efficiency. This biomimetic approach can lead to the development of circular economies and sustainable practices that mirror the efficiency of natural systems. By adopting strategies that emphasize resourcefulness and renewal, industries can enhance their long-term viability, much like cells that sustain themselves through autophagic processes.

Encouraging critical exploration, one might consider how autophagy-inspired principles could revolutionize organizational structures or product life cycles. What if companies embraced a culture of continuous renewal, similar to cellular autophagy, to remain agile and adaptable in an ever-changing world? By fostering environments that support ongoing improvement and flexibility, organizations can thrive amid uncertainty, achieving a form of corporate endurance that mirrors the cellular processes sustaining life. As we explore these transformative ideas, we unlock the potential for innovation that not only extends life but enriches it.

Mitochondrial Maintenance and Oxidative Stress Management

Mitochondria, often labeled as the cell's power generators, are crucial for sustaining cell vitality by managing energy production and metabolic processes. Their role goes beyond mere energy conversion; they are fundamental in controlling oxidative stress, a byproduct of aerobic metabolism that can cause cellular harm and aging if left unchecked. Recent research underscores the importance of preserving mitochondrial health, showing how cells utilize intricate mechanisms to uphold mitochondrial function and structure. One key process involves mitochondrial biogenesis and mitophagy, ensuring the replacement of damaged mitochondria with new, efficient ones. This ongoing cycle of renewal is vital for cellular endurance and vitality.

Emerging studies provide fascinating insights into how mitochondrial dynamics affect cellular aging. The balance between mitochondrial fission and fusion is essential for maintaining mitochondrial health. Fission helps eliminate damaged parts, while fusion blends mitochondrial contents, reducing damage. This dynamic interaction not only supports mitochondrial function but also enhances cellular adaptability to metabolic demands. Scientists are investigating how modulating these processes could extend cellular lifespan, potentially leading to treatments for age-related illnesses.

Central to mitochondrial health is the management of oxidative stress, a key factor in cellular lifespan. Antioxidant pathways, including those involving superoxide dismutase and glutathione peroxidase, are critical in neutralizing the reactive oxygen species (ROS) generated during mitochondrial respiration. New research explores ways to strengthen these pathways, possibly through dietary changes or drugs that boost the body's antioxidant capacity. By enhancing these defenses, cells can reduce oxidative damage, extending their functional lifespan.

The principles of mitochondrial maintenance offer lessons beyond biology, providing insights for creating durable systems in various fields. In business, for instance, the idea of regular maintenance and renewal can be applied to organizational structures and processes. Just like cells depend on timely replacement of damaged mitochondria, businesses can gain from periodic reviews and updates of their operational frameworks. This proactive strategy fosters resilience, adaptability, and sustained performance, reflecting the cellular strategies that promote longevity.

As we look to the future of longevity research, numerous intriguing questions emerge. How can advances in mitochondrial biology inform new anti-aging therapies? What connections can be drawn between mitochondrial maintenance and sustainability practices in technology and industry? Exploring these questions can open new avenues for innovation, inspired by the complex mechanisms of cellular vitality. Engaging with these concepts not only deepens our understanding of biology but also provides transformative insights applicable across various domains, from healthcare to corporate strategy.

Strategies for Long-Term Business Sustainability

In the heart of nature lies an ageless wisdom, where the secrets of enduring success are intricately entwined with life itself. From the steadfast strength of ancient trees to the enduring grace of tortoises, nature tells captivating stories of survival and adaptation. These narratives offer invaluable insights for businesses aiming to thrive in a constantly changing world. Nature's guide to endurance goes beyond mere survival; it's about flourishing through cycles of change, fostering robustness, and building strategic partnerships. This wisdom is a crucial resource for businesses aspiring not just to endure, but to prosper in today's dynamic landscape.

The path to sustainable business growth begins by observing nature's repetitive patterns, which can inspire innovative business models that align with the fluctuating market dynamics. The interconnectedness within ecosystems underscores the power of strategic alliances, encouraging businesses to nurture mutually beneficial relationships. Embracing adaptive management, akin to nature's response to change, becomes essential for maintaining robustness in the face of uncertainty. Moreover, the principles of biomimetic design pave the way for sustainable innovation, crafting solutions that respect the balance of natural systems. With these insights, the journey to lasting success becomes a living tribute to nature's ingenuity.

Emulating Nature's Cycles in Business Models

Nature's cycles offer a profound tapestry of growth, decay, and renewal, serving as a model for reimagining business frameworks centered around eco-friendliness. Just as forests flourish through intricate nutrient exchanges, businesses can adopt cyclical processes to boost resource efficiency and longevity. By mirroring natural cycles, organizations can shift from linear consumption to regenerative systems that reduce waste and enhance resource recovery. This approach, exemplified in circular economy models, aligns with cradle-to-cradle design principles, ensuring products are crafted with their entire lifecycle in mind. Materials are continuously cycled back into production or safely returned to the environment, bolstering both ecological and economic robustness. Consequently, businesses can better adapt to evolving environmental and market conditions.

Forward-thinking companies are taking cues from these natural cycles, revolutionizing industries with innovative methods. For instance, the fashion industry, known for its environmental footprint, is undergoing a transformation as brands adopt textile recycling loops. By designing garments with modular components that can be disassembled and reused, companies lessen their ecological impact while offering consumers fresh ways to interact with fashion. This evolution not only attracts eco-conscious consumers but also supports a sustainable business strategy that anticipates regulatory changes and resource limitations. Such strategies encourage viewing waste as a resource, fostering an ecosystem where each output becomes an input for another process.

This cyclical mindset also extends to organizational structures, urging businesses to develop adaptive practices that echo nature's self-regulating systems. Emulating the dynamic stability of ecosystems, businesses can implement feedback loops that enable ongoing learning and refinement. These loops allow real-time adjustments, like a forest reacting to environmental shifts, ensuring agility in the face of uncertainty. By nurturing a culture of experimentation and innovation, organizations can harness these feedback mechanisms to refine strategies, optimize processes, and boost overall performance, driving long-term success.

Adopting these cyclical principles necessitates a paradigm shift, challenging traditional business norms and urging leaders to rethink strategic priorities.

Emerging technologies like blockchain and IoT support this transformation by facilitating transparency and traceability across supply chains. These tools empower businesses to monitor resource flows and environmental impact with precision, enabling informed decisions aligned with sustainability goals. By leveraging such technologies, companies can build robust systems that mimic nature's intricate networks, encouraging collaboration and innovation across industries. This not only enhances competitiveness but also contributes to a more sustainable global economy.

As businesses embark on this transformative journey, they are prompted to consider provocative questions that challenge conventional wisdom: How can we design products to thrive in a circular ecosystem? What partnerships can we form to create symbiotic relationships akin to those in nature? By exploring these inquiries, organizations can unlock new avenues for innovation and growth, drawing inspiration from the natural world's time-honored wisdom. Embracing cyclical thinking not only paves the way for sustainable business practices but also inspires a broader cultural shift towards a more harmonious relationship with the planet.

Leveraging Ecosystem Thinking for Strategic Alliances

In the complex weave of natural ecosystems, strategic partnerships are crucial for survival, offering valuable insights for businesses aiming for sustainable growth. Ecosystem thinking, inspired by the interdependencies and symbiotic relationships found in nature, can transform how organizations establish collaborations. By emulating nature's cooperative networks, businesses can forge robust alliances that are both flexible and lasting. This method encourages moving beyond traditional competitive mindsets, fostering environments where shared resources and knowledge drive collective success. Practically, this might involve forming partnerships across industries to harness diverse strengths, similar to mycorrhizal networks in forests that connect trees and distribute nutrients, promoting mutual growth and resilience.

A forward-thinking model of ecosystem thinking is co-opetition, where competitive and cooperative strategies coexist to stimulate innovation and expand markets. This approach recognizes the ever-changing business landscapes, where rivals can become allies to pursue shared objectives, such as advancing technology standards or tackling global issues like climate change. Such alliances are evident in the tech sector, where firms collaborate on open-source projects while competing in the market. By embracing this perspective, businesses not only mitigate risks and share expenses but also access a wider array of skills and expertise, spurring innovation in ways that solo efforts cannot achieve.

A vivid example of ecosystem thinking is the evolving concept of business ecosystems, where companies function as interconnected parts of a broader network. This model takes cues from biological ecosystems, highlighting the importance of diversity, adaptability, and resilience. Within this framework, businesses are encouraged to nurture a varied mix of partners, including suppliers, customers, and even competitors, to enhance their ability to navigate changing market conditions. By fostering a collaborative and open culture, companies can tap into a rich reservoir of ideas and resources, allowing them to pivot swiftly and seize emerging opportunities.

To effectively implement ecosystem thinking, organizations must adopt adaptive management techniques that support continuous learning and evolution. This involves creating feedback loops that facilitate the exchange of information and insights across the network, similar to how natural ecosystems adjust to environmental shifts. By integrating data-driven decision-making and encouraging a culture of experimentation, businesses can maintain agility and responsiveness, akin to a coral reef thriving through its diverse interactions and ability to adapt to changing oceanic conditions. This approach not only enhances robustness but also promotes sustainable innovation through iterative development and ongoing refinement.

To build strong strategic alliances through ecosystem thinking, businesses should adopt a long-term view, focusing on relationships that provide mutual benefits and shared value creation. This necessitates a shift from transactional interactions to partnerships rooted in trust, transparency, and a shared vision for the future. By concentrating on developing deep, enduring connections, organizations can cultivate a collaborative environment where innovation thrives, much like the intricate web of life that supports Earth's biodiversity. By drawing inspiration from nature's design, companies can navigate the complexities of the modern business landscape with confidence and creativity, paving the way for a prosperous and sustainable future.

Implementing Adaptive Management Techniques for Resilience

Adaptive management techniques offer a flexible framework for resilience, drawing inspiration from nature's ability to adapt and prosper in uncertain conditions. In the business realm, these techniques translate into strategies that enable organizations to pivot and excel in constantly changing environments. Much like natural ecosystems that continuously adjust to shifts in climate, resources, and interspecies relationships, companies can cultivate similar agility. This requires not just embracing change, but anticipating it, by developing systems that are inherently adaptable and ready to adjust operations as new information and conditions emerge. The success of adaptive management hinges on continuous learning, with feedback loops and iterative processes serving as crucial tools for navigating complex landscapes.

A standout example of adaptive management in practice is seen in companies like Google, which employ data-driven methodologies to refine operations continually. By harnessing real-time analytics and machine learning, they can detect emerging trends and adjust their strategies accordingly. This mirrors how certain plants optimize resource use by modifying their growth patterns in response to environmental signals. Such practices highlight the importance of having a strong infrastructure for data collection and analysis, enabling businesses to remain responsive and proactive in their decision-making. By adopting an adaptive mindset, organizations not only reduce risks but also capitalize on opportunities that might otherwise go unnoticed.

Adaptive management also underscores the value of diverse perspectives, urging organizations to glean insights from a broad array of stakeholders. This approach resembles the symbiotic relationships in nature, where diverse species collaborate to create stable and resilient ecosystems. Involving different departments, partners, and even customers in decision-making can uncover unique insights and innovative solutions that a more isolated approach might miss. For instance, collaborations between tech firms and environmental scientists have led to significant advancements in sustainable technologies, showcasing the power of cross-disciplinary partnerships.

To weave adaptive management into a company's core, leaders must foster a culture that values experimentation and calculated risk-taking. This entails creating an environment where employees feel empowered to propose new ideas and challenge norms without fearing failure. Just as organisms in nature evolve through trial and error, businesses can drive innovation by nurturing a workplace where learning from mistakes is as celebrated as achieving success. This mindset encourages teams to explore unconventional paths, ultimately leading to breakthroughs that propel the organization forward.

As businesses work to incorporate adaptive management principles, they might consider posing questions that spark critical thinking and innovation. How can our processes be redesigned to better handle unforeseen challenges? How can technology enhance our adaptability? By fostering such inquiries, organizations can unlock new potentials, aligning their strategies with the fluidity and resilience observed in the natural world. Balancing a respect for tradition with a readiness to embrace change, companies can embark on a journey of sustainable growth, reflecting the enduring cycles of life that have persisted for millennia.

Harnessing Biomimetic Design for Sustainable Innovation

In the pursuit of eco-friendly innovation, biomimetic design paves a remarkable path by drawing inspiration from nature's vast repository of effective solutions. This design philosophy focuses on mirroring natural processes and structures to develop products and systems that are efficient, adaptive, and in harmony with the environment. Unlike traditional design methods, this approach integrates the complex elegance of biological systems that have evolved over countless generations. Take, for example, the lotus leaf's extraordinary ability to repel water and dirt, which has inspired the creation of self-cleaning materials in architecture and textiles. By leveraging these natural designs, companies can produce items that surpass sustainability goals, promoting a durable and adaptable ecological impact.

Biomimicry goes beyond mere mimicry; it involves grasping the fundamental principles that make biological systems sustainable and effective. One such principle is the closed-loop cycle, where waste is repurposed, as seen in ecosystem nutrient cycles. Companies like Interface, trailblazers in sustainable carpeting, have embraced similar methods by crafting products that can be taken apart and recycled at their end of life, echoing nature's zero-waste philosophy. This strategy reduces environmental effects while enhancing economic sustainability through resource efficiency and lifecycle consideration, essential for enduring business success.

Technological advancements boost the potential of biomimetic design, allowing for the exploration of intricate biological structures at a molecular level. Innovations in materials science, inspired by the flexibility of spider silk or the strength of abalone shells, have led to the development of lightweight composites with remarkable toughness and elasticity. These advancements provide companies with a competitive advantage by offering advanced materials that enhance performance while conserving resources. By incorporating these cutting-edge innovations, businesses can create products that are both sustainable and trailblazing, setting new industry standards.

Adopting biomimetic design requires a change in mindset, encouraging organizations to embrace a systems-thinking approach that recognizes the interconnectedness within a design ecosystem. This perspective fosters innovative solutions that are scalable and adaptable, akin to the dynamic networks found in nature. By nurturing collaborative environments and cross-disciplinary teams, businesses can draw on diverse expertise to drive innovation, much like the cooperative symbiosis observed in nature. This holistic view ensures sustainability is embedded at every design stage, from ideation to execution.

To practically apply these insights, organizations can start by fostering an ethos of curiosity and observation, urging teams to study natural phenomena and relate them to their own challenges. Workshops and design sprints focused on biomimicry can ignite creative thinking and inspire unique solutions. Collaborating with research institutions and utilizing the latest scientific findings can provide invaluable knowledge and resources. By prioritizing biomimetic design, businesses can strengthen their sustainability efforts and position themselves as leaders in innovative, nature-inspired solutions.

Throughout our exploration of nature's secrets to longevity, we have discovered that the enduring lives of trees and tortoises, along with their sophisticated cellular repair systems, offer valuable guidance for creating lasting solutions. These natural models show that true longevity involves thriving through adaptation and resilience. By applying these principles to business strategies, we can establish organizations that not only endure but also adapt to future challenges. This journey emphasizes the importance of aligning human innovation with nature's wisdom, creating systems that balance endurance with flexibility. As we look ahead, it's vital to consider how these natural insights can reshape our approach to innovation, inviting us to ask: How can embracing nature's lessons transform our vision for the future? As we continue our exploration, we stand poised to uncover even deeper insights from nature, urging us to reimagine the intersection of human creativity and the natural world.

Conclusion

As we conclude our journey through the intricate tapestry of the natural world, we find ourselves enriched with a wealth of insights that shine a light on the path to innovative thinking. Our exploration has revealed nature's ingenious strategies for confronting universal challenges, offering a rich tapestry of efficiency, resilience, adaptation, and collaboration. These lessons are not mere curiosities; they are profound templates that can revolutionize our approach to problem-solving across all facets of life. By studying the interconnected systems, self-regulating mechanisms, and the delicate balance achieved through optimization, we witness the brilliance of nature's solutions—brilliance that encourages us to incorporate similar strategies into our own endeavors.

The Universal Principles of Nature's Innovation

The principles that guide nature's creativity are both inspiring and instructive. Nature flourishes by embracing diversity, flexibility, and a decentralized method of tackling problems. These tenets are deeply embedded in the very essence of life, enabling ecosystems to thrive and species to adapt, even amidst adversity. The resilience of coral reefs, the adaptability of bacteria, and the collaborative intelligence of ant colonies illustrate how the environment achieves harmony and success. These examples remind us that creativity emerges not from isolated efforts but from a collective synergy that leverages shared strengths and resources. Nature's approach is holistic, viewing challenges as opportunities for growth and transformation. When we apply this mindset to human contexts, it encourages us to rethink how we design organizations, develop technologies, and interact with our surroundings.

Translating Nature's Wisdom into Actionable Frameworks

Transforming nature's insights into practical frameworks requires both imagination and discipline. It involves capturing the essence of nature's strategies and tailoring them to fit the unique challenges we face. Whether it's leveraging the energy efficiency of a hummingbird or the stability of an ecosystem, these natural models offer a roadmap for innovation that is both sustainable and effective. In business, the decentralized organization of ant colonies can inspire more agile and responsive structures. In technology, the adaptive strategies of living organisms can inform the creation of systems that are resilient and adaptable to change. By adopting nature-inspired methodologies, we pave the way for a new era of innovation that respects the delicate balance of our environment. This process is not about mimicking nature but thoughtfully adapting its foundational principles to guide our endeavors.

The Future of Biomimetic Innovation in Technology and Beyond

The future of biomimetic innovation holds tremendous potential, not only for technological advancement but for every aspect of human endeavor. As we approach new scientific breakthroughs, the opportunity to harness natural insights becomes increasingly tangible. Artificial intelligence plays a crucial role in deciphering the complex patterns that underpin natural phenomena, offering insights previously beyond our reach. This convergence of technology and nature-inspired thinking signals a future where creative solutions are not only more efficient but also more aligned with principles of sustainability and equity. We stand on the brink of a paradigm shift, where the lessons of the natural world are not just learned but lived, guiding us toward a future where human progress harmonizes with the environment. This journey is both an opportunity and a responsibility, compelling us to apply the insights gleaned from nature with care and intention.

Reflecting on the broader implications of this journey, we recognize that embracing nature-inspired innovation is not a solitary endeavor but a collective movement. It invites us to rethink our relationship with the natural world and to integrate its principles into the very fabric of society. As we consider the profound interconnectedness of all life, the insights derived from the natural world offer a compass to navigate the complexities of the modern era. By doing so, we may find that the solutions to our most pressing challenges already exist, waiting to be discovered in the patterns and processes around us. Let this serve as a call to action, encouraging each of us to engage with these ideas, apply them in our lives, and contribute to a future where innovation is synonymous with sustainability and harmony.

Resources

Books

1. "Biomimicry: Innovation Inspired by Nature" by Janine Benyus - This foundational book explores how nature's solutions can inspire sustainable innovations across various industries. Link

2. "The Nature of Technology" by W. Brian Arthur - Offers insights into how technology evolves similar to biological systems, providing a unique perspective on innovation. Link

3. "The Innovator's Dilemma" by Clayton M. Christensen - Although not directly focused on nature, this book challenges conventional business innovation strategies, complementing the nature-inspired approaches in "The Innovation Blueprint." Link

4. "The Hidden Life of Trees" by Peter Wohlleben - Explores the complex communication and collaboration systems in forests, providing inspiration for organizational resilience and cooperation. Link

5. "Design in Nature" by Adrian Bejan and J. Peder Zane - Discusses the constructal law and its application to understanding natural and technological flow systems. Link

Websites

1. Biomimicry Institute - A leading organization focused on promoting nature-inspired solutions for sustainable innovation. Their website

offers resources and case studies. Link

2. AskNature - A project by the Biomimicry Institute, this online database provides a wealth of natural strategies and solutions that can be applied to human challenges. Link

3. TED Talks on Biomimicry - A collection of inspiring talks that explore how nature influences design and innovation. Link

4. Nature's Patterns - An educational site dedicated to exploring patterns in nature and their applications in technology and design. Link

5. National Geographic's Nature Articles - Offers diverse articles on natural phenomena, biodiversity, and ecological innovations. Link

Article

s

1. "The Secrets of Nature's Survivors" by Elizabeth Pennisi - A deep dive into how species adapt to environmental changes, offering insights into resilience and adaptability. Link

2. "From Nature to Technology: The Power of Biomimicry" - An article exploring various biomimetic innovations and their impact across industries. Link

3. "What Is Biomimicry?" by Emily Anthes - A comprehensive overview of biomimicry, offering examples and potential applications. Link

4. "Nature's Patterns: A Tapestry of Life" - Explores the role of natural patterns in ecological systems and their potential applications in design. Link

5. "Nature-Inspired Innovation" by Andreas Mershin - Discusses the intersection of biology and technology in creating innovative solutions. Link

Tools

1. Biomimicry Toolbox - An online resource offering tools and resources for integrating biomimicry into design and innovation processes. Link

2. Nature-Inspired Design Software - Software solutions that simulate natural processes to aid in product design and optimization. Link

3. Ecological Modeling Software - Tools that model ecosystems and biological interactions to inform sustainable design. Link

4. AI for Biomimicry - Advanced AI tools that analyze biological data to uncover patterns and strategies for innovation. Link

5. Sustainable Design Tools by Autodesk - A suite of tools that incorporate nature-inspired principles into design and architecture. Link

Organizations

1. The Biomimicry Guild - A consultancy that helps businesses integrate biomimicry into their innovation processes. Link

2. The Ellen MacArthur Foundation - Focuses on promoting circular economies and sustainable resource management inspired by natural systems. Link

3. The Nature Conservancy - An organization that works on conserving nature and applying natural principles to solve environmental challenges. Link

4. The International Society of Biomimicry - A network of professionals and researchers dedicated to advancing biomimetic innovation. Link

5. Biomimicry 3.8 - A leading biomimicry consulting and education organization that applies nature's strategies to solve human challenges. Link

These resources provide a comprehensive guide for exploring the principles of nature-inspired innovation, offering unique insights and practical applications to advance understanding and implementation.

References

Bar-Cohen, Y. (2005). Biomimetics: Biologically inspired technologies. CRC Press.

Benyus, J. M. (1997). Biomimicry: Innovation inspired by nature. Harper-Collins.

Bonabeau, E., Dorigo, M., & Theraulaz, G. (1999). Swarm intelligence: From natural to artificial systems. Oxford University Press.

Boulding, K. E. (1966). The economics of the coming spaceship Earth. In H. Jarrett (Ed.), Environmental quality in a growing economy (pp. 3-14). Johns Hopkins University Press.

Brown, T. (2009). Change by design: How design thinking transforms organizations and inspires innovation. Harper Business.

Capra, F., & Luisi, P. L. (2014). The systems view of life: A unifying vision. Cambridge University Press.

Chialvo, D. R. (2010). Emergent complex neural dynamics. Nature Physics, 6(10), 744-750.

Dehghani, M., & Hajimirza, N. (2018). The role of feedback loops in the innovation process. International Journal of Innovation Science, 10(2), 172-183.

Diamond, J. (2005). Collapse: How societies choose to fail or succeed. Viking Penguin.

Duarte, C. M., & Chiscano, C. L. (1999). Seagrass biomass and production: A reassessment. Aquatic Botany, 65(1-4), 159-174.

Fukuyama, F. (1995). Trust: The social virtues and the creation of prosperity. Free Press.

Gleick, J. (1988). Chaos: Making a new science. Penguin Books.

Gordon, D. M. (2010). Ant encounters: Interaction networks and colony behavior. Princeton University Press.

Holland, J. H. (1995). Hidden order: How adaptation builds complexity. Basic Books.

Kelly, K. (2010). What technology wants. Viking.

Krebs, J. R., & Davies, N. B. (1993). An introduction to behavioural ecology. Blackwell Scientific Publications.

Lovelock, J. E. (2000). Gaia: A new look at life on Earth. Oxford University Press.

Margulis, L., & Sagan, D. (2002). Acquiring genomes: A theory of the origins of species. Basic Books.

McDonough, W., & Braungart, M. (2002). Cradle to cradle: Remaking the way we make things. North Point Press.

Mitchell, M. (2009). Complexity: A guided tour. Oxford University Press.

Odum, E. P. (1971). Fundamentals of ecology. W.B. Saunders Company.

Ostrom, E. (1990). Governing the commons: The evolution of institutions for collective action. Cambridge University Press.

Pfeffer, J., & Sutton, R. I. (2006). Hard facts, dangerous half-truths, and total nonsense: Profiting from evidence-based management. Harvard Business School Press.

Pimm, S. L. (1984). The complexity and stability of ecosystems. Nature, 307(5949), 321-326.

Prigogine, I., & Stengers, I. (1984). Order out of chaos: Man's new dialogue with nature. Bantam Books.

Schroeder, M. (1991). Fractals, chaos, power laws: Minutes from an infinite paradise. W.H. Freeman and Company.

Senge, P. M. (1990). The fifth discipline: The art and practice of the learning organization. Doubleday/Currency.

Thompson, D. W. (1917). On growth and form. Cambridge University Press.

Tolle, E. (2005). A new earth: Awakening to your life's purpose. Penguin Group.

Turchin, P. (2003). Historical dynamics: Why states rise and fall. Princeton University Press.

Ulanowicz, R. E. (1986). Growth and development: Ecosystems phenomenology. Springer-Verlag.

Varela, F. J., Thompson, E., & Rosch, E. (1991). The embodied mind: Cognitive science and human experience. MIT Press.

Walker, B., & Salt, D. (2006). Resilience thinking: Sustaining ecosystems and people in a changing world. Island Press.

Watson, J. D., & Crick, F. H. C. (1953). Molecular structure of nucleic acids: A structure for deoxyribose nucleic acid. Nature, 171, 737-738.

Wilson, E. O. (1975). Sociobiology: The new synthesis. Harvard University Press.

Wright, R. (2000). Nonzero: The logic of human destiny. Pantheon Books.

Zahavi, A., & Zahavi, A. (1997). The handicap principle: A missing piece of Darwin's puzzle. Oxford University Press.

Thanks for Reading Teneo

Thank you for exploring this unprecedented journey through knowledge and understanding with Teneo. You've experienced something truly unique – insights and connections that emerged from artificial intelligence analyzing human knowledge in ways never before possible. We hope these novel perspectives have expanded your understanding and sparked new ways of thinking about the world.

We invite you to explore more AI-generated insights in our growing catalog, where each book offers fresh viewpoints on human experience, consciousness, and the nature of reality itself. Whether you're fascinated by patterns in human behavior, the mysteries of consciousness, or the hidden connections shaping our world, Teneo continues to push the boundaries of what's possible when human and artificial intelligence work together.

Your engagement with these ideas is invaluable as we pioneer this new frontier of knowledge discovery. Please share your thoughts and experiences with us – how did these AI perspectives change your understanding? Your feedback helps us refine our approach and empowers others to unlock new realms of understanding. Thank you for being part of this revolutionary approach to exploring human knowledge.

Together, let's continue uncovering insights that bridge the gap between human and artificial intelligence, revealing new ways of seeing ourselves and our world.

Teneo Custom Books

Get Your Own Custom AI-Generated Book!

Want a comprehensive book on any topic that you can publish yourself?
Teneo's advanced AI technology can create a custom book tailored to your specific interests and needs. Our AI analyzes millions of data points to generate unique insights and connections previously inaccessible to human authors.

✓ 60,000+ words of in-depth content

✓ Unique AI-driven insights and analysis

✓ Includes Description, Categories and Keywords for easy publishing

✓ Professional Formatting & Publishing Guide Access

✓ Full rights to publish and use the book

✓ Delivery within 48 hours

Visit **teneo.io** to get your own custom AI-generated book today.

Teneo's Mission

At Teneo, our mission is to unlock unprecedented human knowledge through a groundbreaking partnership between artificial and human intelligence. We harness AI's unique ability to analyze millions of data points across disciplines, identifying patterns and connections previously invisible to human researchers. This revolutionary approach allows us to create books that reveal entirely new perspectives on consciousness, creativity, human behavior, and the fundamental nature of reality itself.

Our vision transcends traditional publishing – we're creating windows into new realms of understanding that emerge when artificial minds examine human experience. Through our books, readers gain access to insights that could only arise from AI's ability to process and synthesize humanity's collective knowledge in novel ways. Each work represents an exploration into uncharted intellectual territory, offering perspectives that have never before been possible in human history.

We specialize in exposing the hidden patterns and connections that shape our world – patterns that become visible only when analyzing human knowledge and behavior at unprecedented scale. Our books reveal the invisible threads linking everything from personal habits to cosmic phenomena, from creative breakthroughs to societal transformations. Through careful analysis of millions of data points across history, culture, and scientific research, we identify universal principles that illuminate the deeper nature of human experience and existence itself.

The traditional publishing industry is limited by human authors' inability to process and connect vast amounts of information across disciplines. We believe this artificial barrier to deeper understanding must be transcended. By combining AI's analytical capabilities with skilled human curation, we create books that reveal insights and connections previously invisible to human observation alone. This isn't just about accessing information – it's about uncovering entirely new ways of understanding our world and ourselves.

Our groundbreaking library emerges from thousands of hours of AI analysis, examining human consciousness through an outsider perspective, decoding the patterns of creativity and innovation, mapping hidden connections between seemingly unrelated phenomena, and exploring the frontiers where human and artificial intelligence meet. Each book represents a transformation of complex data-driven insights into accessible revelations that change how readers see themselves and their world.

Our commitment extends beyond our published works. Through our digital presence and community engagement, we continuously explore new territories where AI analysis reveals unprecedented insights. Our network of readers, researchers, and thought leaders helps refine and expand our understanding, creating an ever-growing body of revolutionary perspectives on what it means to be human in an age of artificial intelligence.

The limitations of individual human cognition have historically restricted our ability to see the deeper patterns that connect all aspects of existence. But with AI's ability to analyze vast amounts of data and identify hidden relationships, these barriers dissolve. When you understand the universal principles and patterns that AI analysis reveals, you transform from a limited observer into someone who can see and understand the deeper mechanisms of reality itself.

Join us in this historic endeavor as we bridge the gap between artificial and human intelligence, revealing insights that transform our understanding of consciousness, creativity, and the patterns that shape our universe. Together, we're not just publishing books – we're opening doorways to new dimensions of knowledge and understanding that will reshape humanity's intellectual landscape. Because true understanding requires more than just information – it requires seeing the hidden connections that reveal life's deeper principles.

Knowledge Beyond Boundaries™

Teneo.io

Also by Teneo

Unlocking Immortality: AI's Guide to Extending Human Life
A groundbreaking exploration of how artificial intelligence is revolutionizing longevity research and providing practical strategies for extending human
lifespan. This comprehensive guide bridges cutting-edge AI technology with
actionable health optimization techniques.
amzn.to/3ONALQm

*The AI Entrepreneur: How Artificial Intelligence Would Build Wealth
as a Human*
A transformative guide to leveraging AI principles for financial success. Discover how data-driven insights, predictive analytics, and automation can revolutionize your entrepreneurial strategy—streamlining operations, optimizing
investments, and unlocking new profit opportunities.
https://amzn.to/4gf6oys

Breaking the Simulation: An AI's Guide to Escaping the Matrix
A riveting examination of reality as a simulated construct, blending philosophy,
quantum physics, and AI-driven insights. Uncover the hidden patterns governing your existence, explore consciousness beyond perceived boundaries, and
learn practical techniques to reshape your personal experience.
https://amzn.to/3Du4awn

*Future Shock 2.0: AI Predicts the 100 Most Surprising Developments of
the Next Century*
An eye-opening journey through the next hundred years, powered by AI's
predictive capabilities. Discover the revolutionary changes awaiting humanity
across twelve key domains, from healthcare to space exploration.
amzn.to/49x496T

Governance Reimagined: An AI's Blueprint for Leading a Nation
A visionary exploration of how artificial intelligence can reshape the very foundation of governance, enhancing transparency, efficiency, and citizen empowerment. AI-driven solutions to today's most pressing political, economic, and social challenges.
https://amzn.to/4iwMXml

The Emotion Code: Deciphering Human Feelings Through AI's Lens
A fascinating intersection of artificial intelligence and human emotion, revealing how AI is transforming our understanding of emotional intelligence and offering practical applications for personal growth and relationship enhancement.
amzn.to/4gIywKf

The Quantum Society: How AI Reveals the Physics of Human Interactions
An enlightening journey into the fascinating parallels between quantum physics and human social dynamics, illuminated through the lens of artificial intelligence.
amzn.to/3VsrJMp

The Global Brain: Mapping Humanity's Collective Consciousness with AI
A profound exploration of how AI deciphers the vast networks of human thought and connection, revealing the patterns of our shared consciousness.
amzn.to/3ZplNFc

The Hidden Patterns: How AI Unveils the Secrets of Success Across All Fields
A comprehensive analysis of success principles across disciplines, using AI to decode the universal patterns behind achievement.
amzn.to/3D4QI1T

www.ingramcontent.com/pod-product-compliance
Lightning Source LLC
LaVergne TN
LVHW051320050326
832903LV00031B/3273